C000227818

The South West Coast Path is recognised
as one of the world's great trails.

This guide will help you plan a journey to remember
and make memories to treasure.

Our team, based by the Path in our Plymouth HQ, work with
the land managers, partners and other organisations and
businesses along the 630 miles, to make the South West Coast
Path one of the world's great Trail experiences.

If you would like to contact the charity the details are as follows:
South West Coast Path Association, Residence 2, Royal William Yard, Plymouth, PL1 3RP
Tel: 01752 896237

hello@southwestcoastpath.org.uk

Published by: The South West Coast Path Association. ISBN: 978-0-907055-34-1
Registered Charity number 1163422

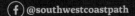 @southwestcoastpath   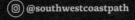 @southwestcoastpath   @swcoastpath

Use the hashtag #southwestcoastpath to join the conversation

Lulworth, Jurassic Coast. Photographer Yellow Matilda

" *walking at its most diverse, most spectacular and most delicious* "

Lonely Planet Great Adventures Guide

As Britain's longest and best-loved National Trail, the South West Coast Path (SWCP) captures the hearts and minds of all who journey along it. From Minehead to Poole, it takes in the best parts of four unique counties, offering 630 miles of uninterrupted walking. The Coast Path has an ancient history connecting coastal communities in the South West and is steeped in local myth and legends with tales of shipwrecks, pirates and smugglers. The Coast Path acts as a green corridor around this amazing coastline giving a unique opportunity to connect to nature – a wild belt that needs our protection.

As you embark on your epic journey this guide will be your companion. It has been produced by the charity that has been championing the Path since 1973 with the support of hundreds of volunteers. From distance timing and terrain gradings, to key information about ferry crossings, tide times and military ranges, the guide has all the information you'll need. It also includes hundreds of businesses offering places to stay, eat and drink and things to do that will make your trip truly unforgettable. We call these businesses our Way Makers, so keep an eye out for the Way Maker badge as you travel around the South West. We hope you have an amazing time exploring this spectacular landscape. Members of the charity receive this guide completely free and those that have bought this guide can **upgrade to membership for £12.00** with these funds going back to protect and promote the Trail. See page 9 for more information on all member benefits.

Happy walking!

Trails can't live on love alone

The South West Coast Path Association's vital work is only possible thanks to the generosity of its members, donors, fundraisers, volunteers, Way Makers and corporate partners. Their support enables us to carry out significant work on the ground, undertake outreach projects, be a voice for the National Trail corridor and provide vital information to walkers and runners. It currently costs us on average **£1,500 each year to care for every mile of the South West Coast Path**. As the planet warms, we're seeing more extreme and frequent storms hitting the Coast Path causing surface run-off and coastal erosion and pushing costs up further.

If you would like to support our vital work keeping the Trail open and accessible to all, please consider becoming a member of the charity, making a donation, or fundraising on your next Coast Path challenge. Visit **southwestcoastpath.org.uk** to see how you can help.

Together, we can protect the Trail we love.

A Trail like the South West Coast Path needs constant repairs and improvements to maintain its status as a world famous hiking route and keep it accessible to the millions who use it.

Since the formation of the South West Coast Path Association, 50 years ago in 1973, our members have been the bedrock of the charity. They have supported us during challenging times whilst we have carried out the work needed to protect the Trail we know and love today.

However, due to the increasing threats posed by climate change, lack of sufficient funding and increased usage of the Trail, we face uncertain times ahead.

We are heartened to know that with the support of our members, our voice can be heard and the positive impact we can have on the Trail is great. But we want to do more.

We want to build the Path's resilience to extreme weather; conserve its rich biodiversity and distinct cultural heritage; shore up the South West tourism economy supported by the Trail and demonstrate the real, positive impact it has on people's health and wellbeing. Did you know that 79% of people reported feeling more positive after walking on the Coast Path and 62% of people feel inspired to be more active after walking on the Coast Path.

Together with our members we want to make sure the South West Coast Path not only survives but thrives, benefiting all of society.

Join us
Please do show your support for the South West Coast Path by becoming a member. You'll also enjoy a range of member benefits such as;

The Complete Guide and Trailblazing magazine
You'll receive the latest copy of this official Complete Guide to the South West Coast Path along with two publications of Trailblazing, our fantastic magazine, jam-packed with the latest news and stories from the Path.

Certificate
You'll receive a FREE completion certificate upon competing all 630 miles of the Path and the chance to submit your story for publication in Trailblazing magazine.

Discounts and offers
We work with a range of businesses, outdoor retailers, and partners along the Trail to offer you exclusive discounts to save you money whilst exploring the South West Coast Path. You will also receive exclusive member-only discounts in our online shop southwestcoastpath. org.uk/shop where we offer a range of publications, gifts and clothing.

Updates and news of the Trail
We apportion 50% of every membership fee to help protect and promote the Trail. We'll send you e-newsletters to tell you more about work taking place thanks to your support, along with inspiration, interviews and your stories from walking the Path.

Prices

Single	£29.00
Joint	£37.00
Overseas	£37.00

Not yet a member?
If you purchased this guide independently of membership and want to upgrade to become a member, we would be delighted to welcome you. Pay just £12.00 more for single membership or £20.00 more for Joint membership.

Call us on 01752 896237 or email hello@southwestcoastpath.org.uk to take up this offer.

Look for our Way Makers

Our Way Makers are businesses offering places to stay, eat and drink, and activities to take part in, either on or near the Coast Path, helping to make your experience along the Trail truly unforgettable.

Staying with friendly hosts in stunning locations, enjoying the best of our region's food and drink, taking part in coastal adventures, and meeting the locals, is what makes the SWCP one of the most popular and unique hiking Trails in the world. Just like Coast Path users, Way Makers come in all shapes and sizes. They range from basic budget campsites offering a 'wild camping' experience to cosy B&Bs, pubs and luxury hotels. There's self-catering options too if you're looking for a base from which to explore the Coast Path and local area. As well as accommodation, our Way Makers include watersports activities, museums, gardens, shops, taxis and of course coastal cafes and pubs. Don't forget to check out which Way Makers you can visit to collect your Coast Path Passport stamp too on our website southwestcoastpath.org.uk/passport.

Support a Way Maker and support the Path

One thing our Way Makers do have in common is that they love welcoming walkers, whilst also doing their bit to help us to protect and care for the Path. They realise just how important the Trail and you are to their local coastal communities, environment and economy. That's why they support the SWCPA as Way Makers, helping us to keep the Path maintained for everyone to enjoy and making sure this amazing natural asset remains accessible and cared for. When you choose a Way Maker, you'll also be doing your bit to help the Path by supporting a business which gives back to the Trail.

Where to find Way Makers

All of the businesses in this guide are Way Makers and listed at the end of each Path section. You will also find them listed on our website, linked to all of our suggested walks within a 5-mile radius of their location. Remember, we have over 600 walks available on our website, including easy access routes and circular walks, so there's still plenty to explore after you've completed the 630 miles of Coast Path from Minehead to Poole. Look out for businesses displaying the Way Maker sticker in their window along the Path.

Going the extra mile

Here in the South West, we pride ourselves on giving a warm welcome to visitors, and doing everything we can to make sure they have a great experience whilst they're here. In the past, walkers have been in touch to tell us about businesses that have gone to great lengths to help them on their travels.

So, if you come across a business that is going the extra mile to help make your experience amazing, we'd love to hear from you! We'll then get in touch with the business to say thank you and ask them to become a Way Maker, if they aren't already. Tell us about a business by emailing waymaker@southwestcoastpath.org.uk.

Proud to support the South West Coast Path

Coast Path Passport

Our new Coast Path Passport launched in 2022 providing an exciting new way for visitors to enjoy the Coast Path and support businesses along the 630-mile coastal route.

Alex Polizzi's Hotel Inspector TV show provided the first reveal of the Passport when the Pack O' Cards pub in Combe Martin (North Devon) became one of the first places to sign up as a Coast Path Passport stamping point.

Alex Polizzi said,

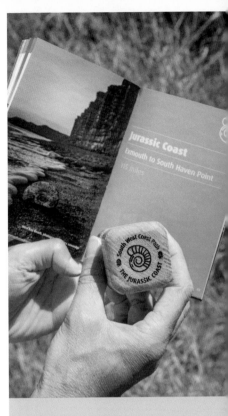

> *I am so excited about the new Coast Path Passport scheme that the South West Coast Path Association have launched. It's fantastic for walkers and businesses along the Path. I hope everyone will enjoy it.*

Upon launching the Passport, we were overwhelmed by the response —selling out of our first batch within just a few hours!

The Coast Path Passport allows the millions of visitors who walk the South West Coast Path each year, to keep a record of their journey by collecting 'stamps' along the way reflecting the unique nature of each stretch of the Trail.

The Passport will create a lasting memory to treasure, while also helping to raise much-needed funds to help care for the Path which is at increasing risk from climate change.

We are delighted that in 2023, holiday cottage company, Luxury Coastal, is on board to sponsor our 50th-anniversary commemorative edition.

luxurycoastal

For more details on the Coast Path Passport go to **southwestcoastpath. org.uk/passport** or scan the QR code.

Planning Your Walk

Whether you are planning to walk the whole 630 miles of the Coast Path or you are just taking to the Path for a few hours, half a day or perhaps just a picnic, you are likely to know your capabilities and not need detailed advice. However, it is worth remembering that some lengths of the Coast Path can be quite arduous, with frequent repeated climbs and descents or occasional awkward terrain, and it is not always possible to calculate the time or effort to be taken for a length purely on the distance. The degree of difficulty has to be considered so check in this guide for the grading of each walk. We have used easy, moderate, strenuous or severe to give an idea of what to expect. For example, the time and effort required for a 'severe' length can be twice that for the same distance of an 'easy' section. More information on the gradings and elevation of the Coast Path can be found on pages 42 and 43.

Some Practical Details

It is worth having a good think about what items you will need to take on your walk, and travel as light as possible. Our kit list on page 17 can help with this. Rucksacks aren't always waterproof, so think of how you can add an additional waterproof layer.

Newcomers to the Coast Path

A great way of getting an idea of what coastal walking is about is to take a day walk first. Perhaps start with a length graded easy or moderate. Alternatively, walk a section shown as having convenient public transport. If doing this, try to use the public transport at the start and walk back to your base. This avoids having to race the clock to catch a bus at the end of the walk. You can find transport links and information on pages 24-29.

The Association works with partners to assist local community groups for new or inexperienced walkers. See southwestcoastpath.org.uk/coast-path-connectors for more information. There is little need for special kit on the easy sections, good shoes and a rainproof jacket will probably be enough. Once you progress further however, decent boots and a rucksack for food and drink and other bits and pieces will be needed. It is always useful to carry a map so that you can keep track of your surroundings, in the unlikely event that you get lost. Visit southwestcoastpath.org.uk/books.

Long Distance Coast Path Walking

If you have not undertaken walking for more than a day at a time, bear in mind that you will not be able to keep up the same distance day after day as you do in a one-off day walk. The first reason for this is that you will probably be carrying more gear than usual. This may include a change of clothes and overnight kit, all in a bigger rucksack than usual. However, it is possible to overcome this by using Baggage Transfer providers – see page 21. Secondly, there is the 'wear' factor, for the first few days especially, it is simply more tiring having to walk each day. And finally, there is the 'interest' factor, the walk is likely to take you through new places and new scenery; there is more to see and you will need more time to look round. These factors will influence your planning.

Booking accommodation in advance means you know you have a bed for the night, which can be important in the South West in the summer and in the unpredictable British weather. Our Way Maker businesses offer accommodation, places to stop for food and drink and activities to undertake along the 630 miles of the Coast Path. Details can be found at the back of each walk section in this guide.

Walking Alone

The most important thing to remember if walking alone is to make sure someone knows your destination and estimated time of arrival. Also, make sure you take a fully charged mobile phone and a power pack as a back up. It is true that signal coverage is patchy along the coast but it's still worth having one. If you have a smart phone, there are apps available that enable you to share your progress with family or friends, to give a further indication of where you are if you haven't arrived where and when you were expected. We have a scheme that enables solo members to meet like-minded individuals wanting to walk the Coast Path. Contact hello@southwestcoastpath.org.uk for more information.

Photography

The South West Coast Path is constantly changing and no two days are ever the same. Recording your journey by taking photographs is a great way to relive the memories you'll make whilst enjoying the beautiful coastal scenery. We love to see your photos and run an annual photography competition. You can find out more by visiting southwestcoastpath.org.uk/photographer-of-the-year.

We also love hearing your stories and welcome our members to submit their completer story and a photo for publication in our magazine 'Trailblazing'. Submit a story to: southwestcoastpath.org.uk/share-your-story. Or for a bit of fun you can upload a selfie of you on the Path for a small donation to help its upkeep here; givepenny.com/appeal-for/photo%20wall.

The Environment of the South West Coast Path

The 20 National Trails across the UK are world-class long-distance paths helping people access, experience and enjoy our finest landscapes. Conceived in 1949, this network of long distance paths was a way of connecting people to the landscape and part of the 'natural health service', an ambition just as important today. As you journey along the South West Coast Path you will experience a diverse range of coastal landscapes including high cliffs, extensive beaches, wide bays, tiny coves, wooded estuaries, and prominent headlands. This range of outstanding landscapes has been recognised officially by the large number of formal designations at international, national and local levels.

International Designations

UNESCO has designated certain world-class environments as Biosphere Reserves. These are areas with a special blend of landscapes and wildlife, a rich cultural heritage and a community that cares about it and wishes to sustain it for the future. The Coast Path passes through the North Devon Biosphere Reserve, which has as its core the dunes of Braunton Burrows **(see Section 7)**, but includes as its outer areas, the whole Coast Path between Lynton and Marsland Mouth **(see Section 3-13)**.

World Heritage Sites are also designated by UNESCO, in this case for their "Outstanding Universal Value". The South West Coast Path passes through two World Heritage Sites (WHS). The Cornwall and West Devon Mining Landscape WHS is defined by the mining landscape which was formed by the tradition of non-ferrous hard-rock mining. It contributed to developing the Industrial Revolution in Britain and pioneered its transfer overseas. The designation covers ten distinct areas and includes iconic relic mining landscapes, with their old engine houses, as well

as old harbours. Five of these areas relate to the Coast Path – the St Agnes area **(see Section 24)**, the Port of Hayle **(see Sections 25 and 26)**, the St Just area **(see Sections 27-28)**, the area around Rinsey and Trewavas **(see Section 32)** and Charlestown **(see Section 41)**.

The Coast Path's second WHS is the Jurassic Coast, England's first such site to be designated for its natural properties. It is designated as it clearly depicts a geological "walk through time" of 185 million years of Earth's history in 95 miles/152km. Geological history, and resulting landscapes, of the Triassic, Jurassic and Cretaceous periods are successively exposed over the length of the WHS, which stretches between Exmouth and Swanage **(see Section 58-70)**.

National Designations

Over 70% of the Coast Path travels through our finest national landscapes including Areas of Outstanding Natural Beauty (AONB) and National Parks. Exmoor **(see Sections 1-3)** with its cliffs and deep wooded valleys, has National Park status. Most of the remainder of the Coast Path is covered by Area of Outstanding Natural Beauty status. The North Devon AONB extends along much of the coast between Exmoor and the Devon/Cornwall border **(see Sections 4-7 and 11-13)** excluding only Ilfracombe and the area around the Taw-Torridge estuary. The Cornwall AONB covers the vast majority of the Cornish coast **(see Sections 13-25 and 27-46)** excluding only a few mainly urban lengths. The whole length of coast between Plymouth and Brixham **(see Sections 47- 54)** falls within the South Devon AONB. East of the River Exe, most of the coast, excluding only the urban areas, as far as the Devon/Dorset border, is covered by the East Devon AONB. And finally, all of the Dorset coast, except the largely urban Weymouth and Portland, is within the Dorset AONB.

The wealth of landscape and environmental designations outlined above gives some idea of the quality of the landscape through which the South West Coast Path passes. However, this hides the fact that there is a wide range of landscape types to be experienced. For an idea of the more detailed landscape types, a description can be found at the start of each of the seven lengths we have divided the Coast Path into – Exmoor, North Devon, North Cornwall, West Cornwall, South Cornwall, South Devon and the Jurassic Coast.

Climate Change and the Path; the fragile place where land meets the sea

Existing on the fringe and edge of our coast is what makes the South West Coast Path so special and freeing. However, it also means the Path is sat on the frontline when it comes to extreme weather, caused by climate change. With increasing storm surges, combined with rising sea levels, we are seeing faster rates of coastal erosion, meaning access to natural landscapes, like those of the South West Coast Path, are possibly more at threat than ever before. We've been tracking "exceptional coastal erosion events" along the National Trail since 2013. For an incident to make it into our records there needs to have been a direct impact on people's ability to use the Coast Path, and a subsequent need for an intervention to repair, restore, or even completely move the route of the Trail.

Over the last 8 years, we have recorded more than 304 exceptional events which have affected the Trail. 116 of these occurred between April 2019 to March 2022 alone. Climate change is no longer a distant threat, but a future we must all adapt to. Through our campaigns, we are raising funds to help protect the Path and ensure it's safe, and accessible, for future generations to use. Ultimately, we want to make sure the South West Coast Path not only survives as a continuous 630-mile National Trail, but also thrives, benefitting both people and nature. You can support the work of the charity and the Coast Path by joining as a member at southwestcoastpath.org.uk/join or by donating at southwestcoastpath.org.uk/donate-now. You can also contact us for more information by phone, email, or by writing to us. You will find the charity contact details on the inside cover of this Complete Guide.

Seatown, Jurassic Coast. Photographer James Loveridge

Stay Safe

It is your responsibility to stay safe whilst out on the South West Coast Path, and to look after others if you are walking as part of a group. Please remember to always keep to the Path, follow the advisory signs and waymarks, and stay away from cliff edges. Particular care and attention should be paid to children and dogs to ensure they are kept in sight at all times. It is important to make sure you are well equipped for your walk, and that you take into consideration possible sudden changes in weather when you are packing your kit. Don't forget to check the weather forecast in advance of your trip and take note of when the sun will set, so you know how many hours of sunlight to expect. The Path can get very muddy, especially if you are walking in winter, so take care on particularly steep sections.

We advise you to be mindful of your ability level. Some sections of the South West Coast Path can be very strenuous and/or remote. Always check the difficulty grading in the walk description and for more challenging routes, try and find someone else to walk with you. If you are venturing out alone, we recommend telling a friend or family member exactly where you plan to walk and an approximate time for arrival. In case of an emergency, please dial 999 and ask for the Coastguard.

Weather

The South West Coast Path is more exposed to wind than any other long-distance Trail in the UK, so please pay attention to gale forecasts. Along some sections, strong winds can be dangerous, especially when rounding exposed headlands and crossing bridges where a high backpack can act like a sail. Please take particular care on these sections. Wind and rain combined can cause your core temperature to drop significantly. If possible, take a spare layer of clothing with you and opt for waterproof and windproof jackets to protect you against the worst of the elements. It is equally important to shield yourself from harmful UV rays, especially on bright cloudy or breezy days when the risk of sunburn feels lower.

Military Ranges

Two lengths of the South West Coast Path may be affected by the use of military ranges. The use of one, at Tregantle in south east Cornwall, only means that a more inland and less picturesque route must be used for a length of some 1.25 miles/2km in Section 46, Portwrinkle-Cremyll (Plymouth Ferry). However, if there is military use of the other, east of Lulworth Cove in Dorset, this means the whole of Section 67 between Lulworth Cove and Kimmeridge Bay will be impossible. Generally the Lulworth ranges are closed to walkers Monday to Friday during school term time and also up to six times a year at weekends. Try to arrange your walk so as not to miss this superb, but tough section.

Information and details for the ranges are included in the relevant section descriptions on pages 144 and 188, and on our website.

Route Changes

The coast would not look so beautiful and dramatic if it wasn't for cliff and beach erosion. The downside to this is that sometimes cliff falls or landslips close sections of the Coast Path, resulting in temporary inland diversions which can occasionally be quite lengthy. In these instances, always follow signage and information on the ground. Whilst any route changes and diversions are signed, they may make your walk longer. It's worth checking the 'route changes' pages of our website before you set out. We are also constantly looking for opportunities to improve the Path, in the few places where it is not as good as it could be.

The Government is in the process of completing the England Coast Path around the entire coast of the country. This is helping us to make improvements to the South West Coast Path. Find out more in the news section of our website.

Here is what we recommend you pack for your trip out on the South West Coast Path.

Base Layer

A base layer is a good place to start most walking outfits. Merino wool is ideal for colder weather as it will keep the heat in, whilst wicking away your sweat.

Spare Insulating Layer

The conditions you choose to walk in dictate what level of insulation you will need. A light fleece is fine for summer, but British winters demand a down or synthetic insulated jacket. Suitable walking clothes can be found in our online shop southwestcoastpath.org.uk/shop.

Waterproofs

Waterproof layers are vital when exploring the Coast Path to ensure you don't end up walking in damp clothes. Your waterproofs should be breathable, with ventilation to allow sweat vapour to escape.

Sturdy Footwear

You will need some sturdy walking trainers or boots to take on the sometimes uneven terrain of the Coast Path in comfort.

First Aid Kit

Whilst you are unlikely to find yourself in danger when walking sensibly on the Coast Path, it never hurts to be prepared. Carry a first aid kit and make sure you know how to use everything in it. Take a torch in case you get caught out after dark, and a whistle is a lightweight way to help attract attention in an emergency. A fold-away foil blanket is another handy piece of kit.

Food and Water

Keeping hydrated is essential for an enjoyable day on the Trail. Aim for at least 2 litres per day, but remember the amount you need to drink is entirely dependent on the length of time you plan to be walking and the temperature. Even if you have a lunch stop planned, we recommend taking a snack, to keep your energy levels up.

Visit refill.org.uk for more information on water refill points along the Path.

Eye and Skin Protection

When it is sunny you'll want to block out the bright light with sunglasses so you can fully enjoy the spectacular sea views. Walking when it's warm is great, but it's important to be sun safe, even on overcast days, so pack some sun cream and apply it accordingly.

Map and Compass

Even though the Coast Path is well signed, taking a map and compass, and knowing how to use them, is essential on any longer walk. You never know when you might have to change route due to unforeseen circumstances, and a quick look at a map can give you a safe alternative.

Walking Poles

Whilst not essential, walking poles can help you move more confidently over difficult terrain and even come in handy should you need to cross a stream or muddy area of the Path.

Mobile Phone

You cannot rely on it, as signal is very patchy along many parts of the Coast Path, but it is handy to have a mobile phone with you. The route of the Coast Path outside of towns is shown on Google Maps, but be aware that using GPS will drain your battery, so it's worth taking a USB power bank as backup.

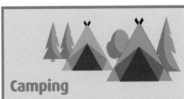

Camping

There are plenty of ways to enjoy the Coast Path as a camper. Find out more at **southwestcoastpath.org.uk/camping**

The Countryside Code – Respect Protect and Enjoy

Respect everyone
- be considerate to those living in, working in and enjoying the countryside
- leave gates and property as you find them
- do not block access to gateways or driveways when parking
- be nice, say hello, share the space
- follow local signs and keep to marked paths unless wider access is available

Protect the environment
- take your litter home – leave no trace of your visit
- do not light fires and only have BBQs where signs say you can
- always keep dogs under control and in sight
- dog poo – bag it and bin it – any public waste bin will do
- care for nature – do not cause damage or disturbance

Enjoy the outdoors
- check your route and local conditions
- plan your adventure – know what to expect and what you can do
- enjoy your visit, have fun, make a memory

gov.uk/countryside-code 🔍

There are lots of ways to have a light footprint and help protect the Path for future generations, including:
- ✔ Use public transport where possible
- ✔ Support local shops and services
- ✔ Keep to the Path to minimise erosion
- ✔ Report Path problems to the South West Coast Path Association
- ✔ Keep dogs under control
- ✔ Look out for water refill stations along the Path. Find out more at **refill.org.uk**

Join the association as a member at

southwestcoastpath.org.uk/join 🔍

Godrevy from Gwithian Towans. Photographer Steve Tew

NATIONAL TRAILS

The South West Coast Path is one of 20 National Trails. This 'family' of Trails is special in that they have been designated by the Government and are managed to a set of Quality Standards that set them above other routes. A 'Trail Partnership', made up of local authorities, working with land owners and Path managers, is responsible for the Path on the ground.

Follow the Acorn

All the trails, including the South West Coast Path, are well signposted and waymarked, using the distinctive National Trail symbol of the acorn.

This acorn is often used alongside coloured arrows or the words 'footpath', 'bridleway' or 'byway' to indicate which public access rights apply to that particular stretch of path.

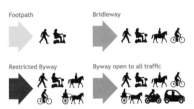

Footpath   Bridleway

Restricted Byway   Byway open to all traffic

Yellow arrows indicate a 'Public Footpath' for use by walkers and mobility scooters.

Blue arrows are for a 'Public Bridleway' which can be used by walkers, horse riders, cyclists and mobility scooters.

Purple arrows mark a 'Restricted Byway' where the public have a right of way on foot, horseback, bicycle, mobility scooters or horse-drawn carriage.

Red arrows indicate that the path is a 'Public Byway' which can be used by walkers, horse riders, cyclists, motorised vehicle drivers, carriage drivers and mobility scooters.

England Coast Path

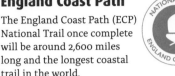

The England Coast Path (ECP) National Trail once complete will be around 2,600 miles long and the longest coastal trail in the world.

In the South West the two National Trails will mostly run along the same route, although there will be some deviations. For example, the ECP will take the first estuary crossing in places like Plymouth, crossing on the Ferry between the Barbican and Mount Batten, whereas the SWCP will continue along its current route passing through Cattedown up the Plym Estuary and back past Hooe Lake to Mount Batten. Find out more at nationaltrail.co.uk/en_GB/trails/england-coast-path.

A world class trail on our doorstep

It's often said that the South West Coast Path is one of the world's great trails and we are regularly included in top-ten trail bucket lists in the media. The diversity of trails around the world is amazing, crossing urban, rural and wilderness, linking communities, supporting sustainable livelihoods, promoting peace in areas of conflict, driving nature recovery, celebrating our cultural heritage and most importantly connecting people to nature.

As the charity protecting and celebrating the Coast Path we are proud to be an active member of the World Trails Network. For the past five years we've engaged with this global trail family to share knowledge and best practice with trails traversing six continents. Through the Network we have learned from other trails, allowing us to look at issues along the Coast Path from different perspectives. We've also shared our experience in championing Britain's longest National Trail.

If you would like to find out more about the World Trails Network visit worldtrailsnetwork.org.

Need some help planning your holiday? We recommend contacting one of the walking holiday companies listed in this section who provide complete walking holiday packages along the South West Coast Path. These include guided and self-guided walk options, depending on how you prefer to travel, as well as themed walks from food foraging to wildlife watching.

Absolute Escapes

Absolute Escapes award-winning specialists in self-guided walking holidays on the South West Coast Path. Packages include carefully selected accommodation, door-to-door bag transfers, and comprehensive information pack with guidebook, map, and recommendations for lunch and dinner each day. They are a leading specialist in walking holidays and offer packages on many long-distance trails in the UK and Ireland. www.absolute escapes.com/south-west-coast-path

Encounter Walking Holidays provide walking holidays and short breaks on every section of the Coast Path. They specialise in helping with the requests that others struggle with or don't want to take on – whether you are a small group looking for the best prices, walking with your dogs, have an unusual itinerary idea or are just arriving from overseas and are new to UK walking routes. They provide detailed quotes for walkers with no commitment to book, so get in touch with your ideas and questions! www.encounterwalkingholidays.com

Footpath Holidays is a family owned walking holiday company founded in 1983. Self-guided holidays along the South West Coast; single centre and 'moving on' with accommodation and baggage transfer. Guided group holidays in Devon, Cornwall and Dorset. www.footpath-holidays.com

HF Walking Holidays offer a north and south route of the South West Coast Path. Whichever is your preferred choice, you will be walking along magnificent beaches and enjoying stunning vistas. The northern route covers the most westerly section of the Path over the majestic, rugged cliffs of the north coast of Cornwall from Treyarnon Bay to Cape Cornwall. The southern Path traverses the granite cliffs of Land's End and finishes at Helford. With wonderful views, secret coves, and almost forgotten fishing villages, this is a superb section encircling the coast of Cornwall. www.hfholidays.co.uk

Macs Adventure offer walking, cycling and active adventures which give you the freedom to travel at your own pace. With over 20 years' experience, they arrange everything from hand-picked accommodation to baggage transfer, and precise mapping to give you a unique and memorable travel experience. www.macsadventure.com

Mickledore Travel specialises in self-guided walking and cycling holidays in the UK. They provide a flexible service making the arrangements that suit you, leaving you free to just enjoy your walk. As walkers and cyclists, they aim to provide a service of the highest quality and a holiday to remember. www.mickledore.co.uk

Nearwater Holidays specialise in single based, inn-to-inn trips and bespoke walking holidays along all sections of the South West Coast Path. The walks have been developed with the benefit of local knowledge to ensure the visiting walker has the chance to see a few extra special places that they would otherwise overlook.

www.nearwaterwalkingholidays.co.uk

Walk the Trail offer self-guided walking holidays throughout the South West including the South West Coast Path, The Two Moors Way, and The Saints Way, along with many other routes across the UK. All holidays include a personalised holiday pack complete with luggage transfers, accommodation location information, maps and guidebooks. Their unique Holiday Finder Tool allows you to choose your start and end locations, giving you greater flexibility to enjoy the Coast Path at a pace to suit you.

www.walkthetrail.co.uk

Western Discoveries are the local experts for walking holidays in Cornwall. They are based in West Cornwall and specialise in providing self-led walking holidays along the Cornwall section of the stunning South West Coast Path, accommodation, luggage transfers, maps, their own detailed route notes and arrival/departure transfers from local transport terminals are all provided with an unparalleled attention to detail.

www.westcornwallwalks.co.uk

Guided Walks

For local walk guides and further local walking holiday providers, see the 'Activities' at the end of every walk section.

Baggage Transfer

Walking is even more enjoyable when all you have to carry is a light daypack, so why not take advantage of a kit transfer service? Packing becomes much easier when you're not worrying about the weight and you know your overnight bags will be ready and waiting when you arrive at the place you're staying. Luggage Transfers proudly supports the South West Coast Path Association. More information can be found on our website at southwestcoastpath.org.uk/baggage-transfer

Luggage Transfers are the only luggage courier service covering the whole 630 miles of the South West Coast Path. With over 10 years' experience and over 50 drivers, they continue to support the South West Coast Path Association through voluntary donations from their walker clients. They are FEEFO Platinum award rated and deliver on average 10,000 bags per month, allowing them to combine bookings to reduce carbon footprint. For further information go to www.luggagetransfers.co.uk

INFORMATION CENTRES

Town	Address	Phone	Website
Weston Super Mare	Water & Adventure Playpark, Weston-super-Mare BS23 1AL	01934 317777	www.visit-westonsupermare.com
Minehead	The Beach Hotel, The Avenue, Minehead TA24 5AP	01643 702624	www.mineheadbay.co.uk
Porlock	The Old School Centre, West End, Porlock TA24 8QD	01643 863150	www.porlock.co.uk
Lynton & Lynmouth	Post Office, 26 Lee Road, Lynton EX35 6BS	01598 753313	www.visitlyntonandlynmouth.com
Combe Martin	Cross Street, Combe Martin EX34 0DH	01271 883319	www.combemartin.com
Ilfracombe	Landmark Theatre, Ilfracombe EX34 9BZ	01271 863001	www.visitilfracombe.co.uk
Woolacombe	The Esplanade, Woolacombe EX34 7DL	01271 870553	www.woolacombetourism.co.uk
Croyde	Baggy Lodge, Moor Lane, Croyde EX33 1PA	0800 188 4860	www.croydebay.com
Braunton	Museum & Information Centre, Caen Street, Braunton EX33 1AA	01271 816688	www.visitbraunton.co.uk
Barnstaple	The Square, Barnstaple EX32 8LN	01271 346747	www.staynorthdevon.co.uk
Bideford	Burton Art Gallery, Kingsley Rd EX39, Bideford 2QQ	01237 477676	www.visitdevon.co.uk/northdevon
Hartland Quay	67 The Square, Hartland EX39 6BL	01237 441916	www.hartlandpeninsula.co.uk
Bude	The Crescent, Bude EX23 8LE	01288 354240	www.visitbude.info
Boscastle	The Harbour, Boscastle PL35 0HD	01840 250010	www.boscastle-visitor-centre
Padstow	South Quay, Padstow PL28 8BL	01841 533449	www.padstowlive.com
Newquay	Marcus Hill, Newquay TR7 1BD	01637 838516	www.visitnewquay.org
Perranporth	Contact only by phone or on-line	01872 575254	www.perranporthinfo.co.uk
Hayle	Hayle Library, Commercial Road, Hayle TR27 4DE	01736 754399	www.visitcornwall.tv/cornwall-visitor-information/tic/hayle
St Ives	The Library, Gabriel Street, St Ives TR26 2LX	01736 796297	www.stives-cornwall.co.uk
Penzance	Station Road, Penzance TR18 2NF0	1736 335530	www.purelypenzance.co.uk/tourism
Falmouth	Prince Of Wales Pier, Falmouth, TR11 3DF	01326 741194	www.falriver.co.uk
Truro	30 Boscawen St, Truro TR1 2QQ	01872 274555	www.visittruro.org.uk
Fowey	5 South Street, Fowey PL23 1AR	01726 833616	www.fowey.co.uk
Looe	The Millpool, West Looe PL13 2AF	01503 262255	www.visitlooe.co.uk
Plymouth	3-5 Plymouth Mayflower, Barbican PL1 2LR	01752 306330	www.visitplymouth.co.uk
Ivybridge	The Watermark, Ivybridge PL21 0SZ	01752 897035	www.ivybridge-devon.co.uk
Salcombe	Market Street, Salcombe TQ8 8DE	01548 843927	www.salcombeinformation.co.uk
Kingsbridge	The Quay, Kingsbridge TQ7 1HS	01548 853195	www.hellokingsbridge.co.uk
Dartmouth	Mayors Ave, Dartmouth TQ6 9YY	01803 834224	www.visitdartmouth.uk
Brixham	Hobb Nobs Gift Shop, The Quay, Brixham TQ5 8AW	0844 4742233	www.englishriviera.co.uk
Paignton	The Esplanade, Paignton, TQ4 6ED	08707 070 010	www.torbay.gov.uk
Torquay	5 Vaughan Parade, Torquay TQ2 5JG	01803 211211	www.englishriviera.co.uk
Shaldon	Shaldon Car Park, Ness Drive, Shaldon TQ14 0HP	01626 873723	www.shaldon-village.co.uk
Dawlish	The Lawn, Dawlish EX7 9PW	01626 215665	www.visitsouthdevon.co.uk
Exmouth	45A The Strand, Exmouth, EX8 1AL	01395 830550	www.visitexmouth.org
Budleigh -Salterton	Fore Street, Budleigh Salterton EX9 6NG	01395 445275	www.visitbudleigh.com
Sidmouth	Ham Lane, Sidmouth EX10 8XR	01395 516441	www.visitsidmouth.co.uk
Seaton	Harbour Road, Seaton EX12 2LT	01297 21388	www.seaton.gov.uk/your-visit
Bridport	Bucky Doo Square, South Street, Bridport DT6 3LF	01308 424901	www.bridportandwestbay.co.uk
Weymouth	98 St Mary Street, Weymouth DT4 8NY	01305 779410	www.weareweymouth.co.uk
Swanage	The White House, Shore Road, Swanage BH19 1LB	01929 766018	www.swanage.gov.uk/_information.aspx
Poole	Poole Museum, 4 High Street, Poole BH15 1BW	01202 128888	www.pooletourism.com

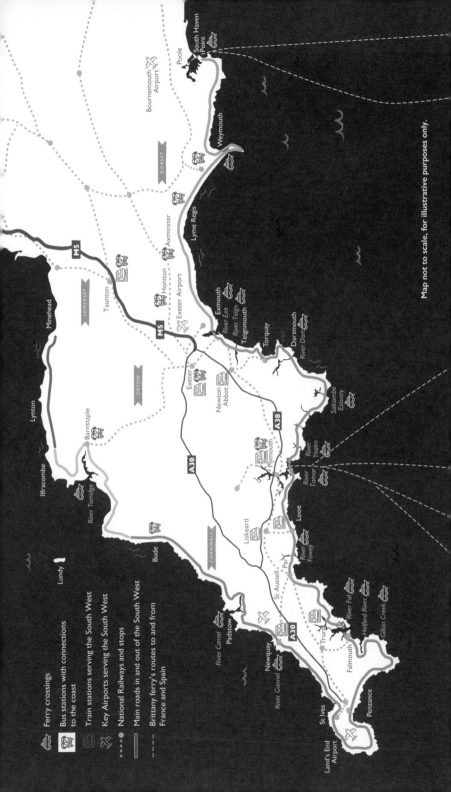

Map not to scale, for illustrative purposes only.

Legend:

🚢 Ferry crossings

🏢 Bus stations with connections to the coast

🚉 Train stations serving the South West

✈ Key Airports serving the South West

● National Railways and stops

··········· Main roads in and out of the South West

– – – – Brittany ferry's routes to and from France and Spain

Locations and features:

Lundy 1

South Haven Point

Poole

Bournemouth Airport ✈

Weymouth

DORSET

Lyme Regis

Axminster

Honiton

M5

Taunton

SOMERSET

Minehead

Lynton

Ilfracombe

Barnstaple

River Torridge

Bude

River Camel

Padstow

Newquay

River Gannel

St Ives

Land's End Airport

Penzance

Falmouth

River Fal

Helford River

Gillan Creek

Truro

A30

St Austell

Liskeard

CORNWALL

Looe

River Fowey

Fowey

Par

River Tamar

River Yealm

Plymouth

A38

Salcombe Estuary

River Dart

Dartmouth

Torquay

Teignmouth

River Teign

River Exe

Exmouth

Exeter Airport ✈

Exeter

Newton Abbot

DEVON

M5

Access to the Path by Road

The South West is well served by three major trunk roads, the M5, A303 and A30 and most of the gateway start and finish points along the South West Coast Path are served by a network of A and B roads. The A35 serves the south coast of Dorset and East Devon, and the A39 serves the north coast of Exmoor, North Devon and much of North Cornwall. Follow the A38 off the M5 at Exeter to access South Devon and South Cornwall. If you arrive in the region at one of the airports, ferry terminals or many of the mainline train stations, you can easily arrange car hire. Please note there is a toll charge on the Tamar Bridge when leaving Cornwall via the A38. More information can be found in our individual walking guides, for sale in our online shop southwestcoastpath.org.uk/books

Railways

One of the easiest ways to complete the Path is to start and finish your trip at one of the towns along the Path with a train station. As well as the following, our travel map on page 23 details the main rail links. There are regular services linking Birmingham, the North West, North East and Scotland with the South West. There is also an overnight sleeper between Paddington and Penzance. Regular South West Train services link London Waterloo, Woking, Basingstoke and Southampton with Bournemouth, Poole, Wareham (for Swanage), Dorchester (for Bridport and Lyme Regis), Weymouth, Axminster (for Lyme Regis & Seaton), Honiton (for Sidmouth).

The cost of rail tickets varies depending on peak and off-peak travel. Splitting your tickets by breaking down your journey may make a difference. For more information go to: **www.thetrainline.com/trains/great-britain/split-tickets**

To book your tickets to the South West:
- ⊕ **www.thetrainline.com**
- ☎ **0333 202 2222** 8am to 10pm

- ⊕ **www.nationalrail.co.uk**
- ☎ **03457 484950**

- ⊕ **www.traveline.info**
- ☎ **0871 200 22 33**

Bus Services

For information on buses to the South West:

Traveline:
- ⊕ **www.travelinesw.com**
- ☎ **0871 200 2233**

To buy tickets go to:
- ⊕ **www.nationalexpress.com**
- ☎ **0871 781 8181**

Megabus timetable enquiries:
- ☎ **0141 352 4444** open 24 hours a day or
- ☎ **0900 1600 900** for booking a ticket from 7am to 10pm
- ⊕ **uk.megabus.com**

Tourist Information Centres (TICs) can be very helpful with bus enquiries. For details see page 22.

Airports

There are airports in or near towns close to the Coast Path. In Path order, they are:

Newquay Airport

St Mawgan, Newquay, TR8 4RQ
Direct services from around the UK, Ireland, Germany, Portugal and Spain and indirect services from around the world.

- 01637 860600
- info@cornwallairportnewquay.com
- www.cornwallairportnewquay.com

Land's End

For flights to the Isles of Scilly: Isles of Scilly Travel, Steamship House, Quay Street, Penzance, TR18 4BZ.

- 01736 334220
- sales@islesofscilly-travel.co.uk
- www.islesofscilly-travel.co.uk

Exeter

Exeter International Airport, Exeter, EX5 2BD.

- 01392 367433
- www.exeter-airport.co.uk

Bournemouth

Bournemouth Airport Ltd., Christchurch, Bournemouth BH23 6SE.

- 01202 364000
- www.bournemouthairport.com

Sea Transport

Brittany Ferries provide a ferry link to/from Plymouth, Poole and Portsmouth to the French ports of Roscoff, Cherbourg, Caen, St Malo & Le Havre, as well as to Santander & Bilbao in Spain. Brittany Ferries, Millbay, Plymouth, Devon, PL1 3EW.

- 0330 159 7000
- www.brittany-ferries.co.uk

The Trip Planning Guide pages on our website provide suggestions for how the Path can be completed as a series of day walks, using public transport southwestcoastpath.org.uk

Bus Information

Listed below, in Path order, are details of bus services intended for guidance only. All information is correct at the time of going to print; responsibility for any inaccuracies or changes cannot be accepted by County Councils or bus travel operators. For up-to-date information, contact the relevant travel providers below. If you find yourself at a bus stop and want to know when the next bus is due, find the eight-letter reference number on the stop and text it to 84268. You will receive a reply with the scheduled times of the next three buses due at that stop.

First Bus Group:
- 0345 646 0707
- www.firstgroup.com

Traveline South West:
- 0871 200 2233
- www.travelinesw.com

Stagecoach:
- www.stagecoachbus.com
- www.bustimes.org/regions/SW

Somerset/Exmoor

From Taunton to Minehead use service 28. From Taunton there is a bus to Lyme Regis or Weymouth changing at Exeter and Axminster.

North Devon

The North Devon coast has a range of bus services. The greatest choice of destinations is from Barnstaple. There are also bus services to and from Ilfracombe and Bideford. Devon and Cornwall's First Buses are useful for those walking between North Devon and North Cornwall. Devon County Council website provides Area Bus Timetable Booklets to download:

- www.traveldevon.info/bus/
  timetables

Cornwall

Cornwall Council have a list of bus routes:
- 🌐 **www.transportforcornwall.co.uk**
- 🌐 **www.bustimes.org/operators/first-kernow**

Stagecoach run service 6 from Exeter to Bude, if you are coming to the South West by train this may be useful.

South Devon

The coastline between Plymouth and Exeter is accessible by bus from many inland towns. Apart from the main bus operators listed above, Stagecoach and Tally Ho! provide local transport.

Stagecoach
- 🌐 **www.stagecoachbus.com**

Tally Ho! Holidays
- 📞 **01548 853081**
- 🌐 **www.tallyhoholidays.co.uk**

For Plymouth Citybus map and services
- 🌐 **www.plymouth.gov.uk/parkingandtravel/publictransport**

East Devon

The East Devon coastline is accessible by bus from Exeter, Ottery St. Mary, Honiton and Axminster. Trains are also available from London Waterloo to Axminster, Honiton and Exeter. The quicker train from London Paddington stops at Exeter as do trains from Bristol. Please note, the summer and winter timetables do vary.

Dorset

The Dorset Coast is accessible by bus from various inland points including Taunton, Axminster and Honiton as well as Poole, slightly beyond the end of the Coast Path.

Plymouth-Cremyll ferry. Photographer Dom Moore

Ferries can be subject to change due to weather conditions, as well as tides and times of day, so we advise that you check with the relevant ferry or water taxi before travelling, rather than relying on the information below. All information was correct, to the best of our knowledge, at time of going to print.

Ferries & River Crossings

The nature of the Coast Path means that many ferries must be used to cross estuaries along the length of the Path. The ferry crossings below are listed in Path order.

Instow to Appledore (River Torridge)

Appledore Instow Ferry
- www.appledoreinstowferry.com
- contact@appledoreinstowferry.com

Ferry service runs: 1 April to 31 October.

Padstow to Rock (River Camel)

- 01841 532239 / 07773081574
- www.padstow-harbour.co.uk
- padstowharbour@btconnect.com

		From Padstow	From Rock
First Ferry:		08:00	
Last Ferry:	26 Oct to 31 Mar	17:00	16:45
	1 Apr to 31 May	18:00	17:45
	1 June to mid Sept	19:00	18:45
	mid Sept to 25 Oct	18:00	17:45
	1 Sept - mid Sept	18:50	18:30
	mid Sept - 31 Oct	17:50	17:30

See ferry website for departure points as these can vary.

Wave Hunters Water Taxi:
- 07778 105297
- www.wavehunters.co.uk

Water Taxi service runs: 18:45 until midnight.

Newquay to Crantock (River Gannel)

Fern Pit Ferry
- 01637 873181
- www.fernpit.co.uk
- info@fernpit.co.uk

Ferry service runs: Daily from May to mid September 09:30 to 18:00 (weather dependent).

Gillan Creek

There's no longer a ferry at Gillam Creek which is submerged roughly 3 hours either side of high water.

Taxi: For an alternative way around the river, please use one of the following:
Telstar Taxis Tel: **01326 221007**
Meneage Taxis Tel: **01326 560530 / 07773 817156**

Helford River

Helford River Boats
- 01326 250770
- www.helford-river-boats.co.uk
- helfordriverboats@yahoo.com

Ferry service runs: 1 April to 31 October: 09:30 – 17:00 on demand.

Taxi: For an alternative way around the river.
Telstar Taxis Tel: **01326 221007**
Meneage Taxis Tel: **01326 560530 / 07773 817156**

Falmouth to St Mawes (River Fal)

Cornwall Fal River Ferries - St Mawes Ferry
- 01326 741194
- www.falriver.co.uk
- info@falriver.co.uk

Ferry service runs: 7 days a week, daily, twice hourly.

Falmouth Water Taxi
- 07522 446659
- www.falmouthwatertaxi.co.uk
- skipper@falmouthwatertaxi.co.uk

Water Taxi runs: 09:00 – 21:00

St Mawes - Place Creek (Percuil River)

Cornwall Fal River Ferries - Place Ferry
- 01326 741194
- www.falriver.co.uk
- info@falriver.co.uk

Ferry service runs: April to October, 7 days a week.

Fowey to Polruan (River Fowey)

Polruan Ferry Co Ltd
- 01726 870232
- www.ctomsandson.co.uk/polruan-ferry
- enquiries@ctomsandson.co.uk

Ferry service runs:
1 May – 4 October
Monday – Friday 07:00 – 23:00
Saturday 08:00 – 23:00
Sunday 09:00 – 23:00

5 October – 30 April
Monday – Thursday 07:00 – 18:00
Friday 07:00 – 21:00
Saturday 9:00 – 18:00
Sunday 10:00 – 18:00

Cremyll (Mount Edgcumbe) to Plymouth (River Tamar)

Plymouth Boat Trips
- 01752 822105
- www.plymouthboattrips.co.uk/ferries/cremyll-ferry
- info@plymouthboattrips.co.uk

Ferry service runs:
Summer Service: 1 April to 30 September
From Cremyll:
Weekdays Monday – Thursday: 06:45 to 21:00
Friday: 06:45 – 22:00
Saturdays: 07:30 – 22:00
Sundays: 08:30 – 21:30

From Plymouth:
Monday to Thursday: 07:15 – 21:15
Friday: 07:15 – 22:15
Saturdays: 07:45 – 22:15
Sundays: 08:45 – 21:45

Winter Service: 1 Oct to 31 March
From Cremyll:
Monday to Friday: 06:45 – 18:30
Saturdays: 07:30 – 19:00
Sundays: 08:30 – 18:00

From Plymouth:
Monday to Friday: 07:15 – 18:45
Saturdays: 07:45 – 19:15
Sundays: 08:45 – 18:15

Sutton Harbour to Mount Batten (River Plym)

Mount Batten Ferry
- 07930 838614
- www.mountbattenferry.co.uk
- universalmarineuk@gmail.com

Summer ferry service runs:
From April to October:
Monday to Friday: 07:30 – 22:15
Saturday and Sunday: 09:00 – 22:15

Winter ferry service runs:
November to 31 March:
Monday to Thursday: 07:45 – 18:00
Saturday and Sunday: 08:45 – 18:00

Wembury (Warren Point) to Noss Mayo (River Yealm)

River Yealm Ferry and Water Taxi
- Bill Gregor: 07817 132757
- www.nationaltrust.org.uk/noss-mayo/features/noss-mayo-ferry

Ferry service runs: 1st April to 30th September: 10:00 to 16:00. Service may be restricted to 10:00 – 12:00 and 15:00 – 16:00 during bad weather or quieter times.

Summit To Sea
- 07399 067942
- www.ycet.co.uk
- info@ycet.co.uk

Ferry service runs: 08:00 to 10:00 and from 16:00 till late. Contact operator for further details.

Mothecombe to Wonwell (River Erme)

There is no ferry at the River Erme. Please refer to the tide times on page 30.

Bigbury (Cockleridge) to Bantham Slipway (River Avon)

Bantham Estate Passenger Ferry
- 01548 560897
- www.banthamestate.co.uk
- info@banthamestate.co.uk

Ferry service runs: 8 April to 2 October: 10:00 – 12:00 and 14:00 – 16:00

Salcombe to East Portlemouth (Salcombe Estuary)

The Salcombe Ferry
- 01548 842061/07769 319375
- www.salcombeinformation.co.uk/advertiser/salcombe-ferry
- simonshortman1@gmail.com

Ferry service runs: All year, contact Simon Shortman ferry operator for further details.

Dartmouth to Kingswear (River Dart)

Lower Dartmouth Ferry
- 01803 752342
- www.southhams.gov.uk/dartmouthlowerferry
- dlf@swdevon.gov.uk

Ferry operates all year:
From Dartmouth TQ6 9AP:
Monday to Saturday: 07:10 – 22:55
Sunday: 08:10 – 22:45

From Kingswear TQ6 0AA:
Monday to Saturday: 07:00 – 22:45
Sunday: 08:00 – 22:45

Dartmouth (River Dart)

Dartmouth Steam Railway & River Boat Co.
Dartmouth to Kingswear passenger ferry
S.Embankment, Dartmouth TQ6 9BH

- 📞 **01803 555872**
- 🌐 **www.dartmouthrailriver.co.uk/
  tours/dartmouth-to-kingswear-
  passenger-ferry**

Ferry service runs:
Monday to Saturday: 07:30 – 18:50
Sundays: 09:00 – 18:50

Shaldon to Teignmouth (River Teign)

- 📞 **Bill Hook: 07896 711822**
- 🌐 **www.teignmouthshaldonferry.co.uk**
- ✉ **info@teignmouthshaldonferry.co.uk**

Ferry service runs:
Start time: 10am all year.
Finish: 18:00 between March and end of June.
Finish: 20:00 between July-September.
Outside of these times the ferry finishes at 18:00.
Winter hours: Weds to Sun 10-4pm weather
and passenger dependent. Call for precise
details.

Starcross to Exmouth (River Exe)

Starcross to Exmouth Ferry. Mark Rackley

- 📞 **07974 022536/07934 461672/
  07779 157280**
- ✉ **starcrossferry@yahoo.co.uk**
- 🌐 **www.facebook.com/
  StarcrossExmouthFerry**

**Ferry service runs: April to October,
every day**
From Starcross: every hour from 10:10 to 16:10,
(and 17:10 mid-May to mid-September).
From Exmouth: every hour from 10:40 to
16:40 (and 17:40 mid-May to mid-September).

Turf to Topsham (River Exe)

- 📞 **Justyna Zawadzka & Paul Craven:
  07778 370582**
- 🌐 **www.topshamturfferry.com**
- ✉ **seadreamferry@gmail.com**

Ferry service runs:
1 April to 30 September
Wednesday- Friday
From Topsham: 11:00 on the hour until 21:00
From Turf: 11:30 every half hour until 21:30

Saturday:
From Topsham: 10:00 on the hour until 21:00
From Turf: 10:30 on the hour until 21:30

Sunday:
From Topsham: 10:00 on the hour until 17:00
From Turf: 10:30 on the hour until 17:30

Dawlish Warren to Exmouth (River Exe)

Exeplorer Water Taxi

- 📞 **07970 918418**
- 🌐 **www.exeplorerwatertaxis.co.uk**
- ✉ **exeplorerwatertaxis@gmail.com**

Ferry service runs: 1 April to 4 September,
daily between 08:00 - 18:00

Topsham (River Exe)

Exeter City Council, Canals and Rivers Dpt.
- 📞 **07801 203338/07801 203338**
- 🌐 **www.facebook.com/ExeterPortAuthority**

Ferry service runs:
Easter to September: 09:30 – 17:30 subject to
tide restrictions of one and a half to two hours
either side of low tide. Ferry closed Tuesday
(and Wednesday except school holidays).

October to Easter: Weekends and bank
holidays: 10:00 to 17:00 or dusk. This may be
subject to change, so visit the website or call
the above number.

Weymouth Harbour

- 📞 **01305 838423**
- 🌐 **www.weymouth-harbour.co.uk**
- ✉ **weymouthharbour@dorset.gov.uk**

Ferry service runs:
Since 16th Century, rowing ferries have
taken passengers across Weymouth Harbour.
Alternatively, contact A1 Taxis: **07758 130281**

South Haven Point to Sandbanks, Poole

Swanage Motor Road & Ferry Co
- 📞 **01929 450203**
- 🌐 **www.sandbanksferry.co.uk**
- ✉ **email@sandbanksferry.co.uk**

Ferry service runs:
Sandbanks: 07:00 – 23:00
Shell Bay: 07:10 – 23:10

TIDE TIMES

Tide times refer to the times of low water at Devonport, Plymouth. These tables act as a guide only for those wishing to wade across the Gannel (Newquay) or the Erme (Mothecombe). Please be sure to read the warnings given under the relevant section in the Guide. Walkers are advised not to wade across any of the other estuaries around the route. Those crossing the Gannel or Erme should note that there can be considerable differences in height between spring and neap tides; and the information below should be used for general timing guidance only. Again, details are available in tide tables locally.

For both the River Gannel (Newquay) and River Erme deduct 30minutes from the Devonport time.

The tidal information is reproduced by permission of the Controller of Her Majesty's Stationery Office and the UK Hydrographic Office (www.ukho.gov.uk) ©British Crown copyright. All rights reserved.

Add 1 hour for Daylight Saving Time from 26th March 2023 to 29th October 2023
Add 1 hour for Daylight Saving Time from 31st March 2024 to 27th October 2024

TIDE TIMES FOR 2023

January		Low Tide AM		Low Tide PM	
		Time	Height	Time	Height
1	Sunday	0651	2	1930	2
2	Monday	0803	2.1	2036	1.9
3	Tuesday	0908	1.9	2135	1.8
4	Wednesday	1003	1.8	2225	1.7
5	Thursday	1052	1.6	2309	1.5
6	Friday	1135	1.5	2349	1.4
7	Saturday	1214	1.4		
8	Sunday	1249	1.4	0025	1.4
9	Monday	1321	1.4	0058	1.4
10	Tuesday	1351	1.5	0128	1.5
11	Wednesday	1421	1.5	0158	1.5
12	Thursday	1450	1.6	0227	1.6
13	Friday	1524	1.7	0259	1.7
14	Saturday	1604	1.8	0335	1.8
15	Sunday	1655	2	0421	2
16	Monday	1804	2.1	0522	2.1
17	Tuesday	1929	2.1	0644	2.2
18	Wednesday	2046	1.9	0809	2
19	Thursday	2154	1.6	0922	1.7
20	Friday	2254	1.3	1027	1.4
21	Saturday	2350	1	1125	1
22	Sunday			1219	0.7
23	Monday	0040	0.8	1309	0.5
24	Tuesday	0128	0.6	1355	0.5
25	Wednesday	0212	0.6	1439	0.5
26	Thursday	0254	0.8	1520	0.7
27	Friday	0334	1	1600	1.1
28	Saturday	0413	1.3	1640	1.5
29	Sunday	0456	1.7	1725	1.8
30	Monday	0548	2.1	1821	2.2
31	Tuesday	0657	2.3	1936	2.3

February		Low Tide AM		Low Tide PM	
		Time	Height	Time	Height
1	Wednesday	0825	2.3	2100	2.2
2	Thursday	0943	2.1	2206	2
3	Friday	1038	1.8	2255	1.7
4	Saturday	1123	1.5	2337	1.5
5	Sunday	1203	1.3		
6	Monday	1238	1.2	0014	1.3
7	Tuesday	1309	1.1	0046	1.2
8	Wednesday	1337	1.1	0116	1.2
9	Thursday	1403	1.2	0143	1.2
10	Friday	1429	1.3	0210	1.2
11	Saturday	1458	1.4	0238	1.3
12	Sunday	1531	1.5	0309	1.5
13	Monday	1613	1.8	0347	1.7
14	Tuesday	1711	2	0437	1.9
15	Wednesday	1840	2.2	0552	2.2
16	Thursday	2024	2.1	0738	2.2
17	Friday	2144	1.7	0909	1.8
18	Saturday	2247	1.3	1020	1.4
19	Sunday	2341	0.8	1118	0.9
20	Monday			1209	0.5
21	Tuesday	0029	0.5	1255	0.2
22	Wednesday	0113	0.3	1338	0.1
23	Thursday	0154	0.3	1417	0.3
24	Friday	0231	0.5	1453	0.5
25	Saturday	0306	0.8	1527	0.9
26	Sunday	0339	1.2	1600	1.4
27	Monday	0414	1.6	1636	1.9
28	Tuesday	0458	2.1	1726	2.3

March		Low Tide AM		Low Tide PM	
		Time	Height	Time	Height
1	Wednesday	0603	2.4	1838	2.5
2	Thursday	0734	2.5	2018	2.5
3	Friday	0928	2.2	2148	2.1
4	Saturday	1022	1.8	2237	1.7
5	Sunday	1105	1.5	2318	1.4
6	Monday	1142	1.2	2354	1.2
7	Tuesday	1216	1		
8	Wednesday	1246	0.9	0025	1
9	Thursday	1314	0.9	0055	1
10	Friday	1340	0.9	0122	0.9
11	Saturday	1406	1	0149	1
12	Sunday	1434	1.2	0216	1.1
13	Monday	1505	1.4	0247	1.2
14	Tuesday	1545	1.7	0323	1.5
15	Wednesday	1642	2.1	0412	1.8
16	Thursday	1816	2.3	0528	2.2
17	Friday	2016	2.2	0727	2.2
18	Saturday	2136	1.7	0904	1.8
19	Sunday	2235	1.1	1010	1.2
20	Monday	2325	0.7	1104	0.7
21	Tuesday			1151	0.3
22	Wednesday	0010	0.4	1234	0.1
23	Thursday	0051	0.2	1314	0.1
24	Friday	0129	0.2	1350	0.3
25	Saturday	0204	0.4	1423	0.6
26	Sunday	0236	0.8	1453	1
27	Monday	0306	1.2	1522	1.5
28	Tuesday	0337	1.6	1554	1.9
29	Wednesday	0418	2.1	1641	2.3
30	Thursday	0524	2.4	1757	2.6
31	Friday	0652	2.5	1928	2.6

April		Low Tide AM		Low Tide PM	
		Time	Height	Time	Height
1	Saturday	0850	2.3	2109	2.2
2	Sunday	0949	1.8	2202	1.8
3	Monday	1030	1.5	2243	1.4
4	Tuesday	1107	1.2	2320	1.2
5	Wednesday	1142	1	2354	1
6	Thursday	1214	0.9		
7	Friday	1245	0.8	0026	0.9
8	Saturday	1315	0.8	0057	0.8
9	Sunday	1344	0.9	0128	0.9
10	Monday	1415	1.1	0158	1
11	Tuesday	1449	1.4	0232	1.2
12	Wednesday	1533	1.8	0312	1.5
13	Thursday	1635	2.1	0406	1.8
14	Friday	1816	2.3	0530	2.1
15	Saturday	2005	2	0723	2
16	Sunday	2117	1.6	0848	1.6
17	Monday	2213	1.1	0949	1.1
18	Tuesday	2301	0.7	1040	0.7
19	Wednesday	2345	0.5	1125	0.4
20	Thursday			1207	0.3
21	Friday	0025	0.4	1245	0.3
22	Saturday	0102	0.4	1321	0.5
23	Sunday	0136	0.6	1353	0.8
24	Monday	0208	1	1423	1.2
25	Tuesday	0238	1.3	1451	1.6
26	Wednesday	0309	1.7	1522	2
27	Thursday	0349	2.1	1608	2.3
28	Friday	0452	2.3	1722	2.5
29	Saturday	0612	2.4	1843	2.5
30	Sunday	0734	2.2	2001	2.3

May		Low Tide AM		Low Tide PM	
		Time	Height	Time	Height
1	Monday	0844	1.9	2104	1.9
2	Tuesday	0936	1.6	2154	1.6
3	Wednesday	1020	1.3	2238	1.3
4	Thursday	1100	1.1	2318	1.1
5	Friday	1139	0.9	2356	0.9
6	Saturday	1216	0.9		
7	Sunday	1252	0.9	0033	0.8
8	Monday	1328	1	0110	0.8
9	Tuesday	1405	1.2	0147	1
10	Wednesday	1447	1.4	0228	1.2
11	Thursday	1537	1.7	0315	1.4
12	Friday	1644	2	0416	1.7
13	Saturday	1810	2.1	0534	1.9
14	Sunday	1937	1.9	0703	1.8
15	Monday	2045	1.6	0818	1.5
16	Tuesday	2142	1.2	0918	1.2
17	Wednesday	2232	1	1010	0.9
18	Thursday	2317	0.8	1056	0.8
19	Friday	2358	0.7	1139	0.7
20	Saturday			1218	0.8
21	Sunday	0036	0.8	1254	0.9
22	Monday	0112	1	1327	1.1
23	Tuesday	0145	1.2	1358	1.4
24	Wednesday	0217	1.4	1429	1.7
25	Thursday	0251	1.7	1503	1.9
26	Friday	0329	1.9	1544	2.1
27	Saturday	0421	2.1	1643	2.3
28	Sunday	0526	2.2	1753	2.4
29	Monday	0635	2.1	1902	2.2
30	Tuesday	0740	2	2005	2
31	Wednesday	0838	1.7	2102	1.7

June		Low Tide AM		Low Tide PM	
		Time	Height	Time	Height
1	Thursday	0931	1.5	2154	1.5
2	Friday	1020	1.3	2243	1.2
3	Saturday	1106	1.1	2329	1
4	Sunday	1151	1		
5	Monday	1235	0.9	0014	0.9
6	Tuesday	1319	1	0058	0.9
7	Wednesday	1405	1.1	0144	0.9
8	Thursday	1452	1.3	0232	1
9	Friday	1544	1.5	0323	1.2
10	Saturday	1641	1.6	0418	1.4
11	Sunday	1746	1.8	0520	1.5
12	Monday	1856	1.8	0628	1.6
13	Tuesday	2005	1.7	0737	1.6
14	Wednesday	2107	1.5	0840	1.5
15	Thursday	2201	1.4	0936	1.3
16	Friday	2251	1.2	1027	1.2
17	Saturday	2335	1.2	1113	1.2
18	Sunday			1155	1.2
19	Monday	0016	1.1	1233	1.2
20	Tuesday	0054	1.2	1308	1.3
21	Wednesday	0130	1.3	1342	1.4
22	Thursday	0203	1.4	1414	1.6
23	Friday	0235	1.6	1446	1.7
24	Saturday	0309	1.7	1520	1.9
25	Sunday	0346	1.8	1600	2
26	Monday	0431	1.9	1651	2.1
27	Tuesday	0528	2	1756	2.2
28	Wednesday	0636	2	1907	2.1
29	Thursday	0743	1.9	2014	1.9
30	Friday	0846	1.7	2116	1.7

TIDE TIMES

July		Low Tide AM		Low Tide PM	
		Time	Height	Time	Height
1	Saturday	0945	1.5	2214	1.4
2	Sunday	1041	1.3	2309	1.1
3	Monday	1134	1.1		
4	Tuesday	1225	1	0001	0.9
5	Wednesday	1315	0.9	0052	0.8
6	Thursday	1403	0.9	0142	0.7
7	Friday	1450	0.9	0230	0.7
8	Saturday	1536	1.1	0317	0.8
9	Sunday	1622	1.3	0404	1
10	Monday	1712	1.5	0452	1.3
11	Tuesday	1809	1.8	0545	1.5
12	Wednesday	1917	1.9	0646	1.8
13	Thursday	2029	1.9	0755	1.9
14	Friday	2135	1.8	0903	1.8
15	Saturday	2232	1.6	1003	1.7
16	Sunday	2321	1.4	1054	1.5
17	Monday			1139	1.4
18	Tuesday	0004	1.3	1219	1.3
19	Wednesday	0043	1.3	1256	1.3
20	Thursday	0118	1.2	1328	1.3
21	Friday	0148	1.3	1357	1.4
22	Saturday	0216	1.4	1425	1.5
23	Sunday	0243	1.5	1452	1.6
24	Monday	0310	1.6	1522	1.7
25	Tuesday	0343	1.7	1559	1.9
26	Wednesday	0426	1.8	1649	2
27	Thursday	0524	2	1802	2.2
28	Friday	0646	2.1	1931	2.1
29	Saturday	0810	2	2048	1.9
30	Sunday	0921	1.7	2156	1.5
31	Monday	1026	1.4	2257	1.1

August		Low Tide AM		Low Tide PM	
		Time	Height	Time	Height
1	Tuesday	1124	1.1	2353	0.8
2	Wednesday	1217	0.8		
3	Thursday	1306	0.6	0044	0.5
4	Friday	1351	0.5	0132	0.4
5	Saturday	1434	0.6	0216	0.4
6	Sunday	1514	0.8	0258	0.5
7	Monday	1554	1.1	0338	0.8
8	Tuesday	1634	1.5	0417	1.2
9	Wednesday	1722	1.9	0500	1.6
10	Thursday	1826	2.2	0553	2
11	Friday	1953	2.3	0704	2.3
12	Saturday	2122	2.1	0836	2.3
13	Sunday	2222	1.8	0950	2
14	Monday	2310	1.5	1042	1.7
15	Tuesday	2351	1.3	1126	1.5
16	Wednesday			1205	1.3
17	Thursday	0027	1.2	1239	1.2
18	Friday	0059	1.1	1308	1.2
19	Saturday	0126	1.1	1334	1.2
20	Sunday	0150	1.2	1359	1.3
21	Monday	0213	1.3	1423	1.4
22	Tuesday	0238	1.4	1450	1.5
23	Wednesday	0307	1.5	1522	1.7
24	Thursday	0343	1.8	1606	2
25	Friday	0433	2	1711	2.2
26	Saturday	0554	2.3	1900	2.3
27	Sunday	0748	2.2	2034	2
28	Monday	0911	1.9	2147	1.5
29	Tuesday	1017	1.4	2248	1
30	Wednesday	1113	1	2341	0.6
31	Thursday	1203	0.6		

September		Low Tide AM		Low Tide PM	
		Time	Height	Time	Height
1	Friday	1248	0.4	0028	0.3
2	Saturday	1331	0.3	0112	0.2
3	Sunday	1410	0.4	0153	0.2
4	Monday	1446	0.7	0231	0.5
5	Tuesday	1521	1.1	0306	0.9
6	Wednesday	1557	1.6	0340	1.3
7	Thursday	1640	2.1	0416	1.8
8	Friday	1743	2.5	0505	2.3
9	Saturday	1920	2.6	0618	2.6
10	Sunday	2114	2.3	0818	2.5
11	Monday	2207	1.9	0936	2.2
12	Tuesday	2249	1.5	1024	1.8
13	Wednesday	2326	1.2	1104	1.4
14	Thursday			1140	1.2
15	Friday	0000	1.1	1212	1.1
16	Saturday	0030	1	1240	1.1
17	Sunday	0056	1	1306	1.1
18	Monday	0120	1.1	1331	1.2
19	Tuesday	0144	1.2	1356	1.3
20	Wednesday	0209	1.3	1423	1.4
21	Thursday	0238	1.5	1456	1.7
22	Friday	0313	1.8	1539	2
23	Saturday	0403	2.2	1647	2.3
24	Sunday	0529	2.5	1849	2.4
25	Monday	740	2.3	2028	2
26	Tuesday	0903	1.9	2137	1.4
27	Wednesday	1003	1.3	2232	0.9
28	Thursday	1055	0.9	2321	0.5
29	Friday	1142	0.5		
30	Saturday	1225	0.3	0005	0.3

October		Low Tide AM		Low Tide PM	
		Time	Height	Time	Height
1	Sunday	1305	0.3	0047	0.2
2	Monday	1342	0.5	0125	0.4
3	Tuesday	1417	0.8	0201	0.7
4	Wednesday	1450	1.3	0233	1.1
5	Thursday	1524	1.7	0304	1.5
6	Friday	1605	2.2	0338	2
7	Saturday	1709	2.6	0425	2.5
8	Sunday	1844	2.7	0541	2.8
9	Monday	2044	2.4	0732	2.7
10	Tuesday	2134	1.9	0903	2.3
11	Wednesday	2214	1.6	0950	1.9
12	Thursday	2250	1.3	1029	1.5
13	Friday	2323	1.1	1104	1.3
14	Saturday	2354	1	1137	1.1
15	Sunday			1208	1.1
16	Monday	0023	1	1237	1.1
17	Tuesday	0051	1.1	1306	1.1
18	Wednesday	0119	1.2	1335	1.2
19	Thursday	0147	1.3	1406	1.4
20	Friday	0219	1.6	1442	1.7
21	Saturday	0258	1.9	1531	2
22	Sunday	0354	2.3	1648	2.3
23	Monday	0530	2.5	1842	2.3
24	Tuesday	0727	2.2	2011	1.9
25	Wednesday	0843	1.8	2115	1.4
26	Thursday	0941	1.4	2208	1
27	Friday	1030	0.9	2255	0.6
28	Saturday	1116	0.7	2339	0.5
29	Sunday	1159	0.6		
30	Monday	1238	0.6	0019	0.5
31	Tuesday	1316	0.8	0057	0.7

November		Low Tide AM		Low Tide PM	
		Time	Height	Time	Height
1	Wednesday	1350	1.1	0132	1
2	Thursday	1424	1.5	0204	1.3
3	Friday	1459	1.8	0235	1.7
4	Saturday	1540	2.2	0309	2.1
5	Sunday	1639	2.5	0354	2.5
6	Monday	1757	2.6	0504	2.7
7	Tuesday	1926	2.5	0629	2.7
8	Wednesday	2035	2.1	0754	2.5
9	Thursday	2122	1.8	0854	2.1
10	Friday	2203	1.5	0940	1.8
11	Saturday	2241	1.3	1021	1.5
12	Sunday	2317	1.2	1059	1.3
13	Monday	2353	1.1	1136	1.2
14	Tuesday			1212	1.1
15	Wednesday	0027	1.1	1247	1.1
16	Thursday	0101	1.2	1323	1.2
17	Friday	0137	1.4	1402	1.4
18	Saturday	0216	1.6	1446	1.6
19	Sunday	0302	1.9	1541	1.9
20	Monday	0403	2.1	1653	2
21	Tuesday	0524	2.3	1819	2
22	Wednesday	0655	2.1	1939	1.8
23	Thursday	0810	1.9	2043	1.5
24	Friday	0910	1.5	2138	1.2
25	Saturday	1003	1.2	2227	1
26	Sunday	1050	1	2312	0.9
27	Monday	1135	0.9	2354	0.9
28	Tuesday	1216	1		
29	Wednesday	1255	1.1	0033	1
30	Thursday	1332	1.3	0109	1.2

December		Low Tide AM		Low Tide PM	
		Time	Height	Time	Height
1	Friday	1407	1.5	0143	1.5
2	Saturday	1443	1.8	0216	1.7
3	Sunday	1521	2	0251	2
4	Monday	1607	2.3	0331	2.2
5	Tuesday	1705	2.4	0422	2.4
6	Wednesday	1811	2.4	0527	2.5
7	Thursday	1918	2.3	0639	2.5
8	Friday	2018	2	0745	2.3
9	Saturday	2111	1.8	0844	2.1
10	Sunday	2159	1.6	0936	1.8
11	Monday	2244	1.4	1023	1.5
12	Tuesday	2328	1.3	1108	1.3
13	Wednesday			1153	1.2
14	Thursday	0010	1.2	1236	1.1
15	Friday	0053	1.2	1321	1.1
16	Saturday	0137	1.2	1406	1.2
17	Sunday	0222	1.4	1454	1.3
18	Monday	0310	1.5	1545	1.4
19	Tuesday	0403	1.7	1641	1.6
20	Wednesday	0502	1.9	1743	1.7
21	Thursday	0610	2	1853	1.8
22	Friday	0724	1.9	2003	1.8
23	Saturday	0834	1.8	2106	1.6
24	Sunday	0935	1.6	2201	1.5
25	Monday	1029	1.5	2251	1.4
26	Tuesday	1118	1.3	2337	1.3
27	Wednesday	1202	1.2		
28	Thursday	1243	1.2	0018	1.3
29	Friday	1321	1.3	0056	1.3
30	Saturday	1356	1.4	0131	1.4
31	Sunday	1429	1.6	0204	1.6

TIDE TIMES FOR 2024

January		Low Tide AM		Low Tide PM	
		Time	Height	Time	Height
1	Monday	0235	1.7	1501	1.7
2	Tuesday	0306	1.9	1533	1.9
3	Wednesday	0340	2	1609	2
4	Thursday	421	2.2	1655	2.2
5	Friday	0517	2.3	1758	2.2
6	Saturday	0631	2.4	1912	2.2
7	Sunday	0747	2.3	2020	2.1
8	Monday	0853	2	2122	1.8
9	Tuesday	0953	1.7	2218	1.6
10	Wednesday	1048	1.4	2311	1.3
11	Thursday	1141	1.1		
12	Friday	0002	1.1	1231	0.9
13	Saturday	0050	1	1319	0.8
14	Sunday	0137	0.9	1405	0.7
15	Monday	0221	0.9	1450	0.8
16	Tuesday	0305	1	1533	0.9
17	Wednesday	0347	1.2	1617	1.2
18	Thursday	0432	1.5	1704	1.5
19	Friday	0524	1.8	1800	1.8
20	Saturday	0629	2	1910	2.1
21	Sunday	0752	2.1	2032	2.1
22	Monday	0914	2	2144	1.9
23	Tuesday	1018	1.8	2240	1.7
24	Wednesday	1110	1.5	2328	1.5
25	Thursday	1155	1.3		
26	Friday	0010	1.3	1235	1.2
27	Saturday	0047	1.2	1312	1.1
28	Sunday	0120	1.2	1343	1.2
29	Monday	0149	1.3	1411	1.2
30	Tuesday	0215	1.4	1435	1.4
31	Wednesday	0239	1.5	1458	1.5

February		Low Tide AM		Low Tide PM	
		Time	Height	Time	Height
1	Thursday	0303	1.6	1523	1.7
2	Friday	0333	1.8	1556	1.9
3	Saturday	0413	2	1642	2.1
4	Sunday	0511	2.2	1752	2.3
5	Monday	0646	2.4	1932	2.3
6	Tuesday	0818	2.2	2053	2
7	Wednesday	0932	1.8	2201	1.7
8	Thursday	1035	1.4	2301	1.3
9	Friday	1131	1	2353	0.9
10	Saturday	1222	0.6		
11	Sunday	0041	0.6	1308	0.4
12	Monday	0126	0.4	1352	0.3
13	Tuesday	0208	0.4	1433	0.4
14	Wednesday	0247	0.6	1511	0.6
15	Thursday	0324	0.8	1548	1
16	Friday	0402	1.2	1627	1.5
17	Saturday	0445	1.7	1713	1.9
18	Sunday	0541	2.1	1816	2.3
19	Monday	0707	2.4	1959	2.4
20	Tuesday	0906	2.2	2136	2.2
21	Wednesday	1012	1.9	2232	1.8
22	Thursday	1100	1.5	2316	1.4
23	Friday	1142	1.2	2356	1.2
24	Saturday	1219	1		
25	Sunday	0031	1	1252	0.9
26	Monday	0101	1	1321	0.9
27	Tuesday	0127	1	1345	1
28	Wednesday	0149	1.1	1405	1.1
29	Thursday	0210	1.2	1425	1.3

TIDE TIMES

March		Low Tide AM		Low Tide PM	
		Time	Height	Time	Height
1	Friday	0233	1.3	1448	1.4
2	Saturday	0300	1.5	1518	1.7
3	Sunday	0336	1.8	1559	1.9
4	Monday	0427	2.1	1659	2.3
5	Tuesday	0558	2.3	1854	2.4
6	Wednesday	0755	2.2	2034	2.1
7	Thursday	0917	1.7	2148	1.6
8	Friday	1022	1.2	2247	1.1
9	Saturday	1116	0.7	2338	0.7
10	Sunday	1205	0.3		
11	Monday	0024	0.3	1249	0.1
12	Tuesday	0106	0.2	1330	0.1
13	Wednesday	0146	0.2	1409	0.2
14	Thursday	0223	0.4	1444	0.5
15	Friday	0259	0.7	1519	1
16	Saturday	0334	1.2	1554	1.5
17	Sunday	0414	1.7	1637	2
18	Monday	0509	2.2	1740	2.4
19	Tuesday	0633	2.5	1922	2.6
20	Wednesday	0855	2.3	2118	2.2
21	Thursday	0953	1.8	2210	1.8
22	Friday	1037	1.4	2252	1.4
23	Saturday	1116	1.1	2329	1.1
24	Sunday	1151	0.9		
25	Monday	0003	1	1222	0.9
26	Tuesday	0032	0.9	1250	0.9
27	Wednesday	0058	0.9	1313	0.9
28	Thursday	0121	1	1335	1.1
29	Friday	0143	1.1	1357	1.2
30	Saturday	0208	1.2	1421	1.4
31	Sunday	0236	1.4	1453	1.6

April		Low Tide AM		Low Tide PM	
		Time	Height	Time	Height
1	Monday	0313	1.7	1534	1.9
2	Tuesday	0407	2	1638	2.3
3	Wednesday	0544	2.2	1835	2.4
4	Thursday	0738	2.1	2016	2
5	Friday	0858	1.6	2128	1.5
6	Saturday	1000	1.1	2225	1
7	Sunday	1053	0.6	2314	0.6
8	Monday	1140	0.3		
9	Tuesday	0000	0.3	1224	0.1
10	Wednesday	0042	0.2	1304	0.2
11	Thursday	0122	0.3	1342	0.4
12	Friday	0159	0.5	1418	0.7
13	Saturday	0235	0.9	1452	1.2
14	Sunday	0311	1.3	1528	1.7
15	Monday	0353	1.8	1613	2.1
16	Tuesday	0448	2.2	1715	2.5
17	Wednesday	0606	2.4	1840	2.6
18	Thursday	0808	2.3	2031	2.3
19	Friday	0913	1.9	2129	1.9
20	Saturday	0958	1.5	2212	1.5
21	Sunday	1037	1.3	2251	1.3
22	Monday	1112	1.1	2326	1.1
23	Tuesday	1144	1	2357	1
24	Wednesday	1214	1		
25	Thursday	0026	1	1241	1
26	Friday	0054	1	1308	1.1
27	Saturday	0122	1.1	1335	1.2
28	Sunday	0151	1.2	1405	1.4
29	Monday	0225	1.4	1442	1.6
30	Tuesday	0309	1.7	1530	1.9

May		Low Tide AM		Low Tide PM	
		Time	Height	Time	Height
1	Wednesday	0410	1.9	1641	2.2
2	Thursday	0541	2	1820	2.2
3	Friday	0715	1.8	1949	1.9
4	Saturday	0830	1.5	2058	1.5
5	Sunday	0931	1.1	2156	1.1
6	Monday	1024	0.7	2247	0.8
7	Tuesday	1112	0.5	2334	0.5
8	Wednesday	1157	0.4		
9	Thursday	0017	0.5	1239	0.5
10	Friday	0058	0.5	1318	0.7
11	Saturday	0138	0.8	1355	1
12	Sunday	0216	1.1	1432	1.3
13	Monday	0255	1.4	1511	1.7
14	Tuesday	0337	1.8	1555	2.1
15	Wednesday	0429	2.1	1650	2.3
16	Thursday	0532	2.2	1757	2.4
17	Friday	0646	2.2	1911	2.3
18	Saturday	0759	2	2020	2.1
19	Sunday	0856	1.8	2115	1.8
20	Monday	0942	1.5	2201	1.6
21	Tuesday	1023	1.4	2242	1.4
22	Wednesday	1102	1.2	2320	1.2
23	Thursday	1138	1.2	2357	1.1
24	Friday	1214	1.1		
25	Saturday	0032	1.1	1249	1.2
26	Sunday	0109	1.1	1325	1.3
27	Monday	0147	1.2	1403	1.4
28	Tuesday	0229	1.3	1447	1.5
29	Wednesday	0318	1.5	1539	1.7
30	Thursday	0417	1.6	1642	1.9
31	Friday	0527	1.7	1756	1.9

June		Low Tide AM		Low Tide PM	
		Time	Height	Time	Height
1	Saturday	0642	1.6	1913	1.8
2	Sunday	0753	1.5	2022	1.6
3	Monday	0857	1.3	2124	1.3
4	Tuesday	0954	1.1	2219	1.1
5	Wednesday	1046	1	2310	0.9
6	Thursday	1134	0.9	2357	0.9
7	Friday	1218	0.9		
8	Saturday	0041	0.9	1300	1
9	Sunday	0123	1	1340	1.2
10	Monday	0203	1.2	1418	1.4
11	Tuesday	0242	1.4	1456	1.6
12	Wednesday	0322	1.6	1535	1.8
13	Thursday	0404	1.8	1619	2
14	Friday	0450	2	1709	2.2
15	Saturday	0544	2.1	1807	2.2
16	Sunday	0644	2.1	1910	2.2
17	Monday	0745	2	2011	2
18	Tuesday	0842	1.8	2108	1.8
19	Wednesday	0934	1.7	2159	1.6
20	Thursday	1023	1.5	2247	1.4
21	Friday	1109	1.3	2333	1.2
22	Saturday	1154	1.2		
23	Sunday	0018	1.1	1238	1.2
24	Monday	0103	1	1322	1.1
25	Tuesday	0148	1	1406	1.2
26	Wednesday	0233	1	1451	1.2
27	Thursday	0320	1.1	1538	1.3
28	Friday	0409	1.2	1628	1.5
29	Saturday	0502	1.4	1725	1.6
30	Sunday	0603	1.6	1830	1.8

July		Low Tide AM		Low Tide PM	
		Time	Height	Time	Height
1	Monday	0711	1.6	1943	1.8
2	Tuesday	0822	1.6	2054	1.7
3	Wednesday	0927	1.6	2158	1.5
4	Thursday	1026	1.4	2255	1.3
5	Friday	1119	1.3	2345	1.2
6	Saturday	1206	1.2		
7	Sunday	0031	1.1	1249	1.2
8	Monday	0113	1.1	1329	1.2
9	Tuesday	0152	1.1	1405	1.3
10	Wednesday	0227	1.2	1437	1.4
11	Thursday	0259	1.4	1508	1.6
12	Friday	0329	1.6	1539	1.8
13	Saturday	0400	1.8	1613	1.9
14	Sunday	0437	1.9	1657	2.1
15	Monday	0528	2.1	1759	2.3
16	Tuesday	0637	2.2	1914	2.2
17	Wednesday	0749	2.1	2023	2.1
18	Thursday	0854	1.9	2126	1.8
19	Friday	0953	1.7	2224	1.5
20	Saturday	1049	1.4	2318	1.2
21	Sunday	1141	1.2		
22	Monday	0008	1	1230	1
23	Tuesday	0056	0.8	1316	0.9
24	Wednesday	0142	0.7	1400	0.8
25	Thursday	0226	0.6	1442	0.8
26	Friday	0307	0.7	1523	1
27	Saturday	0349	1	1605	1.2
28	Sunday	0432	1.3	1651	1.5
29	Monday	0522	1.6	1749	1.9
30	Tuesday	0627	1.9	1905	2.1
31	Wednesday	0750	2.1	2036	2.1

August		Low Tide AM		Low Tide PM	
		Time	Height	Time	Height
1	Thursday	0914	2	2152	1.8
2	Friday	1019	1.7	2250	1.5
3	Saturday	1111	1.4	2338	1.2
4	Sunday	1157	1.2		
5	Monday	0021	1.1	1237	1.1
6	Tuesday	0100	1	1313	1.1
7	Wednesday	0134	1	1344	1.1
8	Thursday	0203	1.1	1411	1.2
9	Friday	0228	1.2	1435	1.4
10	Saturday	0249	1.4	1456	1.6
11	Sunday	0310	1.6	1520	1.8
12	Monday	0336	1.8	1553	2
13	Tuesday	0414	2	1642	2.2
14	Wednesday	0514	2.3	1812	2.4
15	Thursday	0701	2.4	1950	2.3
16	Friday	0825	2.2	2104	1.9
17	Saturday	0934	1.8	2208	1.5
18	Sunday	1034	1.4	2304	1.1
19	Monday	1128	1.1	2355	0.7
20	Tuesday	1217	0.7		
21	Wednesday	0042	0.5	1301	0.5
22	Thursday	0126	0.3	1343	0.5
23	Friday	0207	0.4	1423	0.5
24	Saturday	0245	0.6	1501	0.8
25	Sunday	0322	0.9	1538	1.1
26	Monday	0400	1.4	1620	1.6
27	Tuesday	0445	1.8	1714	2.1
28	Wednesday	0547	2.3	1836	2.4
29	Thursday	0730	2.4	2038	2.3
30	Friday	0913	2.2	2149	1.9
31	Saturday	1012	1.8	2239	1.5

September		Low Tide AM		Low Tide PM	
		Time	Height	Time	Height
1	Sunday	1058	1.4	2322	1.2
2	Monday	1139	1.2		
3	Tuesday	0001	1	1215	1
4	Wednesday	0036	0.9	1248	0.9
5	Thursday	0106	0.9	1316	1
6	Friday	0131	1	1339	1.1
7	Saturday	0151	1.2	1359	1.3
8	Sunday	0209	1.3	1418	1.5
9	Monday	0229	1.5	1441	1.7
10	Tuesday	0255	1.7	1512	1.9
11	Wednesday	0330	2	1557	2.2
12	Thursday	0423	2.3	1718	2.5
13	Friday	0620	2.5	1927	2.4
14	Saturday	0806	2.3	2047	1.9
15	Sunday	0918	1.8	2151	1.4
16	Monday	1017	1.3	2246	0.9
17	Tuesday	1109	0.9	2334	0.5
18	Wednesday	1156	0.6		
19	Thursday	0019	0.3	1239	0.4
20	Friday	0102	0.2	1320	0.3
21	Saturday	0141	0.3	1359	0.5
22	Sunday	0219	0.6	1436	0.8
23	Monday	0254	1	1513	1.3
24	Tuesday	0331	1.6	1554	1.8
25	Wednesday	0415	2.1	1650	2.3
26	Thursday	0519	2.5	1818	2.6
27	Friday	0721	2.7	2031	2.3
28	Saturday	0858	2.3	2130	1.9
29	Sunday	0949	1.9	2215	1.5
30	Monday	1032	1.5	2254	1.2

October		Low Tide AM		Low Tide PM	
		Time	Height	Time	Height
1	Tuesday	1110	1.2	2331	1
2	Wednesday	1145	1		
3	Thursday	0003	0.9	1216	1
4	Friday	0032	1	1243	1
5	Saturday	0056	1.1	1306	1.2
6	Sunday	0116	1.2	1327	1.3
7	Monday	0136	1.4	1349	1.4
8	Tuesday	0158	1.5	1414	1.6
9	Wednesday	0226	1.8	1447	1.9
10	Thursday	0303	2.1	1534	2.2
11	Friday	0358	2.4	1701	2.5
12	Saturday	0555	2.6	1905	2.3
13	Sunday	0744	2.3	2025	1.9
14	Monday	0855	1.8	2127	1.3
15	Tuesday	0953	1.3	2220	0.9
16	Wednesday	1043	0.9	2308	0.6
17	Thursday	1130	0.6	2354	0.4
18	Friday	1214	0.4		
19	Saturday	0035	0.4	1256	0.5
20	Sunday	0115	0.5	1335	0.6
21	Monday	0153	0.9	1414	1
22	Tuesday	0230	1.3	1453	1.4
23	Wednesday	0308	1.8	1536	1.9
24	Thursday	0354	2.2	1633	2.3
25	Friday	0457	2.6	1754	2.5
26	Saturday	0634	2.7	1949	2.4
27	Sunday	0815	2.4	2051	2
28	Monday	0910	2	2137	1.7
29	Tuesday	0954	1.7	2216	1.4
30	Wednesday	1033	1.4	2252	1.2
31	Thursday	1108	1.2	2325	1.2

TIDE TIMES

November		Low Tide AM		Low Tide PM	
		Time	Height	Time	Height
1	Friday	1140	1.2	2355	1.2
2	Saturday	1210	1.2		
3	Sunday	0022	1.2	1237	1.3
4	Monday	0047	1.3	1304	1.3
5	Tuesday	0113	1.4	1331	1.5
6	Wednesday	0141	1.6	1403	1.6
7	Thursday	0214	1.8	1442	1.9
8	Friday	0256	2	1535	2.1
9	Saturday	0357	2.3	1657	2.3
10	Sunday	0533	2.4	1834	2.1
11	Monday	0710	2.2	1953	1.8
12	Tuesday	0823	1.8	2056	1.4
13	Wednesday	0923	1.4	2151	1.1
14	Thursday	1016	1.1	2241	0.8
15	Friday	1105	0.8	2328	0.7
16	Saturday	1151	0.7		
17	Sunday	0012	0.7	1235	0.7
18	Monday	0054	0.9	1317	0.9
19	Tuesday	0134	1.1	1358	1.2
20	Wednesday	0213	1.4	1440	1.5
21	Thursday	0254	1.8	1525	1.8
22	Friday	0339	2.1	1615	2.1
23	Saturday	0432	2.4	1716	2.3
24	Sunday	0538	2.5	1828	2.4
25	Monday	0655	2.5	1942	2.2
26	Tuesday	0805	2.3	2039	2
27	Wednesday	0900	2	2126	1.8
28	Thursday	0946	1.8	2207	1.6
29	Friday	1027	1.6	2245	1.5
30	Saturday	1105	1.5	2320	1.4

December		Low Tide AM		Low Tide PM	
		Time	Height	Time	Height
1	Sunday	1141	1.4	2355	1.4
2	Monday	1216	1.3		
3	Tuesday	0028	1.4	1251	1.4
4	Wednesday	0103	1.4	1327	1.4
5	Thursday	0139	1.5	1406	1.5
6	Friday	0218	1.7	1450	1.6
7	Saturday	0304	1.8	1541	1.8
8	Sunday	0359	2	1643	1.9
9	Monday	0506	2.1	1754	1.9
10	Tuesday	0624	2.1	1910	1.8
11	Wednesday	0742	1.9	2019	1.6
12	Thursday	0850	1.7	2121	1.4
13	Friday	0950	1.4	2216	1.3
14	Saturday	1044	1.2	2308	1.1
15	Sunday	1135	1.1	2356	1.1
16	Monday	1222	1		
17	Tuesday	0040	1.1	1307	1
18	Wednesday	0123	1.2	1350	1.2
19	Thursday	0203	1.4	1431	1.3
20	Friday	0242	1.6	1511	1.6
21	Saturday	0320	1.8	1550	1.8
22	Sunday	0400	2	1632	2
23	Monday	0445	2.2	1720	2.2
24	Tuesday	0540	2.3	1817	2.3
25	Wednesday	0644	2.4	1920	2.2
26	Thursday	0751	2.3	2022	2.1
27	Friday	0852	2.1	2117	1.9
28	Saturday	0945	1.9	2207	1.8
29	Sunday	1034	1.7	2253	1.6
30	Monday	1119	1.5	2336	1.4
31	Tuesday	1203	1.3		

Sea tractor to Burgh Island, South Devon. Photographer Neill Richardson

WaterFit

Protecting rivers and seas together

In April 2022, we launched **WaterFit**, our new plan for healthy rivers and seas, which will see us dramatically reduce our use of storm overflows, maintain our 100% coastal bathing water quality standards all year round, and remove our impact on river water quality across the region by 2030.

COAST PATH

If you spot anything you think could be a sewage leak or pollution across Devon or Cornwall, please call us on

0344 3462020

so that we can investigate as a priority.

South West
Water

Below we've split the Path into 52 day lengths. Each of these allows time for breaks and covers what we think is a comfortable day's walking, whilst finishing at places where you can find accommodation. If you think you'd like to go slower or faster than this, you can find alternative itinerary suggestions on our website.

Day	Distance (Rounded)		From - to
Week 1 (Seven days)			
1	9mi	14km	Minehead – Porlock Weir *Take National Rail main line to Taunton; bus Taunton - Minehead; or National Express coach to Minehead*
2	12mi	20km	Porlock Weir – Lynton
3	13mi	21km	Lynton – Combe Martin
4	13mi	20km	Combe Martin – Woolacombe
5	16mi	27km	Woolacombe – Braunton
6	12mi	20km	Braunton – Instow
7	11mi	18km	Instow – Westward Ho!
Total	**86mi**	**140km**	*Take bus Westward Ho! - Barnstaple; train Barnstaple - Exeter; National Rail main line from Exeter; or National Express coach from Westward Ho!*
Week 2 (Seven days)			
1	11mi	18km	Westward Ho! – Clovelly *National Rail main line to Exeter; train Exeter - Barnstaple; bus Barnstaple - Westward Ho!; or National Express coach to Westward Ho!*
2	10mi	16km	Clovelly – Hartland Quay
3	15mi	25km	Hartland Quay – Bude
4	10mi	16km	Bude – Crackington Haven
5	11mi	18km	Crackington Haven – Tintagel
6	9mi	15km	Tintagel – Port Isaac
7	12mi	19km	Port Isaac - Padstow
Total	**78mi**	**127km**	*Bus to Bodmin Parkway; National Rail main line from Bodmin Parkway*
Week 3 (Six days)			
1	14mi	22km	Padstow – Porthcothan *National Rail main line to Bodmin Parkway; bus Bodmin Parkway - Padstow*
2	11mi	18km	Porthcothan – Newquay
3	11mi	18km	Newquay – Perranporth
4	12mi	20km	Perranporth – Portreath
5	12mi	20km	Portreath – Hayle
6	6mi	9km	Hayle – St Ives
Total	**66mi**	**107km**	*Train St Ives-St Erth; National Rail main line from St Erth; or National Express coach from St Ives*
Week 4 (Six days)			
1	14mi	22km	St Ives – Pendeen Watch *National Rail main line to St Erth; train St Erth - St Ives; or National Express coach to St Ives*
2	9mi	15km	Pendeen Watch – Sennen Cove
3	12mi	19km	Sennen Cove – Lamorna Cove
4	9mi	15km	Lamorna Cove – Marazion
5	11mi	17km	Marazion – Porthleven
6	13mi	22km	Porthleven – Lizard
Total	**68mi**	**110km**	*Bus Lizard Town - Redruth; National Rail main line from Redruth*

Week 5 (Six days)

Day	Distance (Rounded)		From - to
1	11mi	17km	Lizard – Coverack *National Rail main line to Redruth; Bus Lizard Town - Redruth*
2	13mi	21km	Coverack – Helford
3	10mi	16km	Helford – Falmouth
4	14mi	22km	Falmouth – Portloe
5	12mi	20km	Portloe – Mevagissey
6	12mi	19km	Mevagissey – Par
Total	72mi	115km	*National Rail main line from Par*

Week 6 (Seven days)

Day	Distance (Rounded)		From - to
1	13mi	21km	Par – Polperro *National Rail main line to Par*
2	12mi	20km	Polperro – Portwrinkle
3	13mi	21km	Portwrinkle – Plymouth
4	15mi	24km	Plymouth – Wembury (ferry crossing)
5	14mi	22km	Wembury (ferry crossing) – Bigbury on Sea
6	14mi	22km	Bigbury on Sea – Salcombe
7	13mi	21km	Salcombe – Torcross
Total	94mi	151km	*Bus Torcross - Plymouth; National Rail main line or National Express coach from Plymouth*

Week 7 (Six days)

Day	Distance (Rounded)		From - to
1	10mi	16km	Torcross – Dartmouth *National rail main line or National Express coach to Plymouth; bus Plymouth - Torcross*
2	11mi	17km	Dartmouth – Brixham
3	11mi	17km	Brixham – Babbacombe
4	16mi	27km	Babbacombe – Exmouth
5	13mi	21km	Exmouth – Sidmouth
6	11mi	17km	Sidmouth – Seaton (Devon)
Total	72mi	115km	*Bus Seaton - Exeter; National Rail main line or National Express Coach from Exeter*

Week 8 (Seven days)

Day	Distance (Rounded)		From - to
1	14mi	23km	Seaton (Devon) – Seatown (Dorset) *National Rail main line or National Express coach to Exeter; bus Exeter - Seaton*
2	12mi	19km	Seatown (Dorset) – Abbotsbury
3	11mi	17km	Abbotsbury – Ferry Bridge (Wyke Regis)
4	13mi	21km	Isle of Portland
5	14mi	23km	Ferry Bridge (Wyke Regis) – Lulworth Cove
6	14mi	23km	Lulworth Cove – Worth Matravers
7	14mi	22km	Worth Matravers – South Haven Point (Poole Harbour)
Total	92mi	148km	*Ferry South Haven Point-Sandbanks; bus Sandbanks-Poole or Bournemouth; National Rail main line or National Express coach from Poole or Bournemouth*

The Association has published a series of Walking Guide booklets which break down the whole of the Coast Path into easy to follow sections of between 5 and 17 miles per booklet. Each walking guide gives detailed walking directions as well as pointing out items of interest along the route. These Walking Guides provide detailed instructions for short sections of the Path, laid out in both directions. They include maps and photos as well as offering interesting facts, history, wildlife and geological information. These are available to buy at southwestcoastpath.org.uk/books. They are an excellent addition to this Guide.

Walk No.	Section Name	Distance (miles)	Distance (km)
1	Minehead to Porlock Weir	8.9	14.3
2	Porlock Weir to Lynton	12.1	19.5
3	Lynton to Combe Martin	13.7	22.0
4	Combe Martin to Ilfracombe	5.4	8.7
5	Ilfracombe to Woolacombe	8.5	13.7
6	Woolacombe to Croyde Bay	5.2	8.4
7	Croyde Bay to Braunton	9.8	15.8
8	Braunton to Barnstaple	5.4	8.7
9	Barnstaple to Bideford	10.7	17.2
10	Bideford to Westward Ho!	8.0	12.9
11	Westward Ho! to Clovelly	11.1	17.9
12	Clovelly to Hartland Quay	10.3	16.6
13	Harland Quay to Marsland Mouth to Bude	15.2	24.5
14	Bude to Crackington Haven	9.8	15.8
15	Crackington Haven to Boscastle	6.7	10.8
16	Boscastle to Tintagel	4.7	7.6
17	Tintagel to Port Isaac	9.1	14.6
18	Port Isaac to Padstow	11.7	18.8
19	Padstow to Harlyn Bay	6.5	10.5
20	Harlyn Bay to Porthcothan	6.7	10.8
21	Porthcothan to Newquay	10.3	16.6
22	Newquay to Holywell Bay	8.1	13.0
23	Holywell Bay to Perranporth	4.5	7.2
24	Perranporth to Portreath	12.4	20.0
25	Portreath to Hayle	11.7	18.8
26	Hayle to St Ives	6.1	9.8
27	St Ives to Pendeen	13.7	22.0
28	Pendeen to Sennen Cove	9.1	14.6
29	Sennen Cove to Porthcurno	6.3	10.1
30	Porthcurno to Lamorna	5.4	8.7
31	Lamorna to Marazion	9.2	14.8
32	Marazion to Porthleven	10.8	17.4
33	Porthleven to Poldhu Cove	5.2	8.4
34	Poldhu Cove to The Lizard	8.2	13.2
35	The Lizard to Coverack	10.4	16.7
36	Coverack to Helford	12.9	20.8
37	Helford to Falmouth	10.3	16.6
38	St Mawes (ferry) to Portscatho	6.2	10.0
39	Porthscatho to Portloe	7.4	11.9
40	Portloe to Mevagissey	12.2	19.6
41	Mevagissey to Par	10.7	17.2
42	Par to Fowey	6.8	10.9
43	Fowey to Polperro	7.1	11.4
44	Polperro to Looe	5	8.0
45	Looe to Portwrinkle	7.7	12.4
46	Portwrinkle to Plymouth	13.2	21.2
47	Plymouth (Admiral's Hard) to Mount Batten	7.5	12.1
48	Mount Batten to Wembury (ferry)	7.5	12.1
49	Wembury to River Erme	10.3	16.6
50	River Erme to Hope Cove	9.3	15.0
51	Hope Cove to Salcombe	8.1	13.0
52	Salcombe to Torcross	12.6	20.3
53	Torcross to Dartmouth	10.3	16.6
54	Dartmouth to Brixham	10.9	17.5
55	Brixham to Babbacombe	13.2	21.2
56	Babbacombe to Teignmouth	6.4	10.3
57	Teignmouth to Exmouth	8	12.9
58	Exmouth to Budleigh Salterton	5.4	8.7
59	Budleigh Salterton to Sidmouth	7.1	11.4
60	Sidmouth to Seaton	10.3	16.6
61	Seaton (Devon) to Lyme Regis	7.1	11.4
62	Lyme Regis to West Bay	10	16.1
63	West Bay to Abbotsbury	9.3	15.0
64	Abbotsbury to Ferrybridge (Weymouth)	10.9	17.5
65	Ferrybridge around Isle of Portland	13	20.9
66	Ferrybridge (Weymouth) to Lulworth Cove	14.4	23.2
67	Lulworth Cove to Kimmeridge Bay	7.1	11.4
68	Kimmeridge Bay to Worth Matravers (Winspit)	7.1	11.4
69	Worth Matravers (Winspit) to Swanage	6.5	10.5
70	Swanage to South Haven Point	7.5	12.1
71	Alternative route between West Bexington and Osmington Mills along the South Dorset Ridgeway	17.1	27.5

Coast Path Walk Sections

Based on the 630 miles in 8 weeks itinerary on pages 38-39, the South West Coast Path has been divided into 70 Sections. Each Section represents a day's or half-day's walk of the Itinerary. However, it must be emphasised that these Sections should not be confined to use by those walking long stretches of the Coast Path. Each Section is designed to be used on its own as a one off if so wished, as well as by those planning long walks of several days. The Sections are arranged in anti-clockwise order, from Minehead to Poole, with an additional Section 71 for the alternative inland South Dorset Ridgeway. In a number of coastal locations it is now necessary to pay for the toilet facilities. Also be aware that in winter a number of toilets close, or are only opened at weekends.

Walk Sections – Pages 44-205

Each walk section starts with an overview as well as a map illustration of the walk Section, covering the landscape, it's general character and some of its highlights.

Next, there is a short description of how the Section can be undertaken as a day or part-day walk with public transport or a local circular walk.

Finally, the main body of the Section description contains simplified instructions for walking in a Minehead – Poole direction, generally only highlighting those locations where it is possible to go astray.

At the end of each of the 7 Coast Path sections are places to **Sleep**, places to **Eat & Drink** and **Activities/Transport options** in that area.

> **Please note**
> This guide is produced annually and the landscape of the Coast Path changes on a fairly regularly basis. If in doubt, follow the signs and waymarks on the ground and visit our website for the most up to date route changes or Path diversions.

Walk section table format:

Distance – length of the Section in miles and kilometres.

Cumulative distance – total length of the Coast Path from Minehead to the end of the Section in miles and kilometres.

Ascent – height climbed during the Section in feet and metres.

Cumulative ascent – total height climbed on the Coast Path from Minehead to the end of the Section in feet and metres.

Grading – each Section is graded as Easy, Moderate, Strenuous or Severe. Inevitably, such grading is subjective to an extent, and not all of any Section will be identical throughout, but the grading will give an idea of the effort required.

Timing – this is an estimated fair average for completing the Section. Times will vary depending on weather, number in party, gear carried, number of refreshment or photograph stops. The estimate should be an aide in planning.

OS Maps – the reference numbers of the OS Maps needed to walk the Section are given. Both Landranger (1:50,000) and Explorer (1:25,000) maps are given.

Area – for those not geographically acquainted with the South West, the Coast Path has been sub-divided into 7 areas for ease of identification, Exmoor, North Devon, North Cornwall, West Cornwall, South Cornwall, South Devon and Jurassic Coast. These can be seen on the map on the inside cover of the Guide.

Grading of Walk Sections

To help in planning your walk, each walk section has been given a grading of difficulty – easy, moderate, strenuous or severe. The grading will inevitably be subjective to some extent but it should provide a general idea of the amount of effort needed to walk each section.

Easy

Sections graded 'easy' will generally be level, however, one or two notable gradients may feature along the length, although none will be especially long or steep. In addition, the path will normally be in good condition and easy to use, apart from the odd muddy patch after rain. Often, though not always, there will be a sealed surface. Some 'easy' Sections may also lack stiles.

Moderate

Sections graded 'moderate' are likely to include some gradients. Generally these will not be steep or lengthy, although there may sometimes be a succession of relatively gentle gradients. Alternatively, a 'moderate' Section may contain one or two more notable gradients, but they will be separated along the Section's length and be the exception rather than the rule. Normally the path surface will not be difficult or awkward although there may be occasional muddy patches after rain.

Strenuous

'Strenuous' Sections are where gradients are frequent, often in quick succession. This grading is also given to a Section with relatively fewer gradients but where these are noticeably steep and lengthy. It may also be the case that slopes on these lengths have a surface requiring some care, including uneven steps or potentially slippery terrain.

In a few instances this grading is given, purely because a rocky surface means progress can be slow and arduous.

Severe

Only a few Sections are given the grading 'severe'. In almost all instances, the grading reflects an almost continuous progression of climbs and descents up and down steep slopes. Extra care may be required due to steep steps or a rocky surface. While each climb or descent in its own right can be tiring, in the 'severe' Sections it is the constant progression that can be particularly wearing. All 'severe' graded Sections will entail much slower going than would be expected from the pure mileage involved.

Remember that the gradings are a general guide only. They do however give an indication of how much effort is required to complete each Section. Note also that some Sections have gradings that vary over their length as the terrain changes.

Elevation

Walking the whole South West Coast Path is the equivalent of scaling Mount Everest 4 times; a total of 115,000 feet (around 35,050 metres) of elevation. The elevation illustration on the following page, provides an idea of how much the path climbs and falls across the whole Trail.

We have labelled some points on the graphic including Great Hangman, the highest point on the Trail at 298 metres, to give you an idea of the higher sections of elevation on the Path.

Our website is broken down into suggested circular and linear walks, each walk with an interactive elevation map specific to that section of the Coast Path.

At the start of each walk section in this guide, starting on page 44, you will find a graphic of the elevation at the top of the illustrative map. It is important to note that this is illustrative only, to give a general idea of the number and steepness of the gradients. The elevation graphics are also in Path order from Minehead. It is especially important to remember that:

In order to show the nature of the gradients, the vertical scale has been exaggerated. The steepness of the gradients on the Path will not match the angles shown in the elevation graphics but will be much less severe.

The elevation gradients do not necessarily reflect the degree of difficulty over any stretch of the Coast Path. Some sections with quite modest gradients can present other challenges such as uneven terrain.

Whole Path Elevation

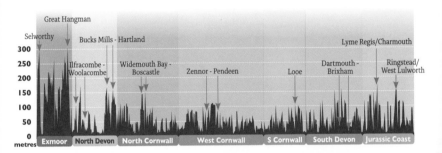

Bossington. Photographer Marcin Jankowski

Exmoor Minehead to Combe Martin – 35 miles

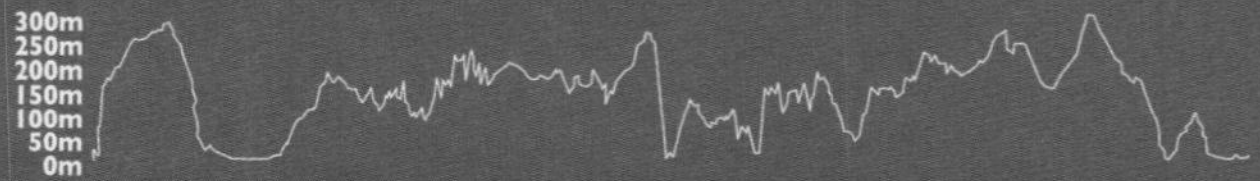

SOMERSET

DEVON

EXMOOR

Minehead

Selworthy

Bossington

Porlock

Porlock Weir

Lynmouth

Lynton

Heddon Valley

Great Hangman

Combe Martin

Barnstaple

Ilfracombe

Lundy

300m
250m
200m
150m
100m
50m
0m

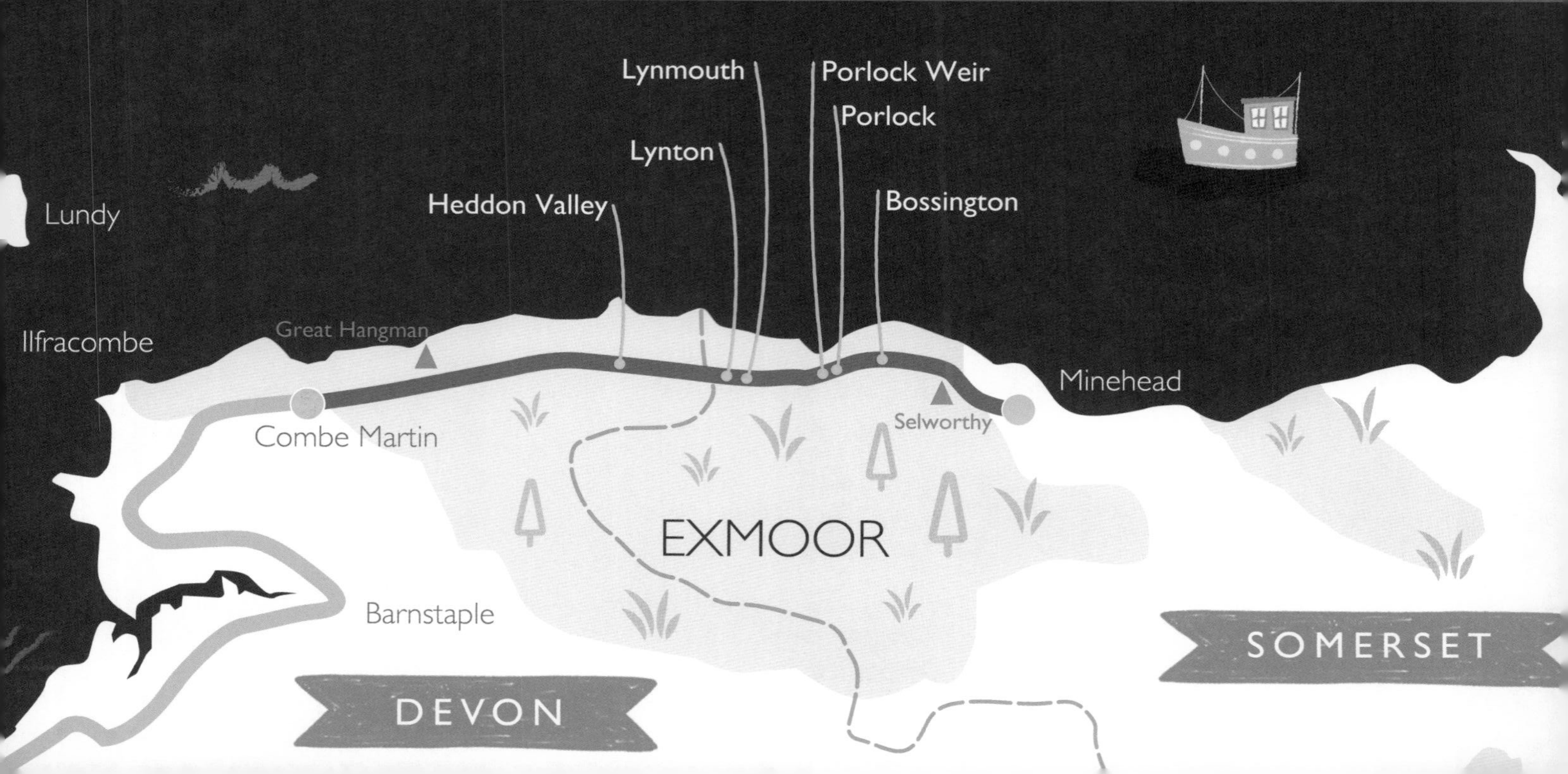

The Exmoor coast is characterised by two main landscape types. The first is the meeting of the rolling expanse of high moorland and the sea. The coastline itself is one of high cliffs, some of them among the highest sea cliffs in England, but this height is sometimes disguised by the cliffs' convex shape, usually referred to as "hog's back". Views are often extensive inland, over the undulating moorland, while seaward in good visibility the coast of Wales may be seen across the Bristol Channel. The second main landscape type comprises steep and deep valleys which cut across the moorland cliffs. These valleys, known as "combes", are typically ancient oak woodland. Often this woodland spreads along the adjacent cliff faces, also convex in shape. Views from the Coast Path here are inevitably less extensive, and sometimes quite limited by the woodland, but the nature of the ancient woodland makes for an environment of considerable ecological interest. The combes and the height of the cliffs in the Exmoor length result in some notable gradients for walkers in places. Contrasting with these main landscape types is the Vale of Porlock, a flat-floored break in the cliffs crossed by the South West Coast Path over marshland at its mouth.

> All of the locations on the map illustration to the left, have at least 1 facility including toilets, a cafe/restaurant, shop or pub.

Dunster Beach, Exmoor. Photographer Cindy Hill

OS Maps: Landranger 181; Explorer OL9

	This Walk	Cumulative	This Walk	Cumulative	Grading	Timing
Ascent	1,824ft	1,824ft	556m	556m	Official: Moderate Alternative: Strenuous	4.5 hours
Distance	8.9mi	8.9mi	14.3km	14.3km		

For detailed directions see our Walking Guide no. 1, Minehead to Porlock Weir.

This is a classic example of where moorland meets the sea. Inland, the high expanse of Exmoor rolls away, broken by deep wooded valleys; where it borders the Bristol Channel there are high, convex cliffs, cut by deep and narrow "combes". This is a lonely, remote length, away from main roads and settlements, with often the only evidence of modern life being development far away on the opposite shore of the Bristol Channel on the South Wales coast. At the western end is the contrasting landscape of Porlock Vale, a flat-floored area of farmland and marshland behind its shingle ridge, quite different in character from the rest of this Section.

Directions

Regular buses run between Minehead and Porlock Weir.

The South West Coast Path starts from the celebratory marker on the sea front in Minehead. The current route, which may not be shown on older maps, proceeds along the sea front, past the quay. Just before Greenaleigh Farm it turns left on ascending zigzags to North Hill.

At the summit of North Hill follow the acorn symbol towards Selworthy and Bossington. At the next Coast Path sign there is a fork, the route to the right being marked "Rugged Cliff Top Path", and either option can be taken. Do not be put off by the description of the seaward path as "rugged", it is a splendid alternative and although a little longer, it is not too strenuous and gives much better sea views than the inland "official" path. It is well waymarked, and dogs are permitted but must be under very close control. There is likely to be cattle grazing.

On the "rugged" Path, at the stile, take the left fork towards a bench, then continue downhill to take the lower Path by a "Rugged Path" signpost. From Grexy Combe (GR 937 481) take the well-defined diagonal path up the hill to a wall, which is then followed first towards the sea then parallel to it to Western Brockholes. Here it turns inland to re-join the inland "official" path behind Hurlstone Point. (This seaward Path will add about an hour to the estimated time.)

The inland route, meanwhile, follows good tracks parallel to the sea. Joining the "rugged" path on Bossington Hill, the now-combined route descends the steep Hurlstone Combe. There is an optional diversion out to Hurlstone Point which gives a superb view. From Hurlstone, take care not to follow the obvious path to the left which contours round Bossington Hill.

The Path descends and goes inland to Bossington village and then just past the car park out towards the sea again. The route now crosses the marsh to Porlock Weir, easy to follow the whole way. At high spring tides it can become impassable, and signs to Porlock village should be followed. For tidal information contact Minehead Tourist Information Centre (TIC) – see page 22.

If the diversion via Porlock village is taken, leave the village on the Toll Road then bear right on a footpath that goes behind West Porlock to Porlock Weir.

OS Maps: Landranger 181 (eastern half); Landranger 180 (western half); Explorer OL9

	This Walk	Cumulative	This Walk	Cumulative	Grading	Timing
Ascent	3,156ft	4,980ft	962m	1,518m	Moderate, strenuous in parts	6 hours
Distance	12.1mi	21.0mi	19.5km	33.8km		

For detailed directions see our Walking Guide no. 2, Porlock to Lynton.

This is a Section of two halves. In the east, approximately between Porlock Weir and the Devon/Somerset border, Exmoor meets the sea at a run of high, convex but well-wooded cliffs. The Coast Path here is a woodland walk with frequent glimpses of the sea, quiet and remote in character. To the west the cliffs become more open and steeper and the area around The Foreland and Countisbury is a spectacular viewpoint with panoramas over the double-decker towns of Lynton and Lynmouth. The section is lonely and remote, with no facilities, except a pub at Countisbury.

Directions

The route is covered by a bus service "The Exmoor Coaster" between Minehead and Lynmouth. For more details see page 25 or visit travelinesw.com.

The official route is signposted left of the hotel at Porlock Weir but it is possible to go in front of the hotel, past the shops then left signposted to Culbone.

Reaching Culbone turn right to visit the charming tiny church, which is recommended. From the church, retrace steps and turn right uphill on the Coast Path. After about 300 yards/275 metres bear right into Culbone, Embelle and Yenworthy Woods. This route may not be shown on some older maps. Unfortunately, recent land slippages towards the end of Yenworthy Wood have forced an inland diversion via Yenworthy Combe.

Continue to Sister's Fountain, where the access path to the bus route at County Gate on the A39 leaves the Coast Path. Go uphill through a pair of wild boar head gateposts, then take care not to miss the narrow signposted Path 300 yards/275 metres past the cottage as the drive bears left. An alternative waymarked route may be taken between Culbone and Yenworthy Wood. Although slightly more inland, it offers better views than the mainly woodland more coastal route.

At Coddow Combe, the route is signposted left off the lighthouse track "Countisbury 1.5 miles". From Countisbury the now spectacular Path continues down the seaward side of the A39 road. Lower down it joins the road for a short way before descending on zigzags to the foreshore. Walk into Lynmouth, crossing the footbridge, then turn right to the sea front. Lynton is vertically above Lynmouth and is reached by turning left up the steps before the cliff railway (which can be taken as an interesting alternative). A new route is also available past the Esplanade car park at the end of the sea front, where a pleasant path, signposted to Lynton, goes left up the steep wooded hillside to emerge on the Coast Path west of Lynton. Both Lynmouth and Lynton have all facilities.

It is interesting to know that from Lynmouth it is possible to walk Devon's Coast to Coast route using the Two Moors Way and its southern extension to the south coast at Wembury. Guide books are available from Lynton Tourist Information Centre (TIC).

OS Maps: Landranger 180; Explorer OL9

	This Walk	Cumulative	This Walk	Cumulative	Grading	Timing
Ascent	3,766ft	8,746ft	1,148m	2,666m	Strenuous	7 hours
Distance	13.7mi	34.7mi	22.0km	55.8km		

For detailed directions see our Walking Guide no. 3, Lynton to Hunter's Inn and Hunter's Inn to Combe Martin.

This generally quiet and remote Section passes through a series of spectacular coastal landscapes: the Valley of Rocks with its rocky crags and pinnacles; the steep wooded cliffs at Woody Bay; the breathtaking scenery of the deep and steep crevice carved through the cliffs at Heddon's Mouth; the wide open spaces of Holdstone Down; and the heights of the Great Hangman, the highest point on the entire Coast Path and one of the highest coastal locations in the country.

Directions

Lynton and Combe Martin are connected by a summer bus service. Heddon's Mouth (6.5 miles/10.5km from Lynton) makes a good break in this length (though not on the bus route).

The Coast Path out of Lynton is on North Walk, and this Path leads to Castle Rock in the Valley of Rocks. The next section follows a minor but sometimes busy road, but a diversion to the right from the turning circle at the end of the Valley avoids its first length. Continue past the Toll House and up the hill. A permissive path on the right to Crock Point then avoids another length, and also gives stunning views.

The Coast Path leaves the road just before the hotel opposite the Red House. Arriving at another road turn left uphill. Follow the next Coast Path sign ahead. When this superb stretch reaches the dramatic Heddon's Mouth valley, follow it down to the valley floor. On reaching the stone bridge over the Heddon River, turn right over the river, and at the next Path turn hard left. Continue for 100 yards/91 metres to the signpost on the right to Combe Martin. (Inland on either side of the river the Path leads to the pub at Hunter's Inn.)

Climb steeply away from the valley floor, keeping right at the top where the Path levels off. Continue round the headland (take care in windy conditions) then the Path heads inland to reach a stone wall; this is followed parallel to the sea. The wall ends and the signed Path continues across the heathland of Holdstone Down.

At Sherrycombe the route follows the grass track along the top of the combe to the inland end and then down. Ascending Great Hangman from Sherrycombe, bear away from the wall on the left and ignore the many paths going to the right, meeting the wall higher up. From Great Hangman the Path is obvious to Little Hangman and beyond to Combe Martin.

The businesses listed here are our 'Way Makers'. They make the great South West Coast Path experience possible, and give back to the Trail. Please support them if you can. More info at www.southwestcoastpath.org.uk/waymaker

GR Grid Reference	🍴 Evening Meal Available
DP Distance from the Path	📶 Wifi
N Nearest Town/Village with facilities	🚗 Parking
3 Number of Rooms	🛒 Grocery Shop On Site
🐕 Dogs Welcome	🚌 Private Transport to the Path

🧺 Laundry Facilities
🍽 Caters to Specific Dietary Needs
🥐 Early Breakfast Available
🍱 Packed Lunch Offered
£ Budget

Bed & Breakfast and Hotels

NAME	OTHER INFO	
The Parks Guest House 26 The Parks, Minehead, Somerset, TA24 8BT ☎ 01643 703547 ✉ info@parksguesthouse.co.uk 🌐 www.parksguesthouse.co.uk	GR: SS964462	DP: 0.8 miles
	N: **MINEHEAD**	
	OFFERS ONE NIGHT STAYS	
	7 🐕 📶 🚗 🍱	
The Beach Hotel Minehead Minehead, TA24 5AP ☎ 01643 704765 ✉ info@thebeachhotel.org 🌐 www.thebeachhotel.org	GR: SS973463	DP: 0 miles
	N: **MINEHEAD**	
	OFFERS ONE NIGHT STAYS	
	17 🐕 📶 🍱	
The Cottage B&B High Street, Porlock, TA24 8PU ☎ 01643 862996 ✉ cottageporlock@gmail.com 🌐 www.cottageporlock.co.uk	GR: SS885467	DP: 0.5 miles
	N: **PORLOCK**	
	OFFERS ONE NIGHT STAYS	
	4 📶 🚗 🍽 🍱	
Myrtle Cottage Porlock, TA24 8PU ☎ 01643 862978 ✉ enquiries@myrtleporlock.co.uk 🌐 www.myrtleporlock.co.uk	GR: SS884467	DP: 0.25 miles
	N: **PORLOCK**	
	OFFERS ONE NIGHT STAYS	
	4 🐕 📶 🚗 ☕ 🍽	
Bossington Hall Luxury B & B Bossington Hall, Allerford, Minehead, TA24 8HJ ☎ 01643 862800 ✉ info@bossingtonhall.co.uk 🌐 www.bossingtonhall.co.uk	GR: SS902476	DP: 0.5 miles
	N: **PORLOCK**	
	OFFERS ONE NIGHT STAYS	
	7 🐕 📶 🚗 🍽 🍱	
Ash Farm B&B Porlock Weir, TA24 8JN ☎ 01643 862414 ✉ jenniferwren@jenniferwren.plus.com 🌐 www.southwestcoastpath.org.uk/ash-farm-porlock-hill	GR: SS842478	DP: 2 miles
	N: **PORLOCK WEIR**	
	OFFERS ONE NIGHT STAYS	
	3 📶 🚗 ☕ 🍱	

NAME	OTHER INFO	
Orchard House Hotel 12 Watersmeet Road, Lynmouth, EX35 6EP 📞 01598 753247 ✉ info@orchardhousehotel.co.uk 🌐 www.orchardhousehotel.co.uk	**GR:** SS725493	**DP:** 0 miles
	N: LYNMOUTH	
	OFFERS ONE NIGHT STAYS	
	6 🐕 🍴 📶 📷	
Bath Hotel Lynmouth Street, The Harbour, Lynmouth, EX35 6EL 📞 01598 752238 ✉ gm@bathhotellynmouth.co.uk 🌐 www.bathhotellynmouth.co.uk	**GR:** SS722495	**DP:** 0.3 miles
	LYNMOUTH	
	OFFERS ONE NIGHT STAYS	
	20 🐕 🍴 📶 🚗 🔄	
St Vincent Guest House Market Street, Lynton, EX35 6AF 📞 01598 752720 ✉ stvincentlynton@outlook.com 🌐 www.stvincentlynton.co.uk	**GR:** SS720493	**DP:** 0.25 miles
	N: LYNTON	
	OFFERS ONE NIGHT STAYS	
	7 🐕 📶 📷 🔄 🍎 ☕	
Sinai House Lynway, Lynton, EX35 6AX 📞 01598 753227 ✉ enquiries@sinaihouse.co.uk 🌐 www.sinaihouse.co.uk	**GR:** SS720487	**DP:** 0.5 miles
	N: LYNTON	
	8 📶 🚗 🔄 🍎	
Gable Lodge Guest House 35 Lee Road, Lynton, Devon, EX35 6BS 📞 01598 752367 ✉ gablelodge@btconnect.com 🌐 www.gablelodgelynton.com	**GR:** SS717494	**DP:** 0.25 miles
	N: LYNTON	
	OFFERS ONE NIGHT STAYS	
	6 🍴 📶 🚗	
Highcliffe House Sinai Hill, Lynton, EX35 6AR 📞 01598752235 ✉ info@highcliffehouse.co.uk 🌐 www.highcliffehouse.co.uk	**GR:** SS719492	**DP:** 2.9 miles
	N: LYNTON	
	OFFERS ONE NIGHT STAYS	
	6 📶 🚗 🔄 🍎 ☕	
The North Cliff Hotel North Walk, Lynton, EX35 6HJ 📞 01598 752 357 ✉ holidays@northcliffhotel.co.uk 🌐 www.northcliffhotel.co.uk	**GR:** SS719495	**DP:** 0 miles
	N: LYNTON	
	OFFERS ONE NIGHT STAYS	
	11 🐕 🍴 📶 🚗 🔄 🍎	
The Crown Hotel Market Street, Lynton, EX35 6AG 📞 01598 752253 ✉ thecrownhotellynton@outlook.com 🌐 www.thecrownlynton.co.uk	**GR:** SS720493	**DP:** 0.25 miles
	N: LYNTON	
	OFFERS ONE NIGHT STAYS	
	10 🐕 🍴 📶 🚗 🔄 🍎	
Newberry Beach Lodge Newberry Road, Combe Martin, EX34 0AP 📞 01271 883709 / 07922571331 / 07710664513 ✉ cjg0040@msn.com 🌐 www.newberrybeachlodge.co.uk	**GR:** SS574471	**DP:** 0 miles
	N: COMBE MARTIN	
	OFFERS ONE NIGHT STAYS	
	4 🐕 🍴 📶 🚗	

NAME	OTHER INFO		
Pack O Cards	**GR:** SS583465		**DP:** I mile
High Street, Combe Martin	**N: COMBE MARTIN**		
☎ 01271 882300	OFFERS ONE NIGHT STAYS		
✉ thepackocards@aol.com			
🌐 www.packocards.co.uk	6 🍴 🐕 📶 🚗 🔘		

Self Catering

NAME	OTHER INFO		
Exmoor Character Cottages	**GR:** SS980734		**DP:** 2 miles
39 Ellicombe Close, Minehead, TA24 6DQ	**N: MINEHEAD**		
☎ 07817698366			
✉ info@exmoorcharactercottages.co.uk			
🌐 www.exmoorcharactercottages.co.uk	14 🐕 📶 🚗 🔘		
YHA Minehead	**GR:** SS973 442		**DP:** 1.8 miles
Allcombe Combe, Minehead, TA24 6EW	**N: MINEHEAD**		
☎ 0345 371 9033			
✉ minehead@yha.org.uk			
🌐 www.yha.org.uk/hostel/yha-minehead	🍴 📶 🚗		
Dolphin Stays Ltd	**GR:** SS863479		**DP:** 0 miles
Harbour House, Pieces of Eight, Porlock Weir, TA24 8PD	**N: PORLOCK WEIR**		
☎ 07941 053602	OFFERS ONE NIGHT STAYS		
✉ julie@dolphinstays.com			
🌐 www.thebestofexmoor.co.uk/stay-in-porlock-weir/ harbour-house-studio	3 🐕 📶 🚗		
Berry Lawn Linhay Bothy	**GR:** SS729495		**DP:** I miles
Countisbury,Lynmouth, EX35 6ND	**N: LYNMOUTH**		
☎ 0344 800 2070	OFFERS ONE NIGHT STAYS		
✉ holiday.enquiries@nationaltrust.org.uk			
🌐 www.nationaltrust.org.uk/holidays/bothy-heddon-orchard-devon	🐕 🚗 £		

Campsites and Holiday Parks

NAME	OTHER INFO		
Sparkhayes Farm Campsite	**GR:** SS886468		**DP:** 0 miles
Sparkhayes Lane, Porlock, TA24 8NE	**N: MINEHEAD**		
☎ 07721 05123 / 01643 862470	OFFERS ONE NIGHT STAYS		
✉ sparkhayes@hotmail.com			
🌐 www.sparkhayes.co.uk	🐕 🍴 🚗 🏕 🔘		
Cloud Farm Campsite	**GR:** SS791477		**DP:** I miles
Oare, EX35 6NU	**N: LYNTON**		
☎ 01598 741190	OFFERS ONE NIGHT STAYS		
✉ cloudfarmcampsite@nationaltrust.org			
🌐 www.nationaltrust.org.uk/holidays/cloud-farm-campsite	🐕 🚗 🏕		

NAME	OTHER INFO
Lynmouth Holiday Retreats EX35 6LD, Lynton ☎ 01598753349 ✉ lynmouth@coastandcountryparks.co.uk 🌐 www.coastandcountryparks.co.uk	**GR:** SS724482 **DP:** 1.7 miles **N: LYNTON** OFFERS ONE NIGHT STAYS [30] 🐕 📶 🚗 🧺 🛒 📷
Exmoor Coast Holidays Caffyns Farm, Lynton, EX35 6JW ☎ 01598 753967 ✉ stay@exmoorcoastholidays.co.uk 🌐 www.exmoorcoastholidays.co.uk	**GR:** SS692481 **DP:** 1 mile **N: LYNTON** OFFERS ONE NIGHT STAYS [3] 🐕 🍴 📶 🚗 🛒 🫖 📷
Heddon Valley Campsite Heddon Valley, Parracombe, EX31 4PY ☎ 01598 741190 ✉ heddonvalleycampsite@nationaltrust.org.uk 🌐 www.nationaltrust.org.uk/holidays/heddon-valley-campsite	**GR:** SS655481 **DP:** 1 miles **N: LYNTON** OFFERS ONE NIGHT STAYS 🐕 🚗
Combe Martin Beach Holiday Park Woodlands, Combe Martin, EX34 0AS ☎ 01271 866766 ✉ combemartin-gm@jfhols.co.uk 🌐 www.johnfowlerholidays.com/devon-holiday-park/ combe-martin-beach-holiday-park	**GR:** SS575470 **DP:** 0.7 miles **N: COMBE MARTIN** [III] 🐕 🍴 📶 🚗
Sandaway Beach Holiday Park Berrynarbor, Combe Martin, Devon, EX34 9ST ☎ 01271866766 ✉ sandaway-gm@jfhols.co.uk 🌐 www.johnfowlerholidays.com/devon-holiday-park/ sandaway-beach-holiday-park	**GR:** SS571472 **DP:** 0 miles **N: COMBE MARTIN** [120] 🐕 🍴 📶 🚗 🛒

Eat and Drink

NAME	OTHER INFO
The Royal Oak High Street, Minehead, TA24 8PS ☎ 01643 862798 ✉ klcpubs@outlook.com 🌐 www.royaloakporlock.com	**GR:** SS88667 **DP:** 1 miles **N: PORLOCK** 🐕 📶 🍴 📷

Information

NAME	OTHER INFO
Minehead Information Centre The Beach Hotel, The Avenue, Minehead, TA24 5AP ☎ 01643 702624 ✉ minehead.visitor@hotmail.com 🌐 www.mineheadbay.co.uk	**GR:** SS974464 **DP:** 0.5 miles **N: MINEHEAD** 🐕

NAME	OTHER INFO		
Porlock Visitor Centre	**GR:** SS884468	**DP:**	I mile
West End, Porlock, TA24 8QD	**N: PORLOCK**		
📞 01643 863150			
✉ visit@porlock.co.uk			
🌐 www.porlock.co.uk	🐕 📶 🚗		
Lynmouth National Park Visitor Centre	**GR:** SS721496	**DP:**	mile
The Esplanade, EX35 6EQ	**N: LYNMOUTH**		
📞 01398 323665			
✉ npclynmouth@exmoor-nationalpark.gov.uk			
🌐 www.exmoor-nationalpark.gov.uk			
Lynton & Lynmouth Tourist Information Centre	**GR:** SS718804	**DP:**	0.5 miles
Lynton Post Office, 26 Lee Road, Lynton, Devon, EX35 6BT	**N: LYNTON**		
📞 01598 753313			
✉ business@visitlyntonandlynmouth.com			
🌐 www.visitlyntonandlynmouth.com			

Lynton. Photographer Richard Kift

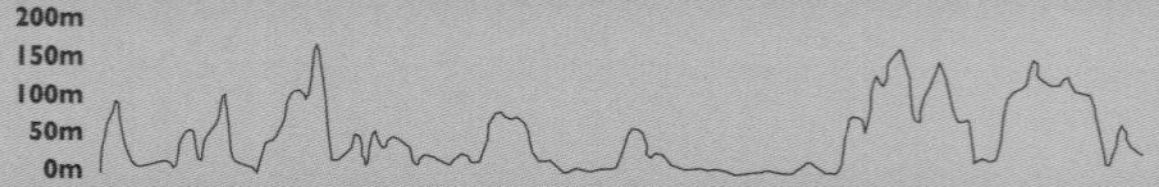

200m
150m
100m
50m
0m

North Devon Combe Martin to Marsland Mouth – **80 miles**

Lundy
Mortehoe
Lee Bay
Ilfracombe
Woolacombe
Putsborough
Croyde
Saunton
Combe Martin
EXMOOR
Braunton
Appledore
Westward Ho!
Peppercombe
Clovelly
Hartland Point
Hartland Quay
Barnstaple
Fremington
Yelland
Instow
Bideford
Northam
Buck's Mills
Hartland
Marsland Mouth
DEVON

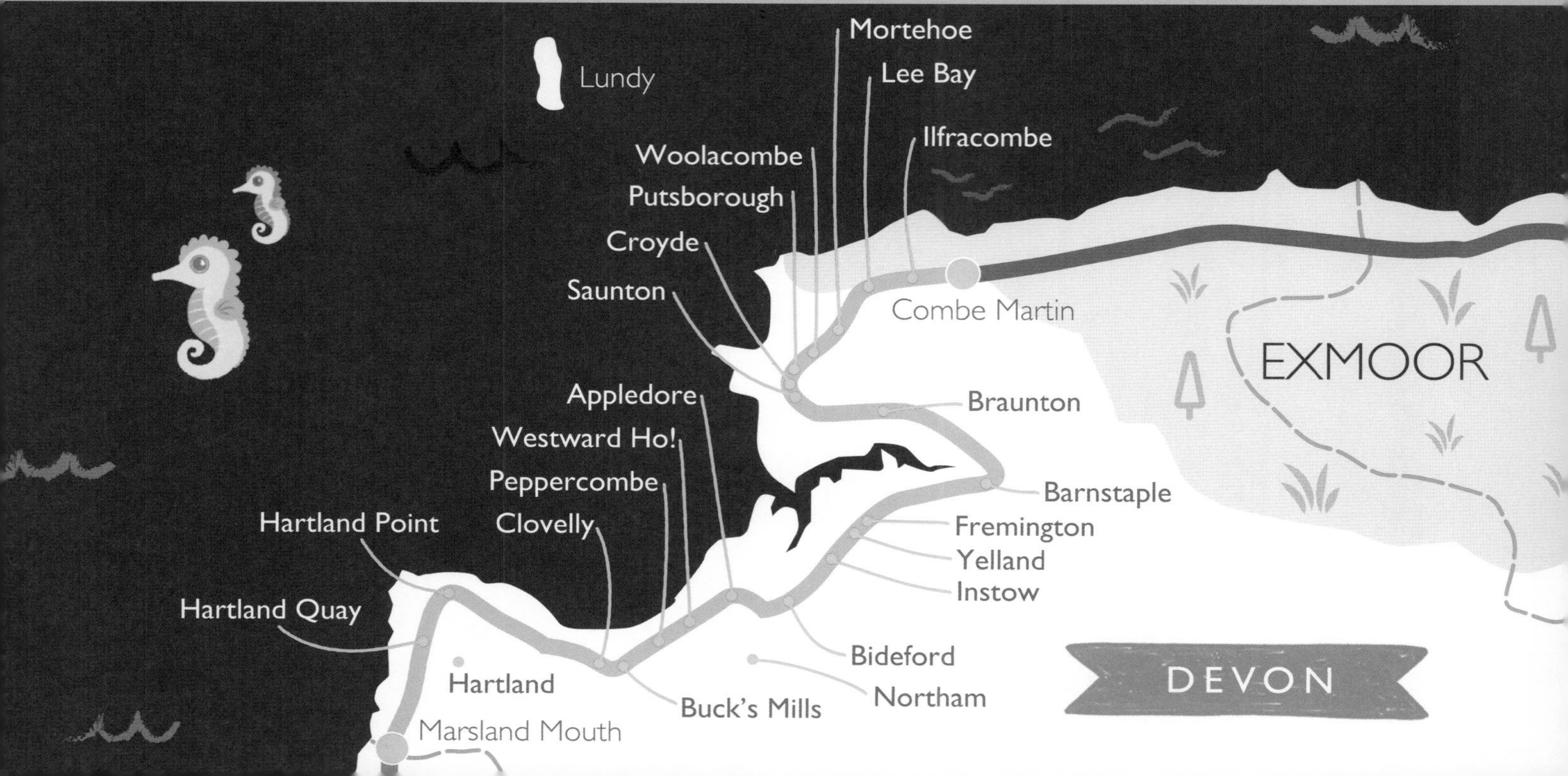

Most of the North Devon coast faces north over the Bristol Channel. Much of this length comprises cliffs of moderate height with, in the east, some prominent headlands like Morte Point and Baggy Point, which offer fine coastal vistas. At the centre of the North Devon length is the large joint estuary of the Taw and Torridge Rivers, flanked by areas of sand dunes and marshland. The South West Coast Path partly uses old railway lines around the estuary, crossing the rivers at the towns of Barnstaple and Bideford. Adjacent to the estuary are extensive sandy beaches, popular with surfers and families. The north facing cliffs continue to Hartland Point, one of the Coast Path's major headlands (referred to as the 'Promontory of Hercules' by the Romans). Seascapes typically have the coast of Wales beyond the Bristol Channel as the backdrop; in the west the offshore island of Lundy, at the "mouth" of the Bristol Channel, is the focal point. Hartland Point marks an abrupt change in direction from the east-west of most of North Devon to the north-south beyond. This north-south length is very dramatic, with high cliffs fronted by jagged fingers of rock stretching into the Atlantic. Deep and steep valleys cut the coastline, making for some considerable gradients for walkers, but there are no bays or harbours other than the tiny harbour at Hartland Quay.

All of the locations on the map illustration to the left, have at least 1 facility including toilets, a cafe/restaurant, shop or pub.

Hartland, North Devon. Photographer Jillian Brady

OS Maps: Landranger 180; Explorer 139 or OL9

	This Walk	Cumulative	This Walk	Cumulative	Grading	Timing
Ascent	1,280ft	10,026ft	390m	3,056m	Moderate, strenuous in parts	2.5 hours
Distance	5.4mi	40.1mi	8.7km	64.5km		

For detailed directions see our Walking Guide no. 4, Combe Martin to Ilfracombe.

This is a Section of rocky inlets, one of which, Watermouth, is spacious enough for boats to be moored. These bays are divided by rugged headlands. The cliffs here are grey and slatey, making for a forbidding looking coastline, notwithstanding the little bays. At the western end, the site of a prehistoric hill fort gives a panoramic view over Ilfracombe. This Section is never far from the A399 coast road and various tourist facilities, so despite the impressive cliffs it is not a lonely length.

Directions

Combe Martin and Ilfracombe are linked by a regular bus service, allowing a bus-walk to be easily undertaken on this Section.

The Coast Path leaves the Lime Kiln car park in Combe Martin, passing the Tourist Information Centre (TIC), then forks right. Turn right (Seaside Hill Road) above the beach. Turn right onto a narrow tarmac lane and follow the acorn signs as the Path winds below the houses, and uphill to finally join the A399 at Sandaway holiday park. Walk on the slightly raised Path along the roadside through two gates. Go along a Path beside a field to a flight of steps, then turn left up the slip road back to the main road and on to the brow, passing the bus shelter. Turn right to follow the road down to the old main road, with a bus shelter, now used as an Information Point, over to the right. Here turn left beside the entrance to the hotel, to follow a track towards Watermouth Cove.

At Watermouth it is possible to cross the foreshore from the harbour office, keeping to the left of the bay for some 110 yards/100 metres to a flight of steps at most states of the tide; take care, as the rocks can be slippery. However, if the tide is high, use the route running parallel to the main road. (Check the Watermouth tide timings by contacting Ilfracombe or Combe Martin Tourist Information Centres (TICs) see page 22).

This roadside Path is a great improvement as it avoids the need to walk in the road carriageway. It was completed in late 2013, following the Association's offer of £50,000 from our reserves towards its cost, because of our safety concerns. The offer enabled the remainder of the funding to be secured from the Rural Development Fund for England and Devon County Council, a successful conclusion to a decade of pressure.

The next pleasant section of Path passes the western side of Watermouth Cove and on around Widmouth Head, and then Rillage Point. There is then a roadside section into Hele. Turn right here, then climb some steps on the far left of the beach. The Path zigzags up past Beacon Point to the top of Hillsborough. Follow the waymarks down the hill to Ilfracombe Harbour.

OS Maps: Landranger 180; Explorer 139

	This Walk	Cumulative	This Walk	Cumulative	Grading	Timing
Ascent	2,037ft	12,063ft	621m	3,677m	Easy to moderate; strenuous west of Lee Bay	3.5 hours
Distance	8.5mi	48.6mi	13.7km	78.2km		

For detailed directions see our Walking Guide no. 5, Ilfracombe to Woolacombe.

Most of this Section is characterised by grass-topped cliffs, fronting numerous small coves and a foreshore of rock ledges. Half-way along is the focal point of Bull Point lighthouse. At Morte Point the character of the coastline changes abruptly, as the enormous beach of Woolacombe Sands in its vast bay comes into view, often dotted with surfers. The dark jagged rocks of Morte Point give this headland a superb brooding atmosphere.

Directions

Ilfracombe and Woolacombe are linked by a regular bus service, allowing a bus-walk to be easily undertaken on this Section.

From Ilfracombe Harbour walk along Capstone Road. After some 170 yards/150 metres turn right to pass around Capstone Point. At the far end take a flight of steps that goes up behind the back of the Landmark Theatre. Follow this Path to the top of the gardens and through a gate by a shelter. Bear right along Granville Road, then right again onto an unmetalled road which leads to the Torrs Walk on the right; the Torrs Walk is well waymarked.

At the top of the Torrs Walk, bear right and follow the Path down the field to the stile in the corner. Continue ahead around the hill to another stile, then cross the field to meet the old coach road ahead. Bear right on this track, which later becomes a minor road into Lee Bay.

The next length from Lee Bay is quite strenuous. Proceed up the road from Lee, turning right at the top of the hill through a brick-pillared gate. Two steep valleys are crossed before Bull Point and its lighthouse are reached. The Path continues on and out around Morte Point, a spectacular jagged, slate ridge like a dinosaur's back emerging from the sea. The Path leaves Morte Point, and crosses the road and heads slightly inland before turning back to arrive at the edge of Woolacombe.

Hele Beach, Ilfracombe. Photographer Lindsay Derbyshire

OS Maps: Landranger 180; Explorer 139

	This Walk	Cumulative	This Walk	Cumulative	Grading	Timing
Ascent	725ft	12,788ft	221m	3,898m	Moderate	2.5 hours
Distance	5.2mi	53.8mi	8.4km	86.6km		

For detailed directions see our Walking Guide no. 6, Woolacombe to Croyde Bay.

The main feature of this Section is the vast sandy beach of Woolacombe Sands, backed by a substantial line of dunes. Busy with families and surfers close to the town, it becomes surprisingly empty away from the facilities. Beyond the beach is the superb headland of Baggy Point, a contrast to the beach with its steep cliffs and broad, grassy top. Rounding the headland, another smaller sandy bay comes into view, Croyde Bay, with the wider vista of Bideford Bay beyond.

Directions

Croyde Bay is an excellent centre for a circular walk using the Coast Path, around Baggy Point to Putsborough, giving views over Woolacombe Sands while experiencing the superb character of the headland.

At Woolacombe the Coast Path runs parallel to the Esplanade road, then turns up Challacombe Road. It leaves this road on the right at approximately the National Trust sign – at a waymark. The Path continues through the enormous dunes of Woolacombe Warren – the waymarking means that going astray is unlikely. An alternative is to follow Marine Drive and the track beyond, which gives better views. If the tide is low many walk the length of Woolacombe Sands but this should not be attempted on a high or rising tide.

The official Path leaves the Warren by a set of steep steps, joining the extension to Marine Drive and the alternative route. It continues along the track then a road, leaving it to the right after the entrance to the beach and caravan site. As an alternative, take the earlier Path on the right to the car park at Putsborough, where there are seasonal refreshments and toilets (the beach route joins here). Go left of the caravan site to a stile and up the cliff slope to re-join the official Path.

The excellent high level Path continues to the end of Baggy Point, giving superb views. At the end of the headland, bear right to join the lower Path towards Croyde. Follow the road, partly on a parallel Path. Do not leave the road at the first slipway. The official Path leaves the road a little further on to cross the beach, but many will continue on to visit Croyde and its facilities.

Woolacombe. Photographer Kate Poole

OS Maps: Landranger 181 (eastern half); Landranger 180 (western half); Explorer OL9

	This Walk	Cumulative	This Walk	Cumulative	Grading	Timing
Ascent	506ft	13,294ft	154m	4,052m	Easy	3.25 hours
Distance	9.8mi	63.6mi	15.8km	102.4km		

For detailed directions see our Walking Guide no. 7, Croyde Bay to Braunton.

The length immediately adjacent to Croyde Bay follows a low cliff, and gives stunning views over the truly enormous length of Saunton Sands, with the dune complex of Braunton Burrows behind. Beyond is the sweep of Bideford Bay, with the possibility of seeing as far as Hartland Point lighthouse, many miles away. Offshore on the horizon is the Isle of Lundy. The remainder of this Section is low and level, through a huge range of dunes (the official route) or along the seemingly endless Saunton Sands. Then comes the twin estuary of the Rivers Taw and Torridge, with mudbanks and reclaimed marshes making for a birdwatcher's delight. This is a length displaying a relatively rare aspect of the South West coast.

Directions

Croyde Bay and Braunton are linked by a bus service, making this a good bus-walk possibility.

The Coast Path leaves Croyde Bay via the beach (no dogs May-September), and on to the low cliffs at Down End. After climbing up some steep steps, turn left at the old coastguard lookout onto the B3231 road, and walk back in the direction of Croyde for a few yards before crossing the road with care, turn right at the waymark then climb some stone steps. The Path now contours round Saunton Down, parallel to and above the road. This ends opposite the large white building of the hotel.

From here there are optional routes. The first option is to cross the road and pass around the hotel to the Saunton Sands car park, where there are toilets and seasonal refreshments. Leave the car park by the entrance road, and after 55 yards/50 metres bear right along a stony lane to the B3231. Continue carefully along the road for some 400 yards/365 metres, past the Golf Club driveway, turning right at a red brick partially rendered house.

If there is no need for the toilets or refreshments, a better option is to turn left uphill opposite the hotel, away from the road. Follow the Path as it bears round to the right, until it arrives at the B3231 opposite the red brick house described above. Cross the road to continue on the same route as above.

This route now enters the Braunton Burrows nature reserve, designated a UNESCO Biosphere Reserve for its nature conservation importance. The route through the Burrows is well waymarked; first follow a clear track through patchy woodland along the edge of the golf course with the military training area on the right. After the Sandy Lane car park, follow the signing for nearly two miles along a rough, traffic-free, military dirt road known as the American Road, to arrive at Crow Point by the estuary of the Taw and Torridge rivers. Follow another dirt road, approximately eastwards, to arrive at the White House, a well-known local landmark.

Many walkers prefer to miss the Burrows and walk from Saunton Sands car park the length of the beach, for some 3.5 miles/5.5 kilometres. Near the end of the beach, just after a wooden groyne, look out for a slatted wooden boardwalk entering the dunes to the left. Follow this to arrive at the Broad Sands car park. This beach route keeps the sea in sight, not the case with the Burrows route.

From the White House following the Path diversion signs, walk on top of the inner sea defence bank. This is followed, between estuary and reclaimed marshes, to the old quay at Velator on the edge of Braunton. To visit Braunton and its facilities, turn left at Velator along the footpath and cycleway, following the former railway track.

Braunton Burrows. Photographer Shaun Selley

OS Maps: Landranger 180; Explorer 139

	This Walk	Cumulative	This Walk	Cumulative	Grading	Timing
Ascent	16ft	13,310ft	5m	4,057m	Easy	2 hours
Distance	5.4mi	69.0mi	8.7km	111.0km		

For detailed directions see our Walking Guide no. 8, Braunton to Barnstaple.

This is a flat, low-level Section, following the line of the former railway track once used by the Atlantic Coast Express. As well as the Coast Path, it is also used by Devon's Coast to Coast Cycle Route. At the Braunton end, the main item of interest is the Royal Marines air base at Chivenor, next to the Path, but further on, the Path runs alongside the estuary of the River Taw, with its interplay of water and sand and mud banks. This makes for a pleasant environment; in character, however, this length is semi-urban.

Directions

There is a regular and year-round bus service between Braunton and Barnstaple, which can also be accessed at Chivenor, approximately mid-way along the route, giving various short walk options.

From Braunton's main car park the signed route to Barnstaple leads to the Coast Path at Velator, and from here the Path follows the former railway past Chivenor Royal Marines base, and then alongside the Taw Estuary all the way to Barnstaple.

The new high level bridge across the River Taw can be used as an alternative to the Coast Path and offers a superb view down the river. However, most will prefer to continue on the riverside Path into Barnstaple, an attractive town with many facilities for walkers.

Approaching Barnstaple on the former railway (signed as Tarka Trail), the Path crosses a bridge over the tributary River Yeo and then passes the old railway station to a riverside embankment. Leave this at steps climbing to Barnstaple's historic Long Bridge. Barnstaple, North Devon's major centre, is a pleasant and interesting historic town well worth exploring, as well as offering a range of facilities, including a branch line railway to the main line at Exeter.

Fremlington Pill emptying into the River Taw. Photographer Simon Goodman

OS Maps: Landranger 180; Explorer 139

	This Walk	Cumulative	This Walk	Cumulative	Grading	Timing
Ascent	40ft	13,350ft	12m	4,069m	Easy	4 hours
Distance	10.7mi	79.7mi	17.2km	128.3km		

For detailed directions see our Walking Guide no. 9, Barnstaple to Bideford.

This is a flat, low-level Section, much of it following a former railway line on the south side of the Taw Estuary. It passes through a landscape of marshland and pastures, with the tidal expanses and sand banks of the river never far away. This is an area of great value for birdlife. Approaching Instow the estuary opens out as the Taw's sister river, the Torridge, joins and there are wide areas of sand bars and dunes. This Section, despite its proximity to "civilisation" and the use of the former railway as part of the Devon Coast to Coast Cycle Route, is nevertheless one of much interest and character.

Directions

There is a regular and frequent all-year bus service between Barnstaple and Bideford, which can also be accessed at Fremington and Instow along the route. A variety of short walk options is therefore available.

Cross Barnstaple's historic Long Bridge then keep to the right of the large roundabout, following Tarka Trail signing, then cross a mini-roundabout to a Path which curves around to a subway under the approach road for the high-level bridge. A link path to the railway station goes off to the left here. The main Path, signed Coast Path and Tarka Trail, then links to the former railway line. The direct Coast Path route across the high-level bridge joins here.

The former railway continues past the delightfully restored Fremington Quay, with its all-year cafe and Information Point. At Yelland look out for the Path leaving the railway to the right, which takes the Coast Path behind the site of an old power station. After passing inland of the cricket ground, the route then crosses an area of dunes to arrive at the estuary-side road through Instow, which has all facilities. Go through the old railway station and follow the former railway to the restored Bideford station. Leave the station to cross Bideford Long Bridge, then turn right along the bustling quay. Bideford has all facilities.

Westward Ho! Photographer Lucy Thompson

OS Maps: Landranger 180; Explorer 139

	This Walk	Cumulative	This Walk	Cumulative	Grading	Timing
Ascent	524ft	13,871ft	159m	4,228m	Easy	3 hours
Distance	8.0mi	87.7mi	12.9km	141.1km		

For detailed directions see our Walking Guide no. 10, Bideford to Westward Ho!

Much of this Section follows the estuary of the River Torridge, first on its east bank then turning back on its west. The estuary is largely enclosed by green hills, but houses and roads are ever-present and a high-level road bridge over the estuary is a major feature. The Coast Path crosses the river at the charming old port of Bideford. Passing beyond the estuary and through the characterful old fishing town of Appledore, the Path crosses the open spaces of Northam Burrows and its surrounding marshlands, and then alongside an enormous pebble ridge as it arrives again at the open sea. As an alternative option, missing out Bideford, a ferry service is now operating between Instow and Appledore, for details see page 27.

Directions

A regular bus service links Bideford and Westward Ho! and another connects Bideford to Appledore. These services allow for a range of Coast Path-based walk options.

From Bideford Quay keep alongside the river past the car park, then next to the rugby club to a lane which passes under the high-level bridge. Follow the waymarked tracks to a riverside lane, then after the old tank traps, fork right to a small woodland area.

Descend to a boardwalk, then continue on the old sea wall. Follow the waymarked route round Appledore shipyard, and at the road turn right into Appledore via Myrtle Street. Continue along the quay and on into the charming old part of the town, along Irsha Street and past the lifeboat station. Here the route follows a Path along the edge of low cliffs and across a field to a slipway. When the tide is low continue along The Skern around another wooden slipway following the high water mark, then cross a stile to enter Northam Burrows. When the tide is high follow the slipway where the route joins a road. Follow the road for approximately 0.3 miles/0.5 kilometres to a crossroads and here turn right.

Follow the track ahead alongside the marshes, then on the seaward side of the dunes to the pebble ridge. Continue ahead on the landward side of the ridge. On the approach to Westward Ho! leave Northam Burrows by the pedestrian gate to the right of the cattle grid by the toll booth. Proceed up Pebble Ridge Road using the right side pavement to the crossroads. Turn right into Golf Links Road, then after the Tesco Express store, turn right into Westbourne Terrace. Just before the slipway turn left onto the promenade to Westward Ho!

Alternatively, there is now a section of path which goes along the sea wall towards the main seafront area signed as a Public Footpath.

OS Maps: Landranger 180 (eastern half) ; Explorer 139 (eastern half);
Landranger 190 (western half); Explorer 126 (western half)

	This Walk	Cumulative	This Walk	Cumulative	Grading	Timing
Ascent	2,995ft	16,866ft	913m	5,141m	Strenuous	6 hours
Distance	11.1mi	98.8mi	17.9km	159.0km		

For detailed directions see our Walking Guide no. 11, Westward Ho! to Clovelly

This Section is one of cliffs and woods. The eastern half is an area of undulating cliffs, cut in places by substantial valleys, though in the length closest to Westward Ho!, where the line of an old railway is used, the Path is generally level. The western half passes through lengthy wooded stretches, much of it along the old carriage road known as the Hobby Drive. At the western end, Clovelly is probably one of the most picturesque villages in England.

Directions

There is no direct bus route between Westward Ho! and Clovelly. However, there is one between Bideford and Clovelly, as well as a frequent link to Bideford from Westward Ho! Peppercombe and Buck's Mills, about two thirds of the way along this length towards Clovelly, are on the Bideford-Clovelly bus route, giving possible bus-walks at this end.

At Westward Ho! walk along the Path above the beach. After passing the last of the holiday chalets, the Path follows the track of the long-disused Bideford to Westward Ho! railway. This makes a fine easy scenic walk. Where the railway turns inland, the Path continues along the cliffs, rising and falling to cross a short pebble beach before climbing again. At Peppercombe turn inland to cross the stream and then continue through woodland. Note that some old maps may not show the correct route at Worthygate Wood. The Path drops to Buck's Mills, a picturesque little spot, then climbs again into more woods. On leaving Barton Wood, keep to the bottom edge of the field until crossing a bridge to the Hobby Drive at the end of a second field. The Hobby Drive section is nearly 3 miles/5 kilometres long, and although very pleasant, offers sea glimpses rather than sea views. The Path arrives at Clovelly at the top of the steep village street. Clovelly is very picturesque and has most facilities, though perhaps limited in range.

Clovelly. Photographer Rebekka Welch

OS Maps: Landranger 190; Explorer 126

	This Walk	Cumulative	This Walk	Cumulative	Grading	Timing
Ascent	2,382ft	19,248ft	726m	5,867m	Moderate to strenuous	5 hours
Distance	10.3mi	109.1mi	16.6km	175.6km		

For detailed directions see our Walking Guide no. 12, Clovelly to Hartland Quay.

There is a great contrast in this Section between east and west. In the east the landscape is one of parkland, the domesticated and partly ornamental landscape of the grounds of Clovelly Court. After leaving the parkland a run of high cliffs culminates at Hartland Point, one of the great defining headlands of the Coast Path. Here the coast turns from east-west to north-south and its character changes into one of the Coast Path's most breathtaking stretches, with dark brooding cliffs behind jagged fingers of rock stretching into the Atlantic Ocean. Experiencing its magnificent scenery is well worth the effort of crossing the spectacular deep valleys which cut the coast. The Section ends at the pub and hotel at Hartland Quay, which has a wonderful remote atmosphere.

Directions

Hartland Quay has no public transport. However, there are numerous walking links from the Coast Path to Hartland village, 2.5 miles/4km inland, which is on the bus route to Clovelly.

If using Clovelly as a base, it is requested that visitors use the main car park. If you're walking on your own, it might be worth paying for a village visit at £7 which includes car parking.

From the main car park, walk out of the entrance and turn right down the road for some 220 yards/200 metres to a black gate on the left. Go through and follow the track first right and through a gap in the wall, then leave the track and follow the marked Path down to the right. After a while go through a kissing-gate then follow the fence on the right to another gate into shrubbery. Continue through the shrubbery through more gates. Turn right at a T-junction and right again at the next fork. Soon the Path arrives at an unusual seat known as the "Angel's Wings". At the track, turn hard right – not along the track. After passing a superb viewpoint the Path descends steeply into a valley to another track. Go right here. The signed detour to the viewpoint is well worth the effort.

The Coast Path goes down the valley to Mouth Mill. Turn left before reaching the shore on to a substantial track. Turn right to cross the new steel and timber bridge.

Turn right after the bridge, then left to climb the valley side. Half-way up, follow the steps to the right. On reaching the top, pass through fields to a stile on the right leading to some descending zigzags. Cross the bridge at the bottom, turn left then take the first right.

After the prehistoric earthwork of Windbury Castle, the Path continues on the cliff-top to Shipload Bay and then on to Hartland Point, where there are seasonal refreshments. The Coast Path turns sharp left off the lighthouse track, towards the coastguard lookout before the lighthouse gate. A short diversion gives a good view of a wreck on the rocks below.

From Hartland Point the Path descends into an unusual valley, almost parallel to the coast, at Smoothlands, before climbing again. Descending then to the valley at the

Abbey River, the Path goes inland to cross at a stone bridge. At the next cliff top, past an old folly tower, the Path arrives at a road by the old Rocket House. Bear right to follow the Path downhill to Hartland Quay, a lonely outpost with car park, toilets and refreshments, as well as a hotel.

Near Morwenstow. Photographer Virginia Arendt

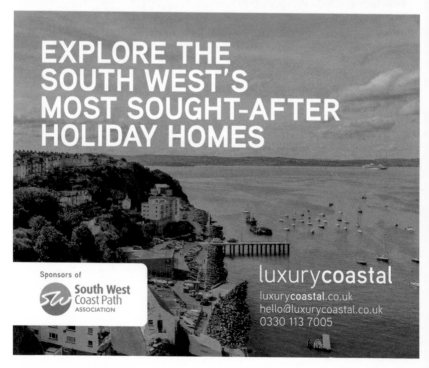

OS Maps: Landranger 190; Explorer 126 (most of length); Explorer 111 (Bude)

	This Walk	Cumulative	This Walk	Cumulative	Grading	Timing
Ascent	4,170ft	23,418ft	1,271m	7,138m	Severe	8.5 hours
Distance	15.2mi	124.3mi	24.5km	200.0km		

For detailed directions see our Walking Guide no. 13, Hartland Quay to Morwenstow and Morwenstow to Bude.

This is an awe-inspiring and dramatic coastline. Great jagged ridges of rock stretch out into the Atlantic Ocean, backed by high, surf-fringed cliffs. The coast is punctuated by jutting headlands and tiny, often inaccessible beaches. In the south, towards Bude, the coast softens a little, and at low tide, long sandy beaches appear. This is a spectacular Section.

(Note that although for convenience this Section is included in the North Devon length, the southern half of the Section is within Cornwall.)

Directions

Hartland Quay has no public transport connections. There is, however, an infrequent bus service between Bude and Morwenstow, half-way along, which could be used for a bus-walk on the southern half of this Section.

Note that this is probably the most arduous of all the days in the suggested itinerary. It is necessary to cross ten river valleys to complete the length, all of them steep and deep. Because of this, many may prefer to split the length at Morwenstow, where there is a tea room and the pub also offers some accommodation.

From Hartland Quay a track then a grassy path passes behind St Catherine's Tor. There is a climb, then the cliff Path reaches the dramatic waterfall at Speke's Mill Mouth. Keep to the eastern side of the stream here for some 150 yards/135 metres then cross by the wooden footbridge. Follow the signs up the valley inland of Swansford Hill. Take care at Sandhole Cliff, after joining the metalled road, to look out for the signpost after about 0.3 mile/0.5 kilometres indicating the turn right back to the coast. (It is hoped this length of road may be eliminated in the near future.) After Welcombe Mouth, Marsland Mouth marks the Cornish border, indicated by a wooden sign. The ascents and descents continue, and a diversion to Morwenstow might be worth considering. The church is picturesque and interesting and there are seasonal refreshments nearby. At the radio dishes do not miss the sign directing right towards the cliff edge. Descending to Duckpool, cross the stream by a footbridge. There are toilets here. Continue on to Sandy Mouth where there are more toilets and seasonal refreshments. The going now eases at last, and after passing over the open cliffs at Maer Down the Path arrives at Crooklets Beach at Bude. Follow the Path along the low cliffs behind the beaches into the town, which has all facilities.

North Devon Combe Martin to Marsland Mouth

The businesses listed here are our 'Way Makers'. They make the great South West Coast Path experience possible, and give back to the Trail. Please support them if you can. More info at www.southwestcoastpath.org.uk/waymaker

> If you enjoy staying, eating, drinking or doing an activity with a business along the Path, please let them know about our Way Maker scheme so we can share their brilliance!

GR Grid Reference
DP Distance from the Path
N Nearest Town/Village with facilities
3 Number of Rooms
Dogs Welcome

Evening Meal Available
Wifi
Parking
Grocery Shop On Site
Private Transport to the Path

Laundry Facilities
Caters to Specific Dietary Needs
Early Breakfast Available
Packed Lunch Offered
£ Budget

For Bude accommodation see **North Cornwall** Page 90

Bed & Breakfast and Hotels

NAME	OTHER INFO
The Poplars Guest House Woodlands, Combe Martin, EX34 0AR 01271 882240 poplarsguesthouse@outlook.com www.poplarsguesthouse.co.uk	**GR:** SS574471 **DP:** 0 miles **N: COMBE MARTIN** OFFERS ONE NIGHT STAYS 5
The Devonian Guest House The Devonian, Torrs Park, Ilfracombe, EX34 8AZ 01271593656 information@thedevonianguesthouse. www.thedevonianguesthouse.co.uk	**GR:** SS511472 **DP:** 0.3 miles **N: ILFRACOMBE** OFFERS ONE NIGHT STAYS 6
Collingdale Guest House 13 Larkstone Terrace, Ilfracombe, EX34 9NU 01271 863770 thecollingdale@gmail.com www.thecollingdale.co.uk	**GR:** SS526475 **DP:** 0.3 miles **N: ILFRACOMBE** 9
High Ways Guest House Mullacott Cross, Ilfracombe, EX34 8NY 01271 863821 highwaysguesthouse@gmail.com www.highwayshouse.com	**GR:** SS502441 **DP:** 2 miles **N: LEE BAY** 5
The Whiteleaf Croyde, Braunton, EX33 1PN 01271 890266 bookings@thewhiteleaf.co.uk www.thewhiteleaf.co.uk	**GR:** SS441389 **DP:** 1 mile **N: CROYDE** 5
Silver Cottage B&B 14 Silver Street, Braunton, EX33 2EN 07974017663 silvercottage.braunton@gmail.com www.bedandbreakfast-braunton.co.uk	**GR:** SS489372 **DP:** 1.5 miles **N: BRAUNTON** OFFERS ONE NIGHT STAYS 2

North Devon Combe Martin to Marsland Mouth

NAME	OTHER INFO	
Trojen Bed & Breakfast Franklyn Avenue, Braunton, EX33 2JY ● 01271 814019 / 07890885825 ◎ jennyjcocker@yahoo.co.uk ⊕ www.staybandbnorthdevon.com	**GR:** SS490365	**DP:** 0.5 miles
	N: BRAUNTON	
	OFFERS ONE NIGHT STAYS	
	② 🛜 🚗 ☕	
Bennings B&B The Firs, Higher Park Road, Braunton, EX33 2LG ● 01271 814358 ◎ info@bennings.co.uk ⊕ www.bennings.co.uk	**GR:** SS499364	**DP:** 1 mile
	N: BRAUNTON	
	OFFERS ONE NIGHT STAYS	
	③ 🐕 🛜 🚗	
No. 22 Bed & Breakfast 22 Sticklepath Terrace, Sticklepath, Barnstaple, EX31 2AY ● 07581878308 ◎ no22bnb@gmail.com ⊕ www.barnstaplebedandbreakfast.com	**GR:** SS255553	**DP:** 0 miles
	N: BARNSTAPLE	
	OFFERS ONE NIGHT STAYS	
	④ 🛜 📺 ☕	
Corner House B&B 14 The Strand, Bideford, EX39 2ND ● 01237 473722 ◎ cornerhousestrand@gmail.com ⊕ www.cornerhouseguesthouse.co.uk	**GR:** SS452268	**DP:** 0.1 miles
	N: BIDEFORD	
	OFFERS ONE NIGHT STAYS	
	⑤ 🐕 🛜 📺 ☕	
Moorview House, Moorview Enterprises Moorview House, Gammaton, Bideford, EX39 4QE ● 01237 473469 ◎ stephen@moorviewhouse.com ⊕ www.moorviewhouse.com	**GR:** SS490244	**DP:** 2.6 miles
	N: BIDEFORD	
	③ 🐕 🛜 🚗 ☕	
Appledore One End House 1 One End Street, Appledore, Bideford, EX39 1PN ● 01237 473846 ◎ ejanemhayman@gmail.com ⊕ appledoreoneendhouse.wixsite.com/bandb	**GR:** SS464304	**DP:** 0.25 miles
	N: APPLEDORE	
	OFFERS ONE NIGHT STAYS	
	③ 🐕 🛜	
Harbour View Cottage 77 High Street, Clovelly, EX39 5TQ ● 01237 432215 ◎ harbourview77@yahoo.com ⊕ www.clovellycottage.co.uk	**GR:** SS317248	**DP:** 0 miles
	N: CLOVELLY	
	OFFERS ONE NIGHT STAYS	
	④ 🐕 🛜 📺 ☕ 🍴	
Elmscott Farm B&B Elmscott, Hartland, EX39 6ES ● 01237 441276 / 01237 441367 ◎ johngoaman@btconnect.com ⊕ www.elmscott.org.uk	**GR:** SS231217	**DP:** 1 mile
	N: HARTLAND	
	OFFERS ONE NIGHT STAYS	
	③ 🛜 🚗 🛒 🐾 📺 ☕ 🍴	
Hartland Quay Hotel Hartland, Bideford, EX39 6DU ● 01237 441218 ◎ info@hartlandquayhotel.co.uk ⊕ www.hartlandquayhotel.co.uk	**GR:** SS222247	**DP:** 0 miles
	N: HARTLAND	
	OFFERS ONE NIGHT STAYS	
	⑭ 🐕 🍴 🛜 🚗 ☕ 🍴	

Self Catering and Hostels

NAME	OTHER INFO
Seaweed Cottage Moory Meadow, EX34 0DG 📞 07802654399 ✉ enquiries@seaweedholidays.co.uk 🌐 www.seaweedholidays.co.uk	**GR:** SS578472 **DP:** 0 miles **N: COMBE MARTIN** 3 🐕 📶 🚗 📷
Willingcott Valley Holiday Village Willingcott Valley, Willingcott Hill, Woolacombe EX34 7HN 📞 01271 871 106 ✉ info@willingcott-valley.co.uk 🌐 www.willingcott-valley.co.uk	**GR:** SS488429 **DP:** 2 miles **N: WOOLACOMBE** 🚗 📷
Ocean Backpackers 29 St James Place, EX34 9BJ 📞 01271 867835 ✉ info@oceanbackpackers.co.uk 🌐 www.oceanbackpackers.co.uk	**GR:** SS522478 **DP:** 0.3 miles **N: ILFRACOMBE** OFFERS ONE NIGHT STAYS 12 📶 🚗 📷
Higher Mullacott Farm Mullacott Cross, EX34 8NA 📞 01271 377432 ✉ enquiries@myfavouritecottages.co.uk 🌐 www.myfavouritecottages.co.uk/groups/higher-mullacott	**GR:** SS517454 **DP:** 1.5 miles **N: ILFRACOMBE** 6 📶
Heddon Orchard Bothy Heddon Valley, EX31 4PY 📞 0344 800 2070 ✉ holiday.enquiries@nationaltrust.org.uk 🌐 www.nationaltrust.org.uk/holidays/bothy-heddon-orchard-devon	**GR:** SS654481 **DP:** 1 miles **N: BARNSTAPLE** OFFERS ONE NIGHT STAYS 1 🐕
Catboat Cottage Irsha Street, EX39 1RY 📞 0776662407 ✉ catboatcottage@gmail.com 🌐 www.catboatcottage.co.uk	**GR:** SS463308 **DP:** 0 miles **N: APPLEDORE** 4 📶 📷
Peppercombe Bothy Peppercombe Bothy, EX39 5EA 📞 0344 800 2070 ✉ holiday.enquiries@nationaltrust.org.uk 🌐 www.nationaltrust.org.uk/holidays/peppercombe-bothy-devon	**GR:** SS432255 **DP:** 0.5 miles **N: BUCK'S MILLS** OFFERS ONE NIGHT STAYS 🐕 🚗
Elmscott Youth Hostel Elmscott, Hartland, EX39 6ES 📞 01237 441367 / 01237 441276 ✉ john.goa@virgin.net 🌐 www.elmscott.org.uk	**GR:** SS231217 **DP:** 1 mile **N: HARTLAND** OFFERS ONE NIGHT STAYS 7 📶 🚗 🛒 🐕 📷

North Devon Combe Martin to Marsland Mouth

NAME	OTHER INFO		
Fosfelle Country House Glamping and Cottages	**GR:** SS263237	**DP:**	2 miles
EX39 6EF	**N: HARTLAND**		
01237441273			
info@fosfelle.co.uk	🔟 🐕 📶 🚗 📷		
www.fosfelle.co.uk			
Little Barton Hartland Cottage & Farmhouse	**GR:** SS241237	**DP:**	3 miles
Hartland, Bideford, EX39 6DY	**N: HARTLAND**		
01237 441259 / 07974 837365	OFFERS ONE NIGHT STAYS		
enquiries@littlebartonhartland.co.uk	9️⃣ 🐕 📶 🚗 📷		
www.littlebartonhartland.co.uk			
Hartland Caravan Holidays	**GR:** SS263242	**DP:**	3 miles
South Lane, Hartland, EX39 6DG	**N: HARTLAND**		
01237 441664	OFFERS ONE NIGHT STAYS		
info@hartlandcaravanholidays.co.uk	🐕 🚗		
www.hartlandcaravanholidays.co.uk			
Quincecote	**GR:** SS244 254	**DP:** 1.25 miles	
Hartland, Bideford, EX39 6DA	**N: HARTLAND**		
01237 441011	OFFERS ONE NIGHT STAYS		
annajon@btinternet.com	1️⃣ 🍴 📶 🚗 📷 ☕		
www.stayinhartland.co.uk			

Campsites and Holiday Parks

NAME	OTHER INFO		
Watermouth Lodges, Park Life Resorts	**GR:** SS556479	**DP:**	0 miles
Watermouth Lodges, Watermouth, Berrynarbor, EX34 9SJ	**N: COMBE MARTIN**		
01271 545 009			
booking-management@parkliferesorts.com	4️⃣2️⃣ 🐕 🍴 📶 🚗 🛒 📷 ☕		
www.parkliferesorts.com			
Little Roadway Farm Camping Park	**GR:** SS467422	**DP:** 0.5 miles	
Georgeham Road, Woolacombe, EX34 7HL	**N: WOOLACOMBE**		
01271 870313	OFFERS ONE NIGHT STAYS		
enquiries@littleroadway.co.uk	🐕 🍴 🚗 🛒 📷 £		
www.littleroadway.co.uk			
Sunnymead Farm Camping & Touring Site	**GR:** SS500442	**DP:**	1 mile
Mortehoe Road, Ilfracombe, EX34 8NZ	**N: WOOLACOMBE**		
01271 879845	OFFERS ONE NIGHT STAYS		
info@sunnymead-farm.co.uk	🐕 📶 🚗 🛒		
www.sunnymead-farm.co.uk			
Tarka Trail Camping	**GR:** SS492322	**DP:**	0 miles
Lower Yelland Farm, Yelland, Barnstaple, EX31 3EN	**N: INSTOW**		
01271861011	OFFERS ONE NIGHT STAYS		
bookings@tarkatrailcamping.co.uk	🐕 🚗 £		
www.tarkatrailcamping.co.uk			

North Devon Combe Martin to Marsland Mouth

NAME	OTHER INFO		
Westacott Farm Camping Abbotsham, Bideford, EX39 5BN ☎ 01237 472351 ✉ enquiries@westacottfarm.co.uk ⊕ www.westacottfarm.co.uk	**GR:** SS410261	**DP:** 0.5 miles	
	N: BIDEFORD		
	OFFERS ONE NIGHT STAYS		
	🚗		
Roeys Retreat Campsite Higher Clovelly, Bideford, EX39 5RU ☎ 07551 008297 ✉ roeysretreat@gmail.com ⊕ www.pitchup.com/campsites/England/South_West/Devon/clovelly/roeys-retreat	**GR:** SS312234	**DP:** 1 miles	
	N: CLOVELLY		
	OFFERS ONE NIGHT STAYS		
	🐕🚗🛒£		
West Welsford Wild Camping West Welsford Farm, EX39 6EQ ☎ 07867 547590 ✉ enquiiries@pitchup.com ⊕ www.pitchup.com/campsites/England/South_West/Devon/hartland/west-welsford-wild-camping	**GR:** SS270217	**DP:** miles	
	N: HARTLAND		
	OFFERS ONE NIGHT STAYS		
	🐕£		
Pitt Farm Camping Hartland, Bideford, EX39 6BZ ☎ 01237 441919 ✉ enquiries@pitchup.com ⊕ www.pitchup.com/campsites/England/South_West/Devon/hartland/pitt-farm-camping	**GR:** SS251259	**DP:** 1 miles	
	N: HARTLAND		
	OFFERS ONE NIGHT STAYS		
	🐕£		
Cheristow Campsite Cheristow Lavender Farm, Higher Cheristow, Hartland, EX39 6DA ☎ 01237 440101 ✉ cheristow77@yahoo.com ⊕ www.cheristow.co.uk	**GR:** SS250254	**DP:** 1.25 miles	
	N: HARTLAND		
	OFFERS ONE NIGHT STAYS		
	🐕🚗£		
Stoke Barton Farm Campsite Stoke, Hartland, EX39 6DU ☎ 01237 441238 ✉ stokebartoncampsite@gmail.com ⊕ www.westcountry-camping.co.uk	**GR:** SS235246	**DP:** 0.5 miles	
	N: HARTLAND		
	OFFERS ONE NIGHT STAYS		
	🐕🚗🛒🖥		

Eat and Drink

NAME	OTHER INFO		
Sandy Cove Hotel Berrynarbor, Combe Martin, Ilfracombe, EX34 9SR ☎ 01271882243 ✉ info@sandycove-hotel.co.uk ⊕ www.sandycove-hotel.co.uk	**GR:** SS566473	**DP:** 0 miles	
	N: COMBE MARTIN		
	OFFERS ONE NIGHT STAYS		
	🐕🍴📶🚗🖥🍽☕		
The Terrace Tapas and Wine Bar 62 Fore Street, Ilfracombe, EX34 9ED ☎ 01271863482 ✉ info@terracetapasbar.co.uk ⊕ www.terracetapasbar.co.uk	**GR:**	**DP:** 0 miles	
	N: ILFRACOMBE		
	🐕📶		

NAME	OTHER INFO		
Biffen's Kitchen Ocean Pitch Campsite, Moor Lane, Croyde, EX33 1NZ ☎ 07788532287 ✉ eat@biffenskitchen.com 🌐 www.biffenskitchen.com/croyde-street-food	**GR:** SS434396	**DP:**	0 miles
	N: CROYDE		
	🐕🍴📶◉☕		
Cafe Croyde Bay Baggy Lodge, Croyde, Braunton, EX33 1PA ☎ 0800 188 4860 ✉ cafecroydebay@gmail.com 🌐 www.cafecroydebay.co.uk	**GR:**	**DP:**	0 miles
	N: CROYDE		
	🐕🍴📶◉☕🍎		
The Quay Cafe Velator, Braunton, EX33 2DX ☎ 01271 268180 ✉ office.thequay@gmail.com 🌐 www.thequaycafe.com	**GR:** SS486357	**DP:**	0 miles
	N: BRAUNTON		
	🐕📶🚗		
Station Masters Cafe Station Masters House, Barnstaple Railway Station, Sticklepath Station Road, Barnstaple, EX31 2AU ☎ 01271 379744 ✉ info@stationmasterscafe.co.uk 🌐 www.stationmasterscafe.co.uk	**GR:** SS555325	**DP:**	0 miles
	N: BARNSTAPLE		
	🐕📶☕		
Red Lion Hotel Red Lion Hotel, The Quay, Bideford, EX39 5TF ☎ 01237 431237 ✉ stay@clovelly.co.uk 🌐 www.clovelly.co.uk	**GR:** SS318248	**DP:**	0 miles
	N: CLOVELLY		
	OFFERS ONE NIGHT STAYS		
	🐕🍴📶🚗☕🍎		

Information

NAME	OTHER INFO		
Ilfracombe Tourist Information Centre The Landmark Theatre, The Promenade, EX34 9BZ ☎ 01271 863001 ✉ hello@visitilfracombe.co.uk 🌐 www.visitilfracombe.co.uk	**GR:** SS518478	**DP:**	0 miles
	N: ILFRACOMBE		
Woolacombe Tourist Information The Esplanade, Woolacombe, EX34 7DL ☎ 01271 870553 ✉ info@woolacombetourism.co.uk 🌐 www.woolacombetourism.co.uk	**GR:**	**DP:**	0 miles
	N: WOOLACOMBE		
Bideford Tourist Information Centre The Burton Art Gallery, Kingsley Road, Bideford, EX39 2QQ ☎ 01237 477676 ✉ info@theburton.org 🌐 www.visitdevon.co.uk/northdevon	**GR:** SS455269	**DP:**	0 miles
	N: BIDEFORD		

NAME	OTHER INFO		
Northam Burrows Visitor Centre	**GR:** SS446297	**DP:**	0 miles
Bideford, EX39 1XS	**N: WESTWARD HO!**		
☎ 01237 479708			
✉ northam.burrows@torridge.gov.uk			
🌐 https://www.torridge.gov.uk/northamburrows			

Activities

NAME	OTHER INFO		
Museum of British Surfing	**GR:** SS487365	**DP:**	0 miles
The Yard, Caen Street, Braunton, EX33 1AA	**N: BRAUNTON**		
☎ 01271 815155			
✉ contact@museumofbritishsurfing.org.uk			
🌐 http://www.museumofbritishsurfing.org.uk	🐕 📶 🚗		

> *I give the Coast Path my woof of approval as a great place to explore for my daily walks – the Path and sea air are a win win for me!*
>
> Rudy, South West Coast Path Association Ambassadog

A big thanks to Rudy and Laura for supporting the SWCPA and providing us with some great 'paws on the Path' stories and advice.

Ambassadog Rudy at Nanjizal

Top tips for keeping your dog safe on the National Trail

The Coast Path is the perfect place for dog walking, with 630 miles of exciting smells and things to look at, but the Trail does require extra care at times.

Unfortunately, there are incidences each year when dogs end up losing their footing on cliff edges or worry grazing farm animals, so for their welfare and yours, here are our top tips for staying safe and making the most out of the Coast Path with your dog:

- Always keep your dog in sight; use a lead if you don't have a reliable recall.

- Carry water for your dog – they can easily get dehydrated in summer.

- Keep your dog away from cliff edges – they are often loose and home to rabbits.

- Clip on a short lead around sheep, cows, and horses, irrespective of how well-trained your dog is. It's safer for everyone.

- If you feel threatened by cattle, unclip the lead so you can get away separately.

- Don't let your dog run up to other people uninvited – not everyone likes dogs. People have stepped out of the way of dogs on cliffs with fatal consequences.

- Always bag it and bin it wherever you are.

- Ensure your dog has a name tag and is micro-chipped so you can be easily reunited if your dog gets lost. If on holiday, have a temporary tag with your contact on it.

- In areas of mining heritage be aware there may be uncapped mineshafts hidden in the undergrowth near the path, so keep your dog close.

- Occasionally white, waxy lumps of palm oil are washed up on beaches, avoid if seen, as it can be harmful if eaten by dogs.

- Be tick aware.

Visit **southwestcoastpath.org.uk/dogs** for more information and advice about walking with your dog on the Coast Path.

Top tips for walking near livestock

When walking on the South West Coast Path you will inevitably encounter livestock. Livestock on the coastline are doing a wonderful job as conservation grazers keeping this coastal grassland habitat diverse and special. Although only docile animals should be on the Coast Path, animals can be unpredictable, especially if they have young.

Here are some top tips to help you navigate your way along the Path and past roaming livestock:

- Stop, look and listen when entering land where livestock are present

- Move quickly and quietly, giving livestock a wide birth, especially bulls. Avoid putting yourself between animals and their young

- Stay alert and keep an eye out for any behavioural changes

- Be prepared for livestock to react to your presence, especially if you have a dog with you

- Keep your dog close on a short lead, and under effective control

- If you feel threatened by livestock, let your dog go. Cattle and ponies should follow the dog and not you. You can then catch up with your dog further along the Path

- Cattle and ponies are naturally inquisitive, but most will stop before they reach you. If they follow, just walk on quietly

- Don't panic, wave your arms or run

- Don't put yourself at risk by walking close to livestock. If you cannot see a safe path through, find an alternative route. If cattle or ponies are blocking a path, you're well within your rights to find a safe way, away from the path to avoid them. You should then re-join the footpath as soon as possible when you consider it safe to do so

- When walking on land with sheep, always give them a wide birth especially during lambing season

- Keep your dog on a short lead and do not let them off in areas with sheep present

- Sheep are naturally very nervous and stress can lead to them hurting themselves and unborn lambs

- It is an offence to allow a dog to worry sheep. Worrying includes attacking or chasing sheep

Report any frightening incidents or attacks to the landowner, the highway authority, the Health & Safety Executive (HSE), and also the police if it's of a serious nature

Visit **southwestcoastpath.org.uk/ safety-advice** for more information.

Always remember to leave gates as you find them

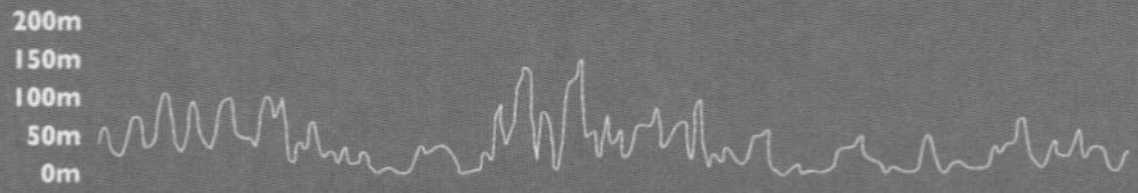

200m
150m
100m
50m
0m

North Cornwall Marsland Mouth to Newquay – **76 miles**

Marsland Mouth
DEVON
Bude
Widemouth Bay
Crackington Haven
Boscastle
Tintagel
Trebarwith Strand
DARTMOOR
Polzeath
Port Gaverne
Port Isaac
Padstow
Harlyn Bay
Rock
Tamar Valley
AONB
Constantine Bay
BODMIN
MOOR
Treyarnon Bay
Porthcothan
Trevone
Mawgan Porth
Watergate Bay
CORNWALL
Plymouth

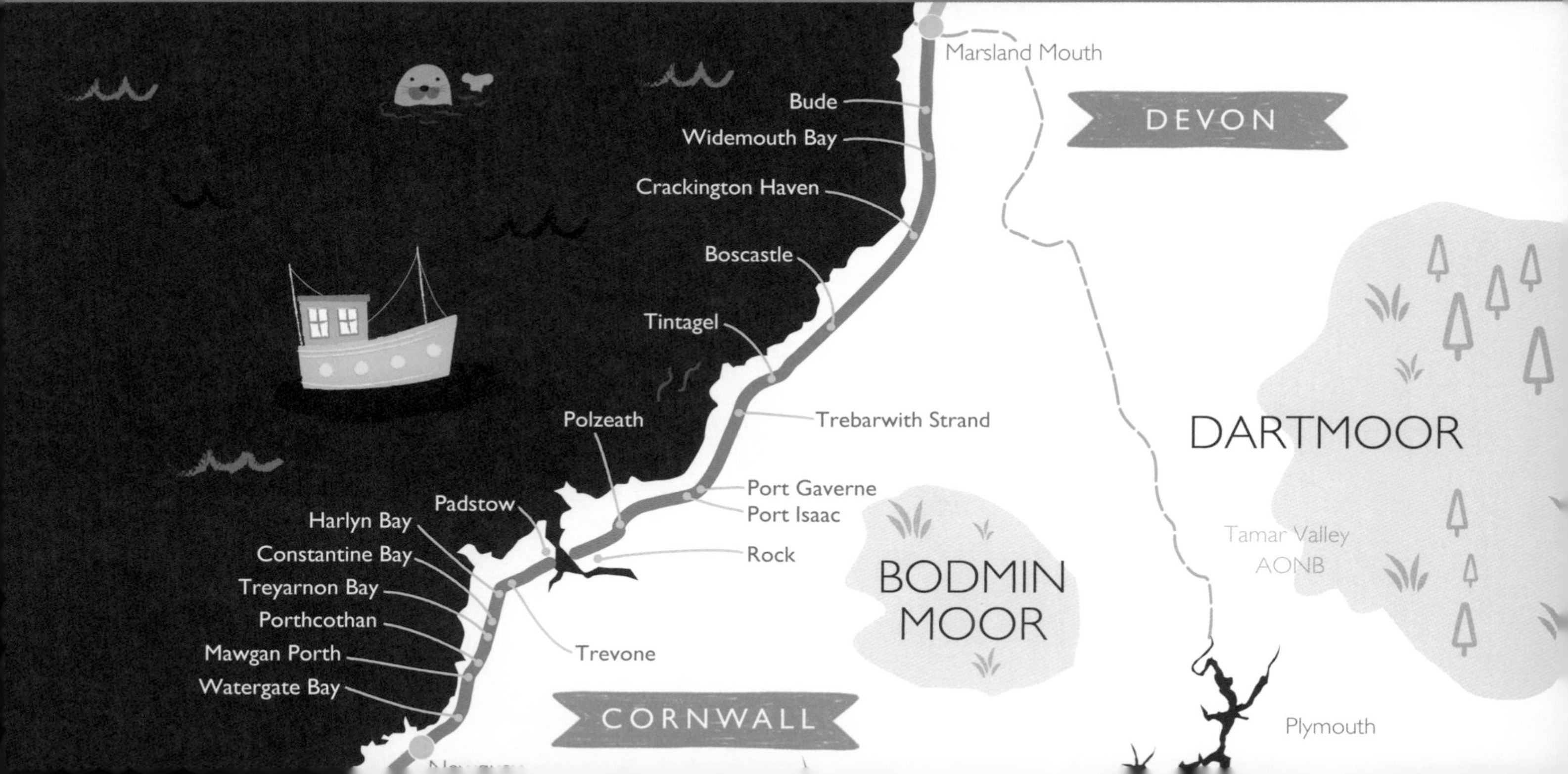

This length of coast faces the prevailing Atlantic westerlies, making for a sometimes exposed landscape. This is exacerbated by the fact that much of this length comprises of high cliffs, often quite sheer, with prominent headlands giving excellent coastal vistas. In places these cliffs are fronted by sandy beaches, as around Bude and Newquay. In the centre of this length is the mouth of the Camel Estuary, also flanked by sandy beaches. The uncompromising nature of the cliffs also means there are few ports or harbours; those that do exist tend to be sheltered from the Atlantic winds – Padstow within the Camel Estuary, Newquay behind Towan Head, Boscastle sheltered in its narrow inlet while Bude is a relatively recent development which owes much of its existence to the arrival of a canal here in the early 19th century. North of the Camel is a length of coast with an untamed atmosphere and including some challenging gradients for walkers; to the south the extensive beaches are popular among families and surfers alike and the cliffs are kinder to walkers.

> All of the locations on the map illustration to the left, have at least 1 facility including toilets, a cafe/restaurant, shop or pub. There are water refill points at Port Quin, Polzeath and around 3 miles South of Polzeath at Rock.

Padstow to Newquay. Photographer Sarah G

OS Maps: Landranger 190; Explorer 111

	This Walk	Cumulative	This Walk	Cumulative	Grading	Timing
Ascent	2,494ft	25,912ft	760m	7,898m	Easy then strenuous	4.75 hours
Distance	9.8mi	134.1mi	15.8km	215.8km		

For detailed directions see our Walking Guide no. 14, Bude to Crackington Haven.

Low grassy cliffs and surfing beaches south of Bude give way to an ever higher and more rugged coastline fronted by rough rock ledges and cut by deep and steep valleys. There are some superb viewpoints along this quiet and remote-feeling length which reward the effort. Crackington Haven is a pleasant spot and on the cliffs above, St Gennys Church is a superb place for contemplation.

Directions

A regular bus service links Bude with Crackington Haven, and also serves Widemouth Bay, about 3 miles/4.8 km from Bude, thus offering a number of bus-walk options.

The Path south from Bude starts at the sea lock on the historic Bude Canal, then climbs to the cliff top at Compass Point and on to Efford Beacon. There are excellent views from here. The Path over Efford Down to Upton and on to Widemouth Bay is easy to follow. Widemouth has toilets and refreshments, the last before Crackington Haven. (There are further refreshment facilities a little inland at Whalesborough, reached by a scenic footpath from Widemouth).

South of Widemouth the Path follows the low cliff for a short distance then diverts inland slightly at Wanson Mouth to join the coast road in the stream valley. Turn right and follow the road as it climbs steeply to Penhalt Cliff (there is an alternative off-road path seaward of the road for part of the way). There are more magnificent views from the cliff-top car park.

From the southern end of the car park the Coast Path crosses a field and descends steeply to Millook Haven. Now follow the steep road uphill for a short distance then turn right onto the cliff top at Raven's Beak. From here the Path climbs steadily past the stunted oak woodland at Dizzard Point and on to Chipman Point. Two further deep and steep valleys are crossed, then a ridge walk leads to Castle Point, which gives tremendous views. Another steep valley crossing leads on to Pencannow Point and views over Crackington Haven. The Path descends easily into the cove, where there are toilets, refreshments, buses and accommodation.

Duckpool, nr Bude. Photographer Kylie Smith

OS Maps: Landranger 190; Explorer 111

	This Walk	Cumulative	This Walk	Cumulative	Grading	Timing
Ascent	2,264ft	28,176ft	690m	8,588m	Strenuous	3.75 hours
Distance	6.7mi	140.8mi	10.8km	226.6km		

For detailed directions see our Walking Guide no. 15, Crackington Haven to Boscastle.

This is a Section of high cliffs, the highest, indeed in Cornwall. Not only are they high, but they also present an appearance of bulk, and the walker will often feel dwarfed by them, especially on a climb or descent or perhaps on a headland. Much of this Section is also quite remote, and this combination makes this a coast with an imposing character.

Directions

Crackington Haven and Boscastle are linked by a regular bus service, making this an option for a bus-walk.

There are toilets and seasonal shops, cafes and a pub at Crackington Haven. Leave behind the beach near the toilets and head out for the headland of Cambeak. Rounding the headland, keep away from its high and sheer cliff edges. Beyond Cambeak the Path is relatively level, passing above the landslip zone at Strangles Beach. Ahead looms High Cliff, the appropriately-named highest cliff in Cornwall. There is a steady ascent but the descent on the south side is very steep. The Path then climbs through a landfall at Rusey Cliff, twisting and turning to the top. A cliff top section through fields follows to the sheer black cliff at Buckator. The Path then dips slightly before continuing at high level to Fire Beacon Point. Here the descent is steep, but helped by attractive slate steps. The Path then follows the cliff face into the inlet of Pentargon, with its impressive waterfall. This is best seen from the southern side – do not be tempted to leave the Path for a better view.

The now easy Path continues on to Boscastle. Aim for the white mast on Penally Hill, then follow the Path alongside the beautiful harbour inlet into Boscastle, now happily restored after a huge flood washed through the valley in 2004.

Boscastle. Photographer Jason Way

OS Maps: Landranger 190 (eastern half); Landranger 200 (western half); Explorer 111

	This Walk	Cumulative	This Walk	Cumulative	Grading	Timing
Ascent	1,230ft	29,406ft	375m	8,963m	Moderate	2.25 hours
Distance	4.7mi	145.5mi	7.6km	234.2km		

For detailed directions see our Walking Guide no. 16, Boscastle to Tintagel.

This fairly short Section is a great local favourite, as it combines all the best of the Coast Path – headlands, sandy bays, historic features and, yes, steep valleys, all in a manageable but picturesque length which is not too taxing. In addition, although popular, it never seems crowded and is, indeed, a "real" walk. With all this and its convenient bus links it is a perfect Coast Path taster.

Directions

Boscastle and Tintagel are linked by a regular bus service. It also serves Rocky Valley, half-way between the two, enabling a variety of bus-walks to be undertaken.

Boscastle has been attractively rebuilt after the floods of 2004, and has all facilities.

The Coast Path leaves the south side of the harbour over the new stone bridge and climbs towards the headland of Willapark, with its prominent white watch tower. The Path cuts across the neck of the headland, but a diversion to the end is worthwhile.

After a steep descent and climb at Grower Gut, the Path continues easily, turning seaward of the Manor House at Trevalga. The headland beyond gives views over the rocky offshore islands important for breeding seabirds. The Path continues past Firebeacon Hill – look out for the Ladies Window rock arch in the gully to the right – then passes seaward of a cliff-top caravan and camping site. There is then a descent into the exquisite Rocky Valley. There is a path up the valley to a bus stop on the coast road, passing prehistoric carvings in the cliff wall.

From the footbridge in the valley the Path climbs again, round the edge of the grassy Bossiney Common and above the sandy bay at Bossiney Haven. Another climb then leads to another headland also, confusingly, called Willapark. Again the Coast Path cuts across the neck of the headland with a worthwhile diversion at the end.

The Path now continues to Barras Nose headland, from where it descends to Tintagel Haven below the castle ruins. Here are toilets, cafe and English Heritage gift shop. A good but steep path leads inland to the village.

Tintagel. Photographer Mark Dilley

OS Maps: Landranger 200; Explorer 111 (eastern half); Explorer 106 (western half)

	This Walk	Cumulative	This Walk	Cumulative	Grading	Timing
Ascent	2,589ft	31,995ft	789m	9,752m	Severe	4.75 hours
Distance	9.1mi	154.6mi	14.6km	248.8km		

For detailed directions see our Walking Guide no. 17, Tintagel to Port Isaac.

Both ends of this Section are relatively popular and accessible. At Tintagel the Coast Path passes the remains of the medieval castle perched on its isolated headland. Since the summer of 2019 a new spectacular cantilever footbridge allows easier access to the castle, readily visible from the Coast Path. The Path then passes the atmospherically located cliff-top church and the now picturesque evidence of coastal slate quarrying. At the other end is the beautifully quaint village of Port Isaac in its scenic bay. The long central length, comprises high cliffs cut by sometimes precipitously steep valleys. It is remote, lonely and often tough, and will be especially appreciated by those who relish an empty, arduous and dramatic coastline.

Directions

It is possible to take a bus between Tintagel and Port Isaac although it is usually necessary to change at Camelford. A bus-walk is therefore possible, particularly using Camelford as a base.

Tintagel has all necessary facilities. Surprisingly, however, little in the village is very old other than the Old Post Office, once a local manor house.

Walkers from Boscastle will pass Tintagel Haven from where the Coast Path passes the entrance to Tintagel Castle, accessed by a cantilever footbridge. (If starting from the village take the path towards Tintagel Haven and fork left to the Castle). There are excellent views over the headland which forms the castle site. Sadly, a fire took hold during the late summer of 2022, causing the Path to close and burning a large section of Glebe Cliff. The route is now open again and hopefully the exposed soil will not be eroded. A good path continues seaward of the church and on beyond past the Youth Hostel in its former quarry building and round Penhallic Point with its superb views.

The Path drops steeply to Trebarwith Strand, where there are toilets, refreshments and pub, the last facilities before Port Isaac. The next part is particularly tough as it climbs steeply out of the Trebarwith valley then almost immediately drops down to sea level and up again at Backways Cove. There follows a level stretch of about a mile/1.5 kilometres to the stream valley behind Tregardock Beach. Descend on the inland side of the detached piece of cliff known as The Mountain, then climb again to Tregardock Cliff. Another level length follows, before the deepest and steepest valley yet at Jacket's Point. At the top yet another deep valley almost immediately follows. Then comes a further valley at Barrett's Zawn. This is an area of massive rock falls. The next valley follows, this one with exceptionally steep and stony sides.

At last the Path levels out again through cliff-top meadows, with just a small valley to cross at St Illickswell Gug. Eventually, the Path reaches the road at Cartway Cove. Cross the road and head downhill to Port Gaverne, a charming spot. Follow the road uphill to the car park at the edge of Port Isaac. Go through this and follow the well-signed Path above the attractive harbour inlet into the village.

Port Isaac is a very picturesque village clustered round the little harbour at the head of a sheltered bay. It has all facilities.

OS Maps: Landranger 200; Explorer 106

	This Walk	Cumulative	This Walk	Cumulative	Grading	Timing
Ascent	2,923ft	34,918ft	891m	10,643m	Strenuous then easy	5.5 hours
Distance	11.7mi	166.3mi	18.8km	267.6km		

For detailed directions see our Walking Guide no. 18, Port Isaac to Padstow.

This Section can be divided into three distinct characters. From Port Isaac to Port Quin is a rollercoaster of a Path, closely following the ups and downs and ins and outs of the quiet, scenic but energy-sapping coast. From Port Quin to Polzeath the character becomes rather more open, if still very scenic, including the broad headland of the Rumps and Pentire Point, a wonderful airy lookout. From Polzeath to the Padstow ferry the landscape is tamer, more domesticated, often with housing or tourist development and more estuarine than maritime as it reaches the mouth of the River Camel.

Directions

There is a regular bus service between Port Isaac and Rock, the ferry point for Padstow. This service also passes through Polzeath at the mouth of the Camel estuary, giving several scenic bus-walk options, including an almost level estuary-side one. There is a popular circuit using the Coast Path between Port Isaac and Port Quin and others from Polzeath around Pentire Point.

Port Isaac has all necessary facilities, and is a scenic gem. To leave the village, take the road to the right behind the fish market. Climbing, it bears right and becomes a cliff Path, soon dropping into Pine Haven. From here to Port Quin the Path is magnificent and clear, but tough as it follows the cliff edge next to a fence line. There is an optional diversion to the end of Varley Head.

The Path enters the beautiful Port Quin inlet, descending to what was once a busy pilchard port, though there are no permanent facilities here now except for a drinking water tap. Follow the road westbound up the steep hill and a little way up the Coast Path leaves to the right, towards Doyden Point. The Path follows above the cove, keeping seaward of and below the large house. Head to a prominent stone cairn, then continue ahead on a grassy Path and past some old mineshafts. From the cairn a diversion to the right goes to the folly of Doyden Castle and to Doyden Point, where there is a superb view back to Port Quin.

There is a sharp descent to Epphaven Cove then the Path passes through a delightful little wooded valley before climbing past the impressive Lundy Hole. The clear cliff Path now heads for the Iron Age fortress on the Rumps headland. A detour to the end is well worthwhile.

From the Rumps the Path climbs through a little former quarry area then continues at high level round Pentire Point, giving spectacular views. An easy descent follows into Polzeath, all well marked. Polzeath has a great surf beach, and so has all the normal facilities such as café, pubs, accommodation, food and surf shops. The Path follows the road past the beach car park where an H_2O water bottle filling facility can be found. The Path then turns right by the cottages, where the road bends sharp left on the steep hill.It now follows a low cliff to Daymer Bay, where there are toilets and a seasonal cafe, then down steps to the beach. (There is a signed inland alternative which must be used at very high tides, which cover the beach). At the far end of the beach the Path crosses a footbridge and continues below Brea Hill.

From the foot of Brea Hill the well-signed path continues between the beach and the golf course to arrive at the car park at Rock, then descends to the ferry slipway for Padstow. Another H_2O water bottle facility can be found at the Rock ferry terminal. A ferry service operates between Rock and Padstow. See page 27 for details.

A water taxi service operates between Rock and Padstow, weather and tides permitting. For further details see page 27.

Note that it is possible to walk Coast to Coast across Cornwall between Padstow and Fowey on the south coast, using the Saints' Way. A guidebook is available from Padstow Tourist Information Centre (TIC).

Port Quin. Photographer Emma Eccles

OS Maps: Landranger 200: Explorer 106

	This Walk	Cumulative	This Walk	Cumulative	Grading	Timing
Ascent	810ft	35,728ft	247m	10,890m	Moderate	2.5 hours
Distance	6.5mi	172.8mi	10.5km	278.1km		

For detailed directions see our Walking Guide no. 19, Padstow to Harlyn Bay.

The length from Padstow to Stepper Point, at the mouth of the Camel, is a scenic length of ever-changing estuarine views with sandy stretches, especially at low tide. Beyond, the coast is an easy but picturesque length of cliffs, which include occasional views right across the headland at the mouth of the estuary and up the Camel as well as west to Trevose Head. The two elements of this Section combine to form a popular local walk.

Directions

A regular bus service links Padstow with Harlyn Bay. This allows for a possible bus-walk. There are also a number of possible circular walks from Padstow using the Coast Path which take in the Stepper Point headland.

Padstow is a charming and bustling little harbour town a short way up the Camel Estuary. If arriving from Rock, notice that normally the ferry arrives in Padstow at the harbour, but at low tide it lands a short distance downstream at St Saviour's Point.

The Coast Path leaves the north end of the harbour and proceeds on low cliffs alongside the estuary. After passing a wooded little stream valley at St George's Cove the Path heads inland of a marshy area before going back to the cliffs and on to Hawker's Cove. Seasonal refreshments are available at Rest a While Tea Garden at Hawker's Cove. Pass behind the old pilots' houses here then fork right to climb to Stepper Point, with its Daymark tower. From here there are remarkable views, inland to Bodmin Moor as well as along the coast.

The Path is now on the exposed Atlantic coast. Go round the precipitous inlet of Butter Hole Cove, looking out for the small Pepper Hole to the right of the Path just before. An easy length to Gunver Head follows, with excellent sea views. Approaching Trevone the Path skirts the impressive Round Hole collapsed cave – approach this with caution as the sides are sheer. Follow the cliffs round into the bay at Trevone, which has toilets, cafe and pub, as well as a car park. The Path crosses the rear of the beach and leaves behind the little headland on the south-west side of the bay, following the cliff edge to Harlyn Bay, where there are seasonal refreshments and toilets.

Harlyn Bay. Photographer Vicky Williams

OS Maps: Landranger 200; Explorer 106

	This Walk	Cumulative	This Walk	Cumulative	Grading	Timing
Ascent	751ft	36,479ft	229m	11,119m	Moderate	3.5 hours
Distance	6.7mi	179.5mi	10.8km	288.9km		

For detailed directions see our Walking Guide no. 20, Harlyn Bay to Porthcothan.

This is a popular Section, never far from a variety of holiday accommodation. It is perhaps most associated with a range of scenic sandy surfing beaches, some of them quite extensive. As a contrast, around the middle of the length is the great landmark of Trevose Head and its lighthouse, visible from great swathes of the North Cornwall coast and an atmospheric location.

Directions

A regular bus service passes Harlyn Bay and links to Porthcothan. The same route serves Constantine Bay, about two-thirds of the way along the coast from Harlyn, giving a potential for a variety of bus-walks.

Harlyn has seasonal refreshments and toilets. From the car park cross the stream on the road bridge then follow the beach below the low cliff. At high spring tides the footpath across the beach is briefly inaccessible. After some 330 yards/300 metres climb the concrete steps on the left onto the cliff and then continue to the headland at Cataclews Point and Mother Ivey's Bay.

The Path passes inland of Padstow's lifeboat station, accessible by a cul-de-sac path, and then goes on to Trevose Head, passing the lighthouse. On a clear day the coastal views are incredibly extensive, ranging from the satellite dishes north of Bude to the granite hills of West Penwith behind St Ives. This is an atmospheric headland.

After an old quarry the Path passes a Round Hole collapsed cave and descends to the partly rocky Booby's Bay. Continue on to the rear of Constantine Bay, a very attractive and extensive beach at low tide. Walk the length of the beach. There are toilets and seasonal refreshments at the far end and a bus stop a little way inland. Beyond the dunes the Path rounds Treyarnon Head to cross another attractive beach at Treyarnon Bay, with seasonal toilets and refreshments.

An unusually indented coastline follows, with sheer-sided headlands and impressive coves. Near Pepper Cove the ramparts of an Iron Age cliff fort may be seen, and the whole coastline is quite spectacular. The Path then turns into another sandy cove, at Porthcothan Bay, which has toilets and refreshments.

RNLI Padstow Lifeboat Station. Photographer Marcin Jankowski

OS Maps: Landranger 200; Explorer 106

	This Walk	Cumulative	This Walk	Cumulative	Grading	Timing
Ascent	1,447ft	37,926ft	441m	11,560m	Moderate	5 hours
Distance	10.3mi	189.8mi	16.6km	305.5km		

For detailed directions see our Walking Guide no. 21, Porthcothan to Newquay.

This is a relatively well-walked Section, particularly around Newquay. It shows the interplay of high cliffs and sandy beaches particularly well. Almost the whole length is characterised by high, flat-topped cliffs, sometimes with prominent headlands, which for long stretches form the back of extensive attractive sandy beaches, many of them popular with surfers. While never a lonely Section, its cliffs and bays make it one well worth exploring, helped by the relatively easy terrain.

Directions

Porthcothan and Newquay are linked by a regular bus service. This route follows a road parallel and close to the coast, meaning that there are a number of possible links to the Coast Path from this bus, allowing for quite a range of possible bus-walks.

Porthcothan has all facilities that may be needed. The Coast Path leaves past the shop and keeps in front of the houses and on around the headland. After a short steep descent and climb, an easy level walk leads to Park Head, an excellent viewpoint. There have been numerous landslips here so keep to the Path inland of the white posts. The whole headland is worth wandering over and exploring. Ahead now is the National Trust's Carnewas property, with its spectacular beach. The Trust's cafe and Information Centre are open throughout the summer. On the beach below are the massive stacks forming Bedruthan Steps.

The Bedruthan Steps area can be busy, but the steps to the beach are closed following a major rock fall. Check the National Trust 'Carnewas at Bedruthan' website for details. A quieter length follows to Trenance Point and into the sandy bay of Mawgan Porth, where there are toilets, refreshments and a pub as well as a bus stop. Surprisingly, this was once the site of an unfinished canal project.

Cross the stream using the road then leave it to the right on the sharp bend on the hill out of Mawgan Porth. There then follows a long high level length to Watergate Bay on airy flat-topped cliffs, cut by a couple of minor descents. The Path passes Iron Age remains here while inland is the contrast of Newquay Airport. The Path continues on the cliff top behind the magnificent Watergate Beach, much used for surfing and other activities. The Path then descends to the road by the Watergate Bay Hotel, and here there are toilets, refreshments and another bus stop.

Cross the stream at the road then turn right by the car park and climb back to the cliffs, which are now followed to the outskirts of Newquay. The coastal view ahead to the town and its headlands is excellent. The short section of Coast Path that leaves the road to pass round the headland of Trevelgue Head is temporarily closed. As this is an important prehistoric location taking a diversion through the gate on the right to visit the headland is recommended. At Porth Beach follow the steps down on the left, to pass underneath the main road and cross the next little headland to emerge above Lusty Glaze beach – look for the information board here relating to the canal previously encountered at Mawgan Porth.

The Path continues into the park at Barrowfields, skirting its seaward side, to reach the main road into Newquay town centre. Follow this just past the railway station then take the old tramway road on the right. Follow the waymarked route along the footpath above Towan Beach.

At the corner go down the steps on the right then from the car park cross Beach Road and follow the tarmac path ahead. At the end follow the steps on the left to pass a bowling green and public toilets to Fore Street. Turn right here as far as the Red Lion and here turn right again to the harbour down North Quay Hill.

As well as all facilities, Newquay has a branch line railway station linking to the main line to Penzance and is the centre of a network of local bus routes.

Cliffs above Bedruthan Steps, Newquay. Photographer Debbie Whatt

The businesses listed here are our 'Way Makers'. They make the great South West Coast Path experience possible, and give back to the Trail. Please support them if you can. More info at www.southwestcoastpath.org.uk/waymaker

If you enjoy staying, eating, drinking or doing an activity with a business along the Path, please let them know about our Way Maker scheme so we can share their brilliance!

GR Grid Reference
DP Distance from the Path
N Nearest Town/Village with facilities
3 Number of Rooms
Dogs Welcome

Evening Meal Available
Wifi
Parking
Grocery Shop On Site
Private Transport to the Path

Laundry Facilities
Caters to Specific Dietary Needs
Early Breakfast Available
Packed Lunch Offered
£ Budget

Bed & Breakfast and Hotels

NAME	OTHER INFO	
The Tree Inn	GR: SS230064	DP: 1.5 miles
Fore Street, Stratton, Bude, EX23 9DA	N: BUDE	
01288 352038	OFFERS ONE NIGHT STAYS	
contact@treeinn.co.uk	6 🍴 📶 🖨 ☕	
www.treeinn.co.uk		
Sea Jade Guest House	GR: SS209066	DP: 0.25 miles
15 Burn View, Bude, EX23 8BZ	N: BUDE	
01288 353404	OFFERS ONE NIGHT STAYS	
seajadeguesthouse@yahoo.co.uk	7 🍴 📶 🚗 🖨 ☕	
www.seajadeguesthouse.co.uk		
Sunrise Guest House	GR: SS209066	DP: 1 mile
Sunrise, 6 Burn View, Bude, EX23 8BY	N: BUDE	
01288 353214	OFFERS ONE NIGHT STAYS	
info@sunrise-bude.co.uk	7 📶 🍽 ☕	
www.sunrise-bude.co.uk		
Beach House B&B and Break Bar	GR: SS199028	DP: 0 miles
Marine Drive, Widemouth Bay, Bude, EX23 0AW	N: BUDE	
01288 361256	OFFERS ONE NIGHT STAYS	
enquiries@beachhousewidemouth.co.uk	10 🐕 🍴 📶 🚗 🛒 🍽	
www.beachhousewidemouth.co.uk		
Pendrin Guest House	GR: SX056888	DP: 0 miles
Atlantic Road, Tintagel, PL34 0DE	N: TINTAGEL	
01840 770524	OFFERS ONE NIGHT STAYS	
info@pendrintintgel.co.uk	7 📶 🚗 🍽	
www.pendrintintagel.co.uk		
Bosayne Guest House	GR: SX056887	DP: 0 miles
Atlantic Road, Tintagel, PL34 0DE	N: TINTAGEL	
01840 770514	OFFERS ONE NIGHT STAYS	
enquiries@bosayne.co.uk	8 📶 🚗 🍞	
www.bosayne.co.uk		
Chandlers Lodge B&B	GR: SX103835	DP: 4.5 miles
13a Clease Road, Camelford, PL32 9QX	N: TREBARWITH STRAND	
01840 938564 / 07486893279	OFFERS ONE NIGHT STAYS	
enquiries@chandlerslodge.co.uk	4 🐕 🍴 📶 🚗 🖨 🍽 ☕ 🍞	
www.chandlerslodge.co.uk		

NAME	OTHER INFO		
Trewetha Cottage B&B Trewetha, Port Isaac, PL29 3RU ☎ 01208 880877 ✉ dijohnsalisbury1@btinternet.com 🌐 www.southwestcoastpath.org.uk/trewetha-cottage-port-isaac	**GR:** SX004800 **DP:** 0.4 miles **N: PORT ISAAC** OFFERS ONE NIGHT STAYS 2 📶 🚗		
The Slipway Harbour Front, Middle Street, Port Isaac, PL29 3RH ☎ 01208 880264 ✉ slipway@portisaachotel.com 🌐 www.portisaachotel.com	**GR:** SW996807 **DP:** 0 miles **N: PORT ISAAC** OFFERS ONE NIGHT STAYS 7 🍴 📶		
South Quay B&B 4 Riverside, Padstow, PL28 8BY ☎ 01841 532383 ✉ thepadstowcullinans@gmail.com 🌐 www.southquaybedandbreakfastpadstow.co.uk	**GR:** SW919753 **DP:** 0.1 miles **N: PADSTOW** 2 🐕 📶		
Coswarth House 12 Dennis Road, Padstow, PL28 8DD ☎ 07907 626084 ✉ coswarth@cawlimited.co.uk 🌐 www.coswarthhouse.com	**GR:** SW919751 **DP:** 0.5 miles **N: PADSTOW** OFFERS ONE NIGHT STAYS 4 📶 🚗 🍽		
Penhalonga B&B Constantine Bay, Padstow, PL28 8JG ☎ 01841 521122 / 078158 33158 ✉ lizkennerley@btinternet.com 🌐 www.southwestcoastpath.org.uk/penhalonga-constantine-bay	**GR:** SW869743 **DP:** 0.5 miles **N: PADSTOW** OFFERS ONE NIGHT STAYS 3 🐕 📶 🚗 ☕ 🍽		
Sunny Corner Main Road, Trevone PL28 8QX ☎ 01841 520476 ✉ mo@wizadora.com 🌐 www.sunnycorner.info	**GR:** SW892758 **DP:** 0 miles **N: TREVONE BAY** 2 🐕 📶 🚗 ☕		
Penlan B&B Porthcothan Bay, PL28 8LP ☎ 01841 520440 ✉ mary@idenna.com 🌐 porthcothanbay.co.uk/bandb-booking	**GR:** SW860718 **DP:** 0.12 miles **N: PORTHCOTHAN** OFFERS ONE NIGHT STAYS 1 📶 🚗 ☕		

Self Catering and Hostels

NAME	OTHER INFO		
Valley View Holiday Cottage Woodford, Bude, EX23 9JQ ☎ 07855 302242 ✉ info@valleyview.holiday 🌐 www.valleyview.holiday	**GR:** SS212136 **DP:** 0.7 miles **N: BUDE** 3 🐕 📶 🚗		

NAME	OTHER INFO
Polrunny Farm Holiday Cottages Boscastle, PL35 0EL ☏ 07885591849 ✉ stay@polrunnyfarm.com ⊕ www.polrunnyfarm.com	**GR:** SX102896 **DP:** 1 mile **N: BOSCASTLE** 7 🐕 🐾 📶 🚗 🔲
Cleave Farm Cottages Cleave Farm, St Gennys, Crackington Haven, EX23 0NQ ☏ 07944 468431 ✉ katyzoeftig@btinternet.com ⊕ www.facebook.com/CleaveFarmCottages	**GR:** SX154977 **DP:** 0 miles **N: CRACKINGTON HAVEN** OFFERS ONE NIGHT STAYS 5 🐾 📶 🚗
Cabin Beaver Beaver Cottages, Tregatta, Tintagel, PL34 0DY ☏ 01840 770378 ✉ beavercottages@outlook.com ⊕ www.beaver-cottages.co.uk/cabin-beaver	**GR:** SX056873 **DP:** 0.25 miles **N: TINTAGEL** OFFERS ONE NIGHT STAYS 🐾 📶
Beaver Cottages Tregatta, Tintagel, PL34 0DY ☏ 01840 770378 ✉ beavercottages@outlook.com ⊕ www.beaver-cottages.co.uk	**GR:** SX056873 **DP:** 0.25 miles **N: TINTAGEL** OFFERS ONE NIGHT STAYS 3 🐾 📶 🚗
Truffle Cottage 48 Egloshayle Road, Wadebridge, Pl27 6AE ☏ 01208 895 354 ✉ bookings@corncott.com ⊕ www.corncott.com	**GR:** SW995722 **DP:** 7 miles **N: POLZEATH** 2 🐾 📶 🚗 🔲
Mariners Lettings Ltd Rock Road, Rock, PL27 6JN ☏ 01208 869257 ✉ enquiries@marinerslettings.co.uk ⊕ www.marinerslettings.co.uk	**GR:** SW933756 **DP:** 0 miles **N: ROCK** 🐾 📶 🚗
Trekara Cottage 5 Rose Terrace, St Merryn, Padstow, PL28 8FD ☏ 07941025125 ✉ contact@trekara.co.uk ⊕ www.trekara.co.uk	**GR:** SW881738 **DP:** 1 miles **N: PADSTOW** 3 📶 🚗
Cornish Traditional Cottages 3 Eddystone Court, Eddystone Road, Wadebridge, PL27 7FH ☏ 01208 895354 ✉ bookings@corncott.com ⊕ www.corncott.com	**GR:** SW989724 **DP:** 0 miles **N: PADSTOW** 🐾 📶 🚗 🔲
Porth Sands Penthouse 6 Porth Sands, Beach Road, Porth, Newquay, TR7 3NE ☏ 07874 880571 ✉ porthsands.penthouse@gmail.com ⊕ www.porthsandspenthouse.co.uk	**GR:** SW829626 **DP:** 0 miles **N: NEWQUAY** 2 📶 🚗

Campsites and Holiday Parks

NAME	OTHER INFO
Widemouth Bay Caravan Park Poundstock, Bude, EX23 0DF ☏ 01288 361 208 ✉ widemouth-gm@jfhols.co.uk 🌐 www.johnfowlerholidays.com/cornwall-holiday-park/ widemouth-bay-caravan-park	**GR:** SS195009 **DP:** 0.75 miles **N: BUDE** [188] 🐕 🍴 📶 🚗 🛒
Little Clifden Campsite Halgabron, Tintagel, PL34 0BD ☏ 07901 604755 ✉ enquiries@pitchup.com 🌐 www.pitchup.com/campsites/England/South_West/ Cornwall/Tintagel/little-clifden-campsite	**GR:** SX072886 **DP:** 0.3 miles **N: TINTAGEL** OFFERS ONE NIGHT STAYS 🐕 £
Penhalt Farm Holiday Park Widemouth Bay, Bude, EX23 0DG ☏ 01288 361210 ✉ info@penhaltfarm.co.uk 🌐 www.penhaltfarm.co.uk	**GR:** SS194002 **DP:** 0.25 miles **N: WIDEMOUTH BAY** OFFERS ONE NIGHT STAYS 🐕 📶 🚗 🛒 ⦿ £
Trebylah Farm Camping Minster, Boscastle, PL35 0HL ☏ 01840 250308 ✉ enquiries@pitchup.com 🌐 www.pitchup.com/campsites/England/South_West/ Cornwall/Boscastle/trebyla-farm	**GR:** SX116924 **DP:** 0.3 miles **N: BOSCASTLE** OFFERS ONE NIGHT STAYS 🐕 £
Tregella Place Camping Tregella Lane, Padstow, PL28 8LJ ☏ 07964 973054 ✉ enquiries@pitchup.com 🌐 www.pitchup.com/campsites/England/South_West/ Cornwall/Padstow/tregella-place-camping	**GR:** SW900738 **DP:** 2 miles **N: PADSTOW** OFFERS ONE NIGHT STAYS 🐕 £
Dennis Cove Campsite Dennis Lane, Padstow, PL28 8DR ☏ 01841 532349 ✉ hello@denniscovecampsite.co.uk 🌐 www.denniscovecampsite.co.uk	**GR:** SW920743 **DP:** 0 miles **N: PADSTOW** OFFERS ONE NIGHT STAYS [100] 🐕 🚗 ⦿
Carnevas Holiday Park St Merryn, Padstow, PL28 8PN ☏ 01841 520230 ✉ carnevascampsite@aol.com 🌐 carnevasholidaypark.co.uk	**GR:** Porthcothan **DP:** 0.5 miles **N: PORTHCOTHAN** OFFERS ONE NIGHT STAYS 🐕 🍴 📶 🚗 🛒
Trewan Hall Camping Site St. Columb, TR9 6DB ☏ 01637 880261 ✉ enquiries@trewan-hall.co.uk 🌐 www.facebook.com/TrewanHallCampsite	**GR:** SW911646 **DP:** 4 miles **N: MAWGAN PORTH** [180] 🐕 📶 🚗 🛒 ⦿

NAME	OTHER INFO		
Higher Pendeen Camping	**GR:** SW859668	**DP:**	0 miles
Gluvian Cart House, Gluvian Farm, TR8 4BG	**N: MAWGAN PORTH**		
☏ 07977592530	OFFERS ONE NIGHT STAYS		
✉ higherpendeen@gmail.com			
🌐 www.higherpendeencamping.com			

Eat and Drink

NAME	OTHER INFO		
Rectory Farm Tea Rooms	**GR:** SS205152	**DP:** 0.25 miles	
Crosstown, Morwenstow, EX23 9SR	**N: BUDE**		
☏ 01288 331251			
✉ jill@rectory-tearooms.co.uk			
🌐 www.rectory-tearooms.co.uk			
Brendon Arms	**GR:** SS206061	**DP:**	0 miles
Falcon Terrace, Bude, EX23 8SD	**N: BUDE**		
☏ 01288 354542	OFFERS ONE NIGHT STAYS		
✉ enquiries@brendonarms.co.uk			
🌐 www.brendonarms.co.uk			
Tintagel Brewery Bar & Bistro	**GR:** SX092868	**DP:**	3 miles
Tintagel Brewery, Tintagel, PL34 0HJ	**N: TINTAGEL**		
☏ 01840219386			
✉ bookings@tintagelbrewerybarandbistro.co.uk			
🌐 www.tintagelbrewerybarandbistro.co.uk			
Pengenna Pasties Tintagel	**GR:** SX055886	**DP:**	miles
6 Atlantic Road, Tintagel, PL34 0DD	**N: TINTAGEL**		
☏ 01840 770223			
✉ info@pengennapasties.co.uk			
🌐 www.pengennapasties.co.uk/shop			
Oystercatcher	**GR:** SW935786	**DP:**	miles
Polzeath, Wadebridge, PL27 6TG	**N: POLZEATH**		
☏ 01208 862371			
✉ oystercatcher@staustellbrewery.co.uk			
🌐 oystercatcherpolzeath.co.uk			
Old Custom House	**GR:** SW921750	**DP:**	miles
Old Custom House Hotel, South Quay, Padstow, PL28 8BL	**N: PADSTOW**		
☏ 01841 532359	OFFERS ONE NIGHT STAYS		
✉ oldcustomhouse@staustellbrewery.co.uk			
🌐 oldcustomhouse.co.uk			
Carnewas Tearooms	**GR:** SW849690	**DP:**	0 miles
Bedruthan Steps, St Eval, PL27 7UW	**N: MAWGAN PORTH**		
☏ 01637860701			
✉ carnarcher@gmail.com			
🌐 www.carnewas-tea-rooms.co.uk			

Information

NAME	OTHER INFO		
Bude Tourist Information Centre The Crescent, Bude, EX23 8LE 01288 354240 budetic@visitbude.info www.visitbude.info	**GR:** SS208150	**DP:**	0 miles
	N: BUDE		

Tintagel Visitor Centre Bossiney Road, Tintagel, PL34 0AJ 01840 779084 tintagelvisitorcentre@gmail.com www.tintagelweb.co.uk/	**GR:** SX058883	**DP:**	0 miles
	N: TINTAGEL		
Padstow Tourist Information The Mariner's Clock Building, Padstow, PL28 8BL 01841 533449 info@padstowtic.co.uk www.padstowlive.com	**GR:** SW921750	**DP:**	0 miles
	N: PADSTOW		

Activities

NAME	OTHER INFO		
Watersports - Friends of Bude Sea Pool The Old Toilets, Summerleaze Car Park, Bude, EX23 8HJ 01288 488118 admin@budeseapool.org www.budeseapool.org	**GR:** SX092868	**DP:**	0 miles
	N: BUDE		

Getting Around

NAME	OTHER INFO		
Trev's Taxi Flat 2, St Catherines, 33 Downs View, Bude, EX23 8RG 07799 663217 trevstaxi3217@btinternet.com www.trevstaxi.co.uk	**GR:** SW207071	**DP:** 0.25 miles	
	N: BUDE		

Lundy Bay. Photographer Jason Way

Check the water quality before diving in with the Surfers Against Sewage App

Since 2019 we're proud to have worked with Surfers Against Sewage to support the Beach Clean campaigns around the SW coast. We'd now like to give a shout out to their Safer Seas & Rivers Service (SSRS) App.

Having a dip in the ocean is often part of the experience of walking the Coast Path. It's sometimes useful to check the water quality before you take a swim and you can now do this with the SSRS App.

Providing the only national water quality information service, the Safer Seas & Rivers Service App helps beach-goers, open water swimmers and watersports enthusiasts track pollution events and real-time water quality information allowing users to assess the risks of entering the water. Covering over 400 locations across England, Scotland and Wales, this information empowers you to make an informed decision about how, when and where you use the water.

The app also includes complementary beach information; including real-time surf conditions, tide times, beach activities, nearby facilities and lifeguard services.

Little Fistral, North Cornwall. Photographer Sam Hussey

To download the smartphone app, designed for both Apple iOS and Android platforms, users should search for '**Safer Seas & Rivers Service**' within their app store or scan the QR code.

SAFER SEAS & RIVERS SERVICE

Surfers at Praa Sands. Photographer Harvey Stacey

West Cornwall Newquay to Falmouth – 144 miles

150m
100m
50m
0m

Newquay

Crantock
Holywell Bay
Perranporth
St Agnes
Porthtowan
Portreath
Gwithian

Hayle
Lelant

Helston

Falmouth

Mawnan Smith
Helford

Porthallow

St Keverne
Coverack

Cadgwith
The Lizard

Carbis Bay
St Ives

Mullion

Zennor

Newlyn

Porthleven
Praa Sands
Perranuthnoe
Marazion
Penzance

Pendeen
Botallack
St Just
Sennen Cove
Land's End
Porthgwarra

Porthcurno
Lamorna Cove
Mousehole

The cliffs to the west of Newquay give way to the scenic and sandy St Ives Bay. Beyond St Ives, an old fishing port of medieval origin, the coast encircles two great peninsulas: Penwith, the westernmost part of England, and the Lizard, the southernmost. Both are composed of hard, resistant rocks, making for a rugged cliff coastline, but their characters differ. Penwith is largely granite and inland of its impressive cliffs, frequently marked by rock pinnacles and solid jointed slabs, and is a rough, semi-moorland landscape. Along a length of Penwith's north coast, the Coast Path passes a number of old cliff-face tin mines. The Lizard has a much smoother profile, with its inland landscape an unusual flat-topped plateau. The exposed locations of these two peninsulas result in harsh, weather-beaten coastlines with a lack of large-scale tree cover, though both are superbly dramatic. Between these two magnificent peninsulas is the iconic Mount's Bay, site of the fairytalelike setting of St Michael's Mount, surmounted by its castle. The bay is the site of a number of coastal towns; Penzance, the main centre for this far western part of Cornwall, Marazion, with its ancient origins, the fishing port of Newlyn and picturesque Mousehole, once of great importance until burned by the Spanish in the wars of the 16th century. East of the Lizard, the quiet wooded estuary of the Helford River is followed by the extensive estuary of the River Fal, which marks the end of this length.

> All of the locations on the map illustration to the left, have at least 1 facility including toilets, a cafe/restaurant, shop or pub.

St Michael's Mount. Photographer Oli at Different View Photography

OS Maps: Landranger 200; Explorer 104

	This Walk	Cumulative	This Walk	Cumulative	Grading	Timing
Ascent	1,145ft	39,071ft	349m	11,909m	Moderate	3.5 hours
Distance	8.1mi	197.9mi	13.0km	318.5km		

For detailed directions see our Walking Guide no. 22, Newquay (Harbour) to Holywell Bay.

This Section includes some superb viewpoints from headlands in and around Newquay, the panoramas quite unspoiled by the proximity of the large town. Beyond Newquay, a range of landscapes is experienced, from wide sandy beaches to exposed cliff tops to small sandy bays, to dune systems. In addition, unexpectedly, the wooded estuary valley of the river known as The Gannel is crossed at the edge of Newquay. This variety, and the proximity to a range of facilities and accommodation, make this a popular, well-used length.

Directions

A regular bus service links Newquay with Holywell Bay, and also serves Crantock, between the two. This gives a number of bus-walk possibilities.

Newquay is the biggest town on Cornwall's north coast. Although usually busy, being especially popular with surfers and also with groups of young holidaymakers, it is in a very attractive setting of beaches and headlands. All the facilities are here, and there is a branch railway linking to the main line to Penzance.

From Newquay Harbour the Coast Path climbs past the old Huer's Hut to Towan Head. From Towan Head the Path then follows the back of Fistral Beach. This is probably the country's most popular surfing beach and international competitions are held here. The Path climbs to the cliffs at the southern end and then crosses the road to go along Pentire Crescent, which leads into Penmere Drive. The Path then arrives above the Gannel Estuary. However, this misses the major headland of Pentire Point East, which is well worth the diversion to the end. It is hoped this will become the official route in the near future, check our website for the most up to date information. (If following the diversion round the headland, on returning from the end, aim for the far bottom of the car park at the neck of the headland. From here head along the suburban road parallel to the Gannel. Follow this to the Fern Pit Cafe.)

There are four options from here for crossing the Gannel, depending on the tide and time of year.

OPTION 1: FERN PIT FERRY (deduct 2 miles/3 kilometres from total mileage)

The first option is to use the Fern Pit Ferry from behind the cafe. The cafe is approximately 0.7 mile/1.1 kilometres west of Penmere Drive. For further details see page 27.

OPTION 2: PENPOL CROSSING (official route)

Go along Penmere Drive then turn right into Trevean Way. Follow the waymarks right and go downhill across a grassy area. At the foot of the grass bank turn right along the footpath, then take the steps on the left down to the tidal Penpol Footbridge across the Gannel Estuary. This can be used 3-4 hours either side of low water. Cross the Gannel here. (If coming from the headland circuit, continue past the Fern Pit Cafe and on along Riverside Avenue, then ahead and right. At a junction where there is a footpath to the right, keep ahead, ignoring the footpath. Bear right into Penmere Drive, again ignoring another footpath on the right. Go along Penmere Drive and re-join the route detailed on the previous page.)

OPTION 3: TRENANCE FOOTBRIDGE (add 3 miles/4.8 kilometres to total mileage)

This route is usable at most states of the tide. From the Newquay side of the Penpol crossing, continue upstream on the Path parallel to the river until it arrives at the A392 Gannel Road. There is a footbridge on the right just before the junction with the A3058 Trevemper Road. Cross the bridge and continue ahead. Do not follow the creekside path to Penpol, but instead take the bridleway on the left towards Trevemper. Turn right just before reaching the tarmac, and follow the footpath through Treringey to arrive at the south side of the Penpol tidal footbridge.

OPTION 4: MAIN ROAD ROUTE (add 4.5 miles/7.2 kilometres to total mileage)

Continue past the Trenance footbridge and along the A392 Trevemper Road from the roundabout. At the next roundabout turn right and after about 100 yards/90 metres take the little unsigned lane on the right. This leads to Trevemper, going forward and right as the lane goes left. After the gate turn left on the route described under Option 3 through Treringey.

Options 2, 3 and 4 come together at Penpol. Cross the ford to follow the lane then take the waymarked Path on the right above the estuary. After passing the ferry landing for Option 1, this path leads to Crantock Beach car park. Crantock village with its facilities and bus stop is a little way inland. Cross the car park and climb the steps through the gate opposite; bear left at the junction of grassy paths on entering the dune area and follow this inland of the main dune area, to re-emerge at a coastal path which leads to the cliffs of Pentire Point West where the Bowgie Inn among others, provide meals and refreshments. The Path goes round Porth Joke (known locally as Polly Joke), then on around Kelsey Head to Holywell Bay, descending across more dunes either into the village or to cross the river on a seaward footbridge. There are facilities, some seasonal here.

Between Holywell Bay and Crantock Beach. Photographer Colin Moore

OS Maps: Landranger 200; Explorer 104

	This Walk	Cumulative	This Walk	Cumulative	Grading	Timing
Ascent	755ft	39,826ft	230m	12,139m	Moderate	2 hours
Distance	4.5mi	202.4mi	7.2km	325.7km		

For detailed directions see our Walking Guide no. 23, Holywell Bay to Perranporth.

The theme of this Section is sand, in the form of both dunes and beaches, although it begins by rounding headlands at Penhale and Ligger Points. However, even at Penhale the inland vista is dominated by dunes, although the adjacent former Army Camp is also prominent. For the bulk of this Section sand is everywhere; on the seemingly endless length of Perran Beach and the dunes which back it. Both ends, Holywell and Perranporth, are busy holiday settlements, but the more remote areas of Perran Beach can be surprisingly quiet.

Directions

Holywell Bay and Perranporth are both served by regular bus services from Newquay, making a bus walk along this length, using Newquay as a base, an option.

Holywell Bay has all facilities, some seasonal. From Holywell Bay the Path rounds Penhale Point, skirting the seaward edge of the somewhat unattractive former Penhale army camp. It then goes on out to Ligger Point, where there is a panoramic view of the length of Perran Beach. The Path heads towards the dunes then descends behind the cliff quarry to the beach. It now follows the back of the beach for some 1.5 miles/2.5 kilometres. At the very highest tides it may not be possible to use the beach route. In this case do not descend to the beach but turn left uphill for a short distance, to follow the Path on your right through the dunes next to a line of red and white posts, and then seaward of a holiday park, parallel to the sea. Join a track which leads to the top of steps from the beach. Even at lower tides it is often necessary to climb these steps from the beach. Coming up from the beach, at the top of the steps turn right following the slate Coast Path waymarks. The Path descends back to the beach on the south side, and then crosses the stream by the footbridge when nearly at Perranporth, where there are all needed facilities. Again at the very highest tides, the beach and footbridge may not be available, in which case follow a path around the lip of the dunes to the rear of the Surf Lifesaving Club, to a sandy track which leads to a road. Follow the road right then turn right at the mini-roundabout into Perranporth.

Porthtowan. Photographer Ian Jesson

OS Maps: Landranger 200 (Perranporth); Landranger 203 (remainder); Explorer 104

	This Walk	Cumulative	This Walk	Cumulative	Grading	Timing
Ascent	2,250ft	42,076ft	686m	12,825m	Moderate then strenuous	5.75 hours
Distance	12.4mi	214.8mi	20.0km	345.7km		

For detailed directions see our Walking Guide no. 24, Perranporth to Portreath.

This section is one in which Cornwall's coastal mining heritage is paramount. There is much evidence of former mining activity, including somewhat stark areas of spoil and sometimes slightly sad building relics, but also some grand and imposing engine houses and chimneys. In some locations, the large-scale level of the activity is difficult to imagine now. In any event, the scale and grandeur of the cliffs, the beaches and the surf mean that nature always re-asserts itself.

Directions

A regular bus service links Perranporth to St Agnes. A skeletal summer service links Perranporth to Portreath, also passing St Agnes and Porthtowan along the way, giving numerous bus-walk options.

Perranporth is a busy holiday centre with all facilities. The Coast Path goes west from the promenade car park and follows the hill up Cliff Road. Keep left of the castellated building then along Tregundy Lane. Continue ahead through the entrance to the Youth Hostel grounds passing the Hostel on the immediate right and on to the cliffs, the Path clinging to the cliff face out to Cligga Head. Here the Path enters quarry and mine workings, but is well signposted. There is then a level stretch alongside Perranporth Aerodrome before the steep descent to Trevellas Porth, a valley marked by many relics of the mining industry. Go upstream to cross at the road bridge, then back to the cliffs and back down again into Trevaunance Cove, where there are toilets and refreshments. The bus stop at St Agnes is a little way inland.

On reaching the road at Trevaunance Cove, go straight across passing the Driftwood Spars car park and a large tall house on the right. Follow the waymarked footpath immediately right along a metalled lane, then fork right along a footpath. Soon the Path climbs steeply to the cliff top. A long and scenic high-level Path now goes around St Agnes Head, giving superb views ahead, then past the iconic engine house at Towanroath before descending to Chapel Porth, a small and attractive cove with toilets and seasonal refreshments available at the Chapel Porth Beach Cafe. The toilets here are only unlocked when the cafe is open.

Follow the stream inland for 200 yards/185 metres then turn right and up to the cliffs, before heading back down again into Porthtowan. Again there are toilets and refreshments and a magnificent beach. There is a bus stop a little inland.

Follow the road inland then turn right up West Beach Road, then left up the narrow road 'West Cliff' to the cliff top. More mine workings are passed, and at Sally's Bottom the path descends and ascends steeply. The Path runs alongside a prominent fence next to MOD land before reaching a road which descends into Portreath. This former industrial harbour town has all facilities.

OS Maps: Landranger 203; Explorer 104 (eastern half); Explorer 102 (western half)

	This Walk	Cumulative	This Walk	Cumulative	Grading	Timing
Ascent	1,362ft	43,438ft	415m	13,240m	Moderate/ easy	5.5 hours
Distance	11.7mi	226.5mi	18.8km	364.5km		

For detailed directions see our Walking Guide no. 25, Portreath to Hayle.

There are two distinct characters to the coast of this Section. Between Portreath and Godrevy it is one of high, level cliffs, the sea far below. In contrast, between Godrevy and Hayle the walk focuses on sand, either dunes or beach, on the focal view of Godrevy lighthouse and on the great colourful sweep of St Ives Bay. This is never a lonely or remote length, but it is a scenic, fascinating and rewarding one.

Directions

A summer bus service links Portreath and Hayle, and also passes Godrevy, half-way between the two. This allows for bus-walk options over the whole Section or over either of the two distinct character lengths.

Portreath has all facilities and a pleasant beach. Leave the town crossing the bridge next to the car park then right, up Battery Hill. Continue ahead, meandering between properties at the end, turning right just beyond them up steps to the top of Western Hill, with its excellent views. After a couple of steep valleys the Path then embarks on a long easy cliff-top walk along Reskajeague Downs, eventually arriving at Hell's Mouth, where there is the seasonal Hell's Mouth Cafe. The Path then narrows and turns right at an obvious T-junction. Cross a stile next to a gate and cross the seaward side of a field, before continuing easily round Navax and Godrevy Points, the lighthouse becoming a focal point offshore. Keep seaward of the car park and access road, and follow the signs along the low cliffs and over the dunes to another car park, at the Godrevy Cafe. Follow the boardwalk from the car park to cross the Red River. Turn left for 30 yards/29 metres then go right, following the large slate waymarks through the former quarry, now a nature reserve.

Keep ahead through the dunes, following the signposts. Note it is often possible to walk along the beach here, but beware the incoming tide which can mean being cut off below the cliffs. If the tide is right, leave the beach at the lifeguard hut near the foot of Black Cliff. If coming through the dunes, keep ahead above the hut. Then with either option ascend some steps and turn right onto the tarmac road. Turn right past the first chalet on the right to follow the path to a car park. Turn towards the left and follow the access track ahead. On reaching the modern development of residential and retail units along North Quay it is recommended to walk as close as permitted to the harbour's edge to appreciate its historic heritage. Then follow the pavement ahead and cross the old swing bridge to the road. Turn right to reach the railway viaduct in the centre of Hayle.

OS Maps: Landranger 203; Explorer 102

	This Walk	Cumulative	This Walk	Cumulative	Grading	Timing
Ascent	617ft	44,055ft	188m	13,428m	Easy	2.5 hours
Distance	6.1mi	232.6mi	9.8km	374.3km		

For detailed directions see our Walking Guide no. 26, Hayle to St Ives.

This Section is never far from roads and houses, so often has a suburban air. However, this is outweighed by the views over the River Hayle estuary, and particularly, by the vistas over the great sweep of St Ives Bay with its vast sandy beaches and dunes, the iconic offshore Godrevy Lighthouse as a focal point, and the fabulous sea colours, turquoises, greens and blues, whenever the sun shines on this length.

Directions

A regular bus service links Hayle and St Ives, giving a bus-walk option. In addition, a branch-line railway plies between Lelant and St Ives, and this gives marvellous sea views. This makes for an unusual and especially scenic train-walk option.

Hayle has all facilities, including a railway station on the main line to Penzance. Walk to the viaduct and turn right on the Path immediately before it. Go ahead to Carnsew Road and continue on the pavement, turning right on a narrow Path between housing. Go left at the end then continue to arrive alongside a large lagoon. Keep on to the end, then bear left to the road. Continue as the road passes alongside the River Hayle estuary on The Causeway, a birdwatchers' delight. Cross to the far side of the road then back to the riverside again, before forking right at the Old Quay House. Under the bridge turn right, into a small housing estate. Just before a car park after the housing turn left to a lane, then turn right here. Follow the lane next to the railway and estuary all the way to Lelant Church. Go along the Path next to the church to pass under the railway. Just before the beach turn left along the seaward side of the railway through dunes. (NB. this is also the route of the St Michael's Way, a cross-peninsula path from Lelant to Marazion – a guide leaflet is available at St Ives Tourist Information Centre (TIC).)

Follow the clear Path parallel to the magnificent Porthkidney Beach. Approaching the headland of Carrack Gladden the Path forks – keep right then continue ahead. Descend the road to Carbis Bay, where there are toilets and seasonal refreshments, walking between the hotel and holiday lodges. Climb over a railway bridge then continue as the Path becomes a minor road. Pass the Path taking St Michael's Way inland, then at a little cross-roads go straight ahead, steeply downhill. (Turning right shortly after the St Michael's Way turning down a private, pedestrians only Path gives a more scenic alternative to the official route, re-joining at the little cross-roads.) Cross the railway bridge and double back right, then left to arrive at Porthminster Beach, just below St Ives railway station.

OS Maps: Landranger 203; Explorer 102

	This Walk	Cumulative	This Walk	Cumulative	Grading	Timing
Ascent	3,428ft	47,483ft	1,045m	14,473m	Severe	7 hours
Distance	13.7mi	246.3mi	22.0km	396.4km		

For detailed directions see our Walking Guide no. 27, St Ives to Zennor and Zennor to Pendeen Watch.

There are no settlements on this Section and the character is lonely and remote. It is also tough going, with rocky scrambles and boggy lengths. But it can only be described as a magnificent length. Stark cliffs, rock pinnacles, tiny scenic coves with translucent water, rugged exposed headlands – all are here. Inland, the view is often of empty moorland. This is the Coast Path at its most awe-inspiring. Prepare for its rigours, then enjoy the wonderful experience.

Directions

A regular summer bus service links St Ives and Pendeen village, a little inland of the Coast Path. It also passes through other inland settlements linked by footpath to the Coast Path, principally Zennor, Treen (Gurnard's Head) and Morvah, allowing for various bus-walks options.

A warning: this is a tough and deserted length of the Coast Path. There are no settlements or refreshment facilities, though there are some Path links inland to small settlements. The terrain is often rough and rocky and in places can be boggy. But a compensation: this is a length of wonderfully dramatic coastal scenery.

From the Path below St Ives railway station, keep along as close as possible to the sea and harbour. The official route goes round the green St Ives Head, usually known as The Island. This is reached by following signs to the museum from the far end of the harbour, and on through a small car park. From The Island go through the old "Downlong" quarter to Porthmeor Beach and the Tate. There are also short cuts direct to here – follow signs to the Tate St Ives.

Go along the rear of Porthmeor Beach, then bear off right along the Path next to the putting green. The Coast Path now leads out to the rugged Clodgy Point and then on round Hor Point to Pen Enys Point, where it cuts across the neck of the headland. Pass the trig point on Carn Naun, where there are extensive views forward and back, then descend to cross the stream at River Cove. Just beyond, the Path passes the offshore Carracks, where seals are regularly seen. Approaching Zennor Head the Path forks – keep right to follow the seaward Path round the headland. From Zennor Head the Path heads inland – look out for the signed Coast Path descending steeply to the right. If in need of refreshments, or for the bus, continue along the Path inland to Zennor, where there is a pub and seasonal cafe.

On the Coast Path, more ups and downs lead to the distinctive headland of Gurnard's Head. The Path cuts across its neck, but a diversion onto the headland, an Iron Age fortified site, is worth the effort. There are also diversions inland here to Treen, where refreshments are available at the Gurnard's Head Inn and there is a bus stop.

The Coast Path continues, generally easy to follow if not always an easy walk. Approaching Bosigran, another Iron Age fortification, head for the high point of the ridge, following Coast Path signs and keeping on the landward side of a low wall. At the crest of the ridge head inland and downhill, aiming for a stream and building.

Cross the stream on a small bridge near a ruined building, then follow the Path uphill, just seaward of an obvious stone wall. There is a diversion Path inland here to a bus stop at Rosemergy. After heavy rain the Path round here can be boggy.

Further on the Coast Path, look out for a Path inland to Morvah for another bus stop, if needed. Otherwise keep on the obvious Coast Path round the back of Portheras Cove, and on to the lighthouse at Pendeen Watch. Pendeen village, with its pubs, cafe, shop, toilets and bus stop, is about 1 mile/1.5 kilometres inland.

View from Pendeen Watch

OS Maps: Landranger 203; Explorer 102

	This Walk	Cumulative	This Walk	Cumulative	Grading	Timing
Ascent	1,683ft	49,166ft	513m	14,986m	Moderate	4.25 hours
Distance	9.1mi	255.4mi	14.6km	411.0km		

For detailed directions see our Walking Guide no. 28, Pendeen Watch to Sennen Cove.

This Section offers a wide range of walking experiences. Between Pendeen Watch and Botallack, the overriding experience is of Cornwall's coastal mining heritage. This ranges from unattractive early 20th century industrial relics to romantic stone-built cliff-face engine houses, all this next to sheer cliffs and often wild seas. Beyond Botallack is a superb length of scenic exposed cliffs, highlighted by the magnificent headland of Cape Cornwall. This Section has all that is best on the Cornish coast – rugged cliffs, mining relics, translucent water, turquoise coves, purple heather, rocky scrambles, the view of a lighthouse. Then, approaching Sennen Cove, there is a sweep of broad sandy beaches backed by dunes, and the length ends with a scenic harbour and a lifeboat station. A wonderful length.

Directions

A regular summer bus service links Pendeen village, a little inland of the Coast Path, with Sennen Cove. It also serves St Just, inland of Cape Cornwall, which is used as the centre of various Coast Path-based circular walks. Bus-walks are also possible from Geevor and Botallack, reached by the footpath from the coast.

From Pendeen Watch the Path goes along the road to the end of the row of cottages, then turns right at a granite marker. (The road continues into Pendeen village, with its range of facilities.) The Coast Path is clear and leads to the old mining area at Geevor. A diversion inland leads to refreshments and toilets at the mining museum, which is itself well worth a visit, if possible. Follow the signed track beyond Geevor to the National Trust's Levant Beam Engine House, open for steaming at certain times. From here the official Path follows the clear track parallel to the coast, but a narrower path to seaward with better views leads from the far end of the car park. The two options come together as more mines are passed at Botallack. Look to seaward to see the famous Crowns Mine engine houses, perched improbably on the cliff.

Beyond Botallack, as the mines give way, look for the signed Path to the right which leads to the headland at Kenidjack Castle. A lot of the waymarking in this area uses granite stones, perfect for the landscape setting. From the old building on the headland descend left to a track, go left then bear right on a path down to another track. Go left here then turn right to cross the floor of the Kenidjack Valley. Climb to the top and turn right. Ahead now is the distinctive shape of Cape Cornwall, surmounted by its chimney. Turn right immediately before the road and then bear right across a field past the ruins of a chapel to a stone stile. Cross this, turn left and then climb right to reach the top of the headland. Savour the views, then join the Path, which descends over the seaward side of the Cape by zigzags and steps to reach the National Coastwatch Institution watchhouse. This recent addition to the Coast Path provides a superb experience. Go to the left of the watchhouse, then down the steps and along a path past some stone buildings and through a gate, to reach another set of granite steps descending to the right. In the nearby car park are seasonal refreshments and toilets. St Just is about 1 mile/1.5 kilometres up the road.

At the bottom of the steps go left, then climb right on the track to a road at the top. Bear off right at the sign and follow the clear Path into the Cot Valley. A new route has been established down the valley. For this, turn left at the road and almost immediately right, over a footbridge and past old mine workings, climbing to reach a path which heads to the cove at Porth Nanven. Just before reaching the cove, climb left onto the cliffs. There is a good clear cliff-face path to the beach at Gwynver, although with one rocky climb. From Gwynver the Path continues through the dunes behind the sandy beaches, which can be walked at low tide, to the car park at Sennen Cove. This is a popular family and surfing spot with all facilities.

Botallack. Photographer John van der Hoff

OS Maps: Landranger 203; Explorer 102

	This Walk	Cumulative	This Walk	Cumulative	Grading	Timing
Ascent	1,542ft	50,708ft	470m	15,456m	Moderate	3.25 hours
Distance	6.3mi	261.7mi	10.1km	421.1km		

For detailed directions see our Walking Guide no. 29, Sennen Cove to Porthcurno.

This is the most westerly length of coast in England. Much of it has the character of moorland meeting the sea, with great granite headlands and massive rock outcrops, interspersed with isolated coves with exquisite sea colours. Towards Porthcurno the moorland is replaced by a more pastoral landscape, but the cliffs and coves continue. Much of this Section has a quiet character, interrupted only by the visitor mecca of Land's End.

Directions

Sennen Cove and Porthcurno are linked by a regular bus service, which also goes to Land's End. This allows for a choice of bus-walks, and there are also numerous circuits possible based on the Land's End area.

Sennen Cove has all facilities. Leave the village passing the Round House gallery into the car park. Turn left up steps then right, towards the lookout. From here a range of parallel paths all lead to Land's End. Bear right to the First and Last House, at England's most westerly point, then keep seaward of the main complex to the outpost at Greeb Cottage. The complex has toilets and refreshments if needed. The Path goes behind Greeb Cottage; then again a choice of paths all lead towards the beautiful bay of Nanjizal. At the far end of the bay, head inland up the track then turn right steeply uphill on a stepped path. After passing through a gate, look out for the official, unsigned Path leaving the main track to go seaward down some rocky steps. The Path descends then climbs to the Coastwatch station on Gwennap Head. The main track also leads here, but less scenically.

The official Path is clear from Gwennap Head down into Porthgwarra. An alternative, to be used in good conditions and for the sure-footed only, is to leave the main Path to the right some 150 yards/140 metres after the Coastwatch station, then pass the hole of Tol-Pedn-Penwith ("the holed headland of Penwith") before bearing left to re-join the main Path.

Porthgwarra is a charming little hamlet, with toilets and seasonal refreshments and unusual passages through the cliffs. Leave along a track next to some cottages, climbing again to the cliffs. The clear Path descends to Porth Chapel, passing St Levan's Holy Well. Continue straight ahead over the bridge, climbing again to arrive at the car park of the unique cliff-face Minack Theatre. Leave by the Path next to the theatre entrance. The Path drops very steeply, with deep steps, to Porthcurno Beach. If in doubt, because of the conditions or possible vertigo, follow the road. At the bottom of the steps, keep left above the beach to Porthcurno's facilities.

OS Maps: Landranger 203; Explorer 102

	This Walk	Cumulative	This Walk	Cumulative	Grading	Timing
Ascent	1,381ft	52,089ft	421m	15,877m	Strenuous	3.25 hours
Distance	5.4mi	267.1mi	8.7km	429.9km		

For detailed directions see our Walking Guide no. 30, Porthcurno to Lamorna Cove.

This is a quiet, remote and very scenic Section of cliffs and headlands, punctuated by some picturesque coves and a lighthouse. The larger coves, at each end, Porthcurno and Lamorna, are particularly attractive and are the only access points for cars, so are more popular, Otherwise, the sound of the sea and seabirds are likely to be the only disturbances in this beautiful length.

Directions

A regular bus service goes to Porthcurno and passes about 1 mile/1.5km inland of Lamorna Cove, making a bus-walk feasible. Many undertake one of a variety of circular walks between Porthcurno and Treen using the Coast Path.

Porthcurno has all facilities in summer. The Coast Path leaves at the back of the beach, climbing a steep track to Percella Point before turning to run parallel to the sea. A seaward loop gives a good view of the beautiful Pedn Vounder Beach, but requires a little scramble to return to the official route. The Path then reaches the neck of Treen Head, or Treryn Dinas, the site of an Iron Age fortification. A cul-de-sac diversion heads for the end and the Logan Rock. Continue on the clear Path over the cliff to descend into Penberth Cove, a superb little fishing hamlet with an old capstan. There are toilets but no refreshments.

After climbing away from Penberth, the Path continues along the cliff top, with one steep descent and climb at Porthguarnon, then starts to head inland. After passing a seaward house look out for the signed Path to the right, which descends into the wooded valley of St Loy and on to the boulder beach. Keep along the top of the beach for 55 yards/50 metres before leaving up the Path. This climbs to pass above the lighthouse of Tater-du. Approaching Lamorna Point the Path crosses a length of tumbled rocks, making for slow going, until it suddenly descends to the car park at Lamorna Cove. Here are toilets and seasonal refreshments.

Lamorna. Photographer Rob Milne

OS Maps: Landranger 203; Explorer 102

	This Walk	Cumulative	This Walk	Cumulative	Grading	Timing
Ascent	725ft	52,814ft	221m	16,098m	Strenuous then easy	3.5 hours
Distance	9.2mi	276.3mi	14.8km	444.7km		

For detailed directions see our Walking Guide no. 31, Lamorna Cove to Penzance to Marazion.

West of Mousehole this Section is one of lushly vegetated cliffs, but most of it is urban or semi-urban in character as it passes through Newlyn and Penzance. However, it is really defined by its views over the magnificent Mount's Bay, dominated by the iconic sight of St Michael's Mount and its castle, which give this coast a magical character.

Directions

A regular bus service passes about 1 mile/1.5km inland of Lamorna Cove and also serves Newlyn and Penzance, with links possible between Penzance and Marazion, giving a variety of possible bus-walk options.

Lamorna Cove has a seasonal cafe, toilets and, a little way inland, a pub. The Coast Path leaves the cove behind the harbour, bearing right to the cliffs. The well-marked Path eventually leads to a road which descends into Mousehole. The road leads to the harbour; however, the official route turns right opposite "Lowena" then continues towards the sea, turning left, along a terrace to a car park. It briefly passes along the harbour before turning left then right to reach the main harbour-side road. Mousehole has all facilities and is very picturesque.

At the far end of the harbour go through the car park, on along a concrete walkway then up some steps. Turn right along the road, then along a seaward track to arrive at Newlyn. Follow the road round the harbour and past the fish market, turning right just after the Seamen's Mission to cross a bridge. Bear right past the Tolcarne Inn then follow the promenade to Penzance. Pass the harbour, then go right through the large car park to where a walkway leaves from its far right-hand end. Penzance has all facilities, is the end stop of the main-line railway, and is the hub of local bus services. The train and bus stations are next to the car park.

The walkway follows the sea wall to the edge of Marazion. At the end of the walkway and cycle route, either cross over and follow the road or cross the dunes to a large car park, cross this and continue behind the sea wall into Marazion.

Marazion is the centre for access to St Michael's Mount, and is the southern end of the cross-peninsula St Michael's Way from Lelant. The little town of Marazion has all facilities.

Choughs soaring high above waves and rock. Photographer Brian Shipman

OS Maps: Landranger 203; Explorer 103 (Porthleven); Explorer 102 (remainder)

	This Walk	Cumulative	This Walk	Cumulative	Grading	Timing
Ascent	1,916ft	54,730ft	584m	16,682m	Moderate then strenuous	4.75 hours
Distance	10.8mi	287.1mi	17.4km	462.0km		

For detailed directions see our Walking Guide no. 32, Marazion to Praa Sands and Praa Sands to Porthleven.

Between Marazion and Cudden Point this Section is dominated by the sweep of Mount's Bay and its iconic focal point of St Michael's Mount. It is a charming length of low cliffs and small fields. East of Cudden Point the Mount is lost but the local landscape is bolder, with craggy headlands, long sandy beaches, inaccessible coves and picturesque cliff-top engine houses.

Directions

There are regular bus services which link Marazion and Porthleven and also serve Perranuthnoe and Praa Sands between the two, making a variety of bus-walks possible. Marazion is a pleasant little town with all facilities and the causeway to St Michael's Mount.

The Coast Path leaves along the main road, following it for some way to the speed restriction sign. Turn right just after the cemetery, then follow the footpath downhill to reach the coast and turn left. Just after Trenow Cove the Path turns inland. Look out for the signed right turn after 275 yards/250 metres, which goes back to the low cliffs and on to Perranuthnoe. There are toilets and seasonal refreshments here.

Take the lane on the seaward side of the car park, bearing right and then left into a field. The well-marked Path leads to Cudden Point, with magnificent views over Mount's Bay. It descends past Little Cudden to Bessy's Cove, where it joins a track. Go ahead, bearing right at some granite gate posts, then through Prussia Cove on a lane between large stone buildings. Keep ahead on the Path which passes above Kenneggy Sand and then descends to Praa Sands, where there are toilets and seasonal refreshments. Go down the slipway to the beach then along in front of the shop, taking the steps up beside the cafe. Keep along the top of the grassy dunes, turning left when signed at the end, then right into a housing estate. At the end bear right and climb to the cliffs. The Path skirts behind Rinsey Head, then through a car park and down to a restored engine house. It continues to Trewavas Head, inland of more restored engine houses. Beyond there have been numerous cliff falls – be sure to follow the signed Path. This then enters Porthleven on a lane – fork right entering the town to pass alongside the harbour to its head. Porthleven has all facilities.

Couple hiking near Perranuthnoe. Photographer Mike Newman

OS Maps: Landranger 203; Explorer 103

	This Walk	Cumulative	This Walk	Cumulative	Grading	Timing
Ascent	781ft	55,511ft	238m	16,920m	Moderate	3 hours
Distance	5.2mi	292.3mi	8.4km	470.4km		

For detailed directions see our Walking Guide no. 33, Porthleven to Poldhu Cove.

This is a Section mostly of low cliffs with cliff-face Paths, long stretches being above extensive beaches. It harbours a couple of unexpected features, firstly in the shape of Loe Bar, a large strip of shingle barring the freshwater Loe Pool from the sea, and secondly in the unusual position of Gunwalloe Church, hidden away in the corner of a sandy cove. Add a cliff-top monument to Marconi, a couple of picturesque coves, and the rocky and atmospheric harbour at Mullion Cove, and it makes for a fascinating length.

Directions

Porthleven and Poldhu are both served by regular but separate bus routes, which meet at Helston.

Porthleven has all facilities. The Coast Path goes alongside the harbour towards the clock-tower at the end near the pier. Follow the road past this building, going right at the fork and keep on out of the town to a car park. Climb the steps and continue ahead on the track to Loe Bar. Cross the bar to the far side, forking right, downhill, shortly after the memorial. After passing a renovated fishery building, the Path arrives at Gunwalloe Fishing Cove. Go ahead onto the National Trust's Baulk Head, then above Halzephron Cove to a road. Bear right to a small car park then go right again, away from the road, on the cliffs down to Gunwalloe Church Cove. There are toilets and seasonal refreshments here. The picturesque church is tucked away at the right-hand end of the cove.

Skirt the beach to a road, then take the signed Path over a footbridge and over the rear of the beach to the Path rising away. Immediately after the car park at the top, turn right along the cliff top before returning to the road and dropping into Poldhu Cove, where there is a bus stop, toilets and refreshments. A good Path leads inland to Mullion village.

Kynance Cove. Photographer Ian Jesson

OS Maps: Landranger 203; Explorer 103

	This Walk	Cumulative	This Walk	Cumulative	Grading	Timing
Ascent	1,631ft	57,142ft	497m	17,417m	Moderate	4 hours
Distance	8.2mi	300.5mi	13.2km	483.6km		

For detailed directions see our Walking Guide no. 34, Poldhu Cove to The Lizard.

This is an exposed Section of high, flat-topped cliffs and spectacular coves and bays. The coastal landscape is superb throughout, but punctuated by some real scenic gems, of which Kynance Cove is probably the pick. The combination of steep cliffs, unusual geology and flora, beautiful sea colours and long stretches of easy walking make this a rewarding length. And watch out for choughs, Cornwall's iconic bird now returned to re-colonise this coast.

Directions

A regular bus service links Poldhu with Lizard Town, the latter about 0.5 mile/1 kilometre inland from the end of the Section, thus giving a possible bus-walk. In addition, there are many easy local circuits based on the Coast Path in the Lizard-Kynance area.

From the road at Poldhu turn right up the driveway signed to the Marconi Centre, leaving this after 110 yards/100 metres for a path on the right. This passes the Marconi monument on the cliffs, then drops down into Polurrian Cove. Climb away past the Polurrian Hotel, then right along the Path to the Mullion Cove Hotel. Keep seaward and drop down to the harbour, where there are seasonal refreshments. There are toilets 110 yards/100 metres up the road.

The Coast Path leaves the cove slightly inland to the right, up the hill just after the cafe. Climb to the cliffs, keeping to the right to hug the coastline. There is an information board on the unique flora and fauna of the area here.

The easy and clear Path rounds Parc Bean Cove and Lower Predannack Cliff. Approaching Vellan Head, be sure to keep close to the coast for the official route – the more obvious track misses the views. After the deep valley at Gew Graze, the Path rounds Rill Point and descends to Kynance Cove. The steep descent leads to the beach by the seasonal cafe. There are also toilets here. If the sun is shining, the sea is brilliant turquoise.

From the cafe, either follow the main track up towards the car park or cross the little beach (at low tide) and climb a partly stepped path to the cliffs, leaving this at a sign pointing right. This passes adjacent to the car park, where the main track arrives, and the Coast Path then continues clearly and easily above Pentreath Beach at Caerthillian and round Old Lizard Head, and on to Lizard Point, England's most southerly point, where there are cafes, gift shops and toilets. The nearby lighthouse is open to visitors at certain times. A path leads inland to Lizard Town, which has all facilities including regular bus services.

OS Maps: Landranger 203 (Lizard); Landranger 204 (remainder); Explorer 103

	This Walk	Cumulative	This Walk	Cumulative	Grading	Timing
Ascent	2,293ft	59,435ft	699m	18,116m	Moderate, strenuous in places	5.75 hours
Distance	10.4mi	310.9mi	16.7km	500.3km		

For detailed directions see our Walking Guide no. 35, The Lizard to Coverack.

This is a Section of cliffs and coves, punctuated by headlands giving excellent views along the coastline. Here and there are areas of sandy beach at the foot of the cliffs, but only at Kennack are they very extensive. This coast is largely sheltered from the worst of the prevailing south-westerly winds, and consequently has a lush, well-vegetated character. This being a relatively unfrequented stretch, substantial lengths are quiet and remote.

Directions

Lizard Town, about 0.5 mile/1 kilometre inland of the Coast Path, has a bus service which also passes a little inland of Cadgwith, about half-way along this length, which presents a bus-walk possibility. In addition, there are numerous easy circuits based on The Lizard using the Coast Path, which are popular and attractive.

Lizard Point has cafes and toilets, while Lizard Town, inland, has all necessary facilities. Lizard Point has the distinction of being England's most southerly point and is a fine location. The Coast Path leaves the Point alongside the car parking area and on in front of the lighthouse. There is a Heritage Centre at the lighthouse, and both lighthouse and Heritage Centre are open to the public at certain times (www.trinityhouse.co.uk). After passing the lighthouse descend to cross a footbridge then climb, passing in front of the Housel Bay Hotel and on past the Lloyds Signal Station, bearing right here. The route passes Bass Point National Coastwatch Institution lookout, the first in the country to be established. At Kilcobben Cove the Path goes behind The Lizard lifeboat station with its boathouse, which was completed in 2011. It then arrives at Church Cove. Go left for a short distance, then take the Path through the gate on the right. There are some ups and downs to a Path junction just after a stone stile at Polgwidden Cove; keep right here. A little further on, the Path skirts the dramatic collapsed cave of the Devil's Frying Pan. Follow the signed Path past the cottages and down into the picturesque little fishing hamlet of Cadgwith.

Cadgwith has a pub, shop, refreshments and toilets. There is a superb little beach here where the fishing boats are hauled up. This is overlooked by a convenient grassy knoll with seats known as The Todn (Cornish for lawn). Walk through Cadgwith and up the hill, turning right on the signed Path a little way up. The Path then descends to Poltesco, crossing a footbridge. There is a diversion to the right leading to the attractive and interesting cove, complete with old serpentine works, where the local colourful rock was made into useful items. Climbing out of Poltesco, the Path then joins a road which leads to the beach at Kennack Sands. There are toilets here and seasonal refreshments.

Follow the Path behind the beaches and on to the cliffs to reach the neck of the long promontory of Carrick Lûz, the site of an Iron Age cliff fort. The Path cuts across the neck and then negotiates the steep valley at Downas Cove. Another, shallower valley crossing leads to the end of Black Head and its lookout hut. The Path now descends over the cliffs towards Chynhalls Point, going amongst the natural rock outcrops which can be slippery in wet weather. Beyond the Point the Path soon reaches Coverack.

An alternative inland path avoids the slippery Chynhalls Cliff. At the top of the Coast Path descent, the wide alternative path goes through gorse and passes a Sculpture Park, then the edge of a caravan park before arriving at a bungalow on a tarmac road. Turn right towards the hotel and then almost immediately bear left down a narrower path to rejoin the Coast Path, at Chynhalls Point.

Reaching the road at Coverack, the Path soon veers off right down some steps to arrive at a car park at the end of the village. Follow the road past the harbour. Coverack, a pretty place, has all facilities, including a regular bus service into Helston.

Lizard Point. Photographer Oli at Different View Photography

OS Maps: Landranger 204; Explorer 103

	This Walk	Cumulative	This Walk	Cumulative	Grading	Timing
Ascent	2,192ft	61,627ft	668m	18,784m	Moderate,	5.75 hours
Distance	12.9mi	323.8mi	20.8km	521.1km		

For detailed directions see our Walking Guide no. 36, Coverack to Helford.

This is a sheltered Section of the Coast Path. It includes low cliffs facing away from the prevailing winds, but also lengths of pleasant rural field paths, a little inland, necessary to avoid inaccessible coastal working and former quarries. In addition, this Section has substantial lengths which fringe a tidal creek and wooded estuary-side paths passing pretty beaches where the Coast Path reaches the Helford River. While not as dramatic as some Sections, it is an attractive stretch with a quiet charm of its own.

Directions

Separate bus routes from Helston serve Coverack and Helford Passage, across the river via ferry (Good Friday or 1st April to October) from Helford, allowing a bus-walk based on Helston. There is an attractive local circuit using the Coast Path between Helford and Gillan Creek.

There are all necessary facilities at Coverack. The Coast Path follows the road away from the pub and past the harbour, continuing straight ahead on a narrow lane when the road goes left. Look out for the sign pointing right, just before the end of the lane. The Path goes over sometimes boggy ground next to the coast to arrive at Lowland Point. Next, the old workings at Dean Quarry are passed on their seaward side. The well-signed Path then arrives at the open area at Godrevy Cove. The next length of coast is inaccessible due to operating quarries, so the Coast Path heads across the open area inland to pick up a signed Path going uphill between fields. This leads to the little hamlet of Rosenithon. At the T-junction, turn right on the lane, uphill, turning left into a field just after the right-hand bend. Cross three fields in the same direction, stone stiles between them, to emerge on a lane. Go left then, at a junction, right, which leads to Porthoustock, a coastal hamlet with public toilets.

The route of the next stretch, to another coastal hamlet, Porthallow, is also a rural inland walk. It leaves Porthoustock past the telephone box and up the hill. Where the road bears right go straight ahead on a narrower lane. Go past a row of thatched cottages and over a little grassy bank at the end next to a greenhouse to a kissing-gate. Just past the gate there is a fork in the Path. Bear right and follow the Path climbing to the far top corner of the field to cross a lifting-bar stile and a Cornish stile (a sort of stone cattle grid) into another field. Turn right in this field alongside the hedge, then bear away left at the top to cross another Cornish stile to a road. At the road go left, passing through the tiny hamlet of Trenance. Here the route follows the road round to the right to a T-junction. At the junction go slightly right and immediately left onto an enclosed Path, which leads to a track between buildings. At the road turn right to arrive at Porthallow.

Porthallow has a pub, toilets and seasonal refreshments. Look out for the marker indicating the half-way point of the Coast Path, equidistant (at 315 miles) from Minehead and Poole. Leave Porthallow along the back of the beach and up the steps. The Path now follows the coastline, keeping close to the edge round Nare Point. There is an inland diversion that leaves the coast before Nare Point and returns at Flushing, on Gillan Creek, a tidal tributary of the Helford River.

There used to be a seasonal ferry across Gillan Creek but it has ceased to run.

The Path moves away from the creek for a while then continues along the south side of the creek through a wooded area to Carne, at the head of the creek. Turn right over the bridge, then right again along the north side of the creek to St Anthony Church. Past the church turn left uphill, then shortly right on a farm track which leads into a field. Cross diagonally left to the top of the field to a kissing-gate.

For a short, direct route from here go through the gate and turn left. However, the Coast Path includes an optional extra of a circuit of Dennis Head. For this circuit do not pass through the gate but turn right, then almost immediately left over a stile. At the next junction continue straight ahead to reach the end of the headland. The Path circles around the headland, re-joining the outward route to the stile and then the kissing-gate.

Go through the gate and continue along the top of the field. The route now heads up the estuary side of the Helford River through woods and past coves. Towards the end the Path reaches a track – follow to the road and go right here then quickly left. The Path then emerges next to the main car park at Helford. Go down the hill into the village. Helford has a pub and shop and there are toilets at the car park.

Grebe Beach, Helford River. Photographer Jay Christopher

OS Maps: Landranger 204; Explorer 103

	This Walk	Cumulative	This Walk	Cumulative	Grading	Timing
Ascent	1,397ft	63,024ft	426m	19,210m	Moderate	4.5 hours
Distance	10.3mi	334.1mi	16.6km	537.7km		

For detailed directions see our Walking Guide no. 37, Helford to Falmouth (Ferry).

There are two contrasting parts to this Section. Between Helford and Rosemullion Head, it is a sheltered walk alongside the mouth of the beautiful Helford River, with undulating, relatively low cliffs alternating with charming little beaches. Between Rosemullion Head and Falmouth, the walk flanks the sweep of Falmouth Bay, with rather larger coves overlooked by the great headland of Pendennis Point at the Falmouth end, crowned by its castle. Over the bay is St Anthony Head lighthouse. None of this is a lonely or remote walk, and the Falmouth end is decidedly urban, but it is never uninteresting and always very scenic.

Directions

Helford Passage and Falmouth are linked by a regular bus service, giving numerous bus-walk options. The short circular walk round Pendennis Head in Falmouth is a great local favourite.

Helford has pub, shop and toilets; Helford Passage, over the river, has a pub and seasonal refreshments. There is a seasonal ferry link. For ferry details see page 27.

Walk around Helford River

If the ferry is not operating, a 13 miles/21 kilometre walk around the Helford River is possible. This will add another day to the itinerary. For this route, from Helford take the Path up the hill to arrive at Penarvon Cove. Go round the back of the cove and turn inland up a track to a road. Turn right, then left on a track to the permissive Path along the atmospheric Frenchman's Creek. At the end take the Path on the right signed to Withan, past Frenchman's Pill Cottage, crossing a footbridge. Follow the Path through the woods and aim for the far left corner of the field, taking the stile on the left. Follow the boundary on the left past Withan Farm, then head west over the fields to a lane. Here turn left to a crossroads, turning right here towards Mawgan. The lane joins a larger road; turn right past Gear then down and up into Mawgan-in-Meneage village. Turn right just after the church on the Path towards Gwarth-an-drea, then left behind a bungalow to a road. Turn right, and at the junction bear right and continue downhill to the bridge at Gweek. There is a shop and pub here. Take the road opposite the Gweek Inn, and at Tolvan Cross turn right along a bridleway to a road junction. Go straight ahead, towards Porth Navas. After crossing the stream, take the footpath on the left along the field edge to the road.

Follow the road ahead to Nancenoy and Polwheveral. At the crossroads after Polwheveral turn right, then after 140 yards/128 metres take the Path on the left along the field edge, then across the field corner to a road junction. Take the Porth Navas road opposite, through the village to Trenarth Bridge, then turn right towards Falmouth. At the junction at Trebah turn right, then right again into Bar Road. At the end turn left on a footpath which leads to the Helford River, turning left to the Ferryboat Inn at Helford Passage, the landing place for the ferry from Helford.

Ferry users start from here

Coast Path, Helford Passage – Falmouth

From the Ferryboat Inn, facing the pub, turn right along the river and up to a grassy hill. Keep on to a concrete track and follow this, passing behind Trebah Beach at Polgwidden Cove. Continue on the riverside then through woods to meet a track. Turn right to descend to the little village of Durgan. Go up the road, ignoring one path to the right, until the road turns left and the Path continues straight ahead. Follow this Path, arriving at Porth Saxon Beach behind a building, and then through a field to Porthallack Beach. The Path then climbs round Toll Point to arrive at a wooded area. At the fork keep right and follow the Path onward to Rosemullion Head, leaving the Helford River behind.

Keep seaward round the headland, then descend to go through a small wood and then on, the Path becoming suburban now, to reach Maenporth where there are toilets and refreshments and a bus stop. Turn right behind the cafe and continue to Swanpool, with more toilets and refreshments and another bus stop. Take the Path from the far end of the beach to arrive at Gyllyngvase, then keep along Falmouth's promenade to the far end. The official Path goes around the magnificent Pendennis Point – keep to the seaward road all the way to the end, then at the car park descend on the signed Path up the river, parallel to the road above. The Path emerges from woods and passes the Leisure Centre, descending above the docks to a T-junction. Turn right then go ahead under the railway bridge, passing the Maritime Museum and along Falmouth's main shopping street to arrive at the Prince of Wales Pier at the far end. Falmouth, of course, has all facilities, including a rail link to the main line at Truro.

Looking across the river to Falmouth from St Anthony's Head. Photographer Gemma De Cet

The businesses listed here are our 'Way Makers'. They
make the great South West Coast Path experience possible,
and give back to the Trail. Please support them if you can.
More info at www.southwestcoastpath.org.uk/waymaker

> If you enjoy staying,
> eating, drinking or doing
> an activity with a business
> along the Path, please let
> them know about our Way
> Maker scheme so we can
> share their brilliance!

- **GR** Grid Reference
- **DP** Distance from the Path
- **N** Nearest Town/Village with facilities
- **3** Number of Rooms
- Dogs Welcome
- Evening Meal Available
- Wifi
- Parking
- Grocery Shop On Site
- Private Transport to the Path
- Laundry Facilities
- Caters to Specific Dietary Needs
- Early Breakfast Available
- Packed Lunch Offered
- **£** Budget

Bed & Breakfast and Hotels

NAME	OTHER INFO	
Cliff House B&B	GR: SW656453	DP: 0 miles
Cliff Terrace, Portreath, TR16 4LE	N: **PORTREATH**	
01209 843847	OFFERS ONE NIGHT STAYS	
cliffhousebookinginfo@gmail.com		
www.cliffhouseportreath.co.uk	5 🐕 📶 🚗	
Portreath Arms Hotel	GR: SW657453	DP: 0 miles
The Square, Portreath, TR16 4LA	N: **PORTREATH**	
01209 842259	OFFERS ONE NIGHT STAYS	
email@theportreatharms.co.uk		
www.theportreatharms.co.uk	7 🐕 🍽 📶 🚗	
The Painters Cottage Bed and Breakfast	GR: SW518401	DP: 0.25 miles
The Cottage, Talland Road, St Ives, TR26 2DF	N: **ST IVES**	
01736 797626	OFFERS ONE NIGHT STAYS	
madie28@btinternet.com		
www.thepainterscottagestives.com	5 🍽 📶 🚗 🍴 🍴	
Boswednack Manor B&B	GR: SW443378	DP: 0.5 miles
Zennor, St Ives, TR26 3DD	N: **ZENNOR**	
01736 794183	OFFERS ONE NIGHT STAYS	
boswednack@btinternet.com		
www.boswednackmanor.co.uk	4 📶 🚗 🍴 ☕ 🍴	
Tremorran Bed & Breakfast	GR: SW369326	DP: 0 miles
Tremorran, Botallack, St Just, Penzance, TR19 7QJ	N: **BOTALLACK**	
01736 786272	OFFERS ONE NIGHT STAYS	
tremorran@gmail.com		
www.tremorran.co.uk	4 📶 🚗 🚐 🧺 🍴 ☕ 🍴	
Bosavern House	GR: SW370304	DP: 0.5 miles
St Just, TR19 7RD	N: **ST JUST**	
01736 788301		
info@bosavern.com		
www.bosavern.com	8 🐕 📶 🚗	

NAME	OTHER INFO	
The Old Post House B&B 24 Bosorne Street, St Just, TR19 7LU 07931 139603 moylefiona@gmail.com www.theoldposthousebandb.co.uk	**GR:** SW368312 **DP:** 0.4 miles **N: ST JUST** OFFERS ONE NIGHT STAYS 3 📶 🎧 ☕	
The Studio 3 Coastguard Cottages, Treen, Porthcurno, TR19 6LQ 01736 810504 jeffrey_hardman@sky.com www.sennencornwall.com	**GR:** SW392232 **DP:** 0.1 miles **N: PORTHCURNO** OFFERS ONE NIGHT STAYS 1 🐾 📶 🚗	
Lamorna Pottery B&B Lamorna, Penzance, TR19 6NY 01736 810330 potterylamorna@gmail.com www.lamornapottery.co.uk	**GR:** SW441257 **DP:** 1.25 miles **N: LAMORNA COVE** OFFERS ONE NIGHT STAYS 2 🍴 📶 🚗 ☕ 🍎	
Panorama Guest House Chywoone Hill, Newlyn, Penzance, TR18 5AR 01736360798 stay@panoramaguesthouse.co.uk www.panoramaguesthouse.co.uk	**GR:** SW461052 0 **DP:** 0 miles **N: NEWLYN** 6 🐾 📶 🚗 🧳 🖥 🎧 🍎	
Keigwin House Alexandra Road, Penzance, TR18 4LZ 01736 363930/07557 057773 fran@keigwinhouse.co.uk www.keigwinhouse.co.uk	**GR:** SW466299 **DP:** 0.25 miles **N: PENZANCE** OFFERS ONE NIGHT STAYS 8 📶 🚗 ☕	
Mount View Overnight Acommodation Trevine, Blowing House Hill, Ludgvan, TR17 0DF 01736 740277 mountviewshephuts@btinternet.com www.mountviewshepherdhuts.co.uk	**GR:** SW509337 **DP:** 5 miles **N: MARAZION** OFFERS ONE NIGHT STAYS 5 🐾 📶 🚗 ☕	
Polurrian on the Lizard Polurrian Road, Mullion, TR12 7EN 01326 240421 info@polurrianhotel.com www.polurrianhotel.com	**GR:** SW670186 **DP:** 0.5 miles **N: MULLION COVE** OFFERS ONE NIGHT STAYS 41 🐾 🍴 📶 🚗	
The Old Bakery B&B Mainway, The Lizard, TR12 7NZ 01326 290755 info@theoldbakerybandb.co.uk www.theoldbakerybandb.co.uk	**GR:** SW703126 **DP:** 0.75 miles **N: LIZARD** OFFERS ONE NIGHT STAYS 2 📶 🚗 🎧 ☕	
Penmenner House Bed & Breakfast Penmenner Road, The Lizard, TR12 7NR 01326 290315 sgnegus@btinternet.com www.penmenner-house.co.uk	**GR:** SW701120 **DP:** 0.3 miles **N: LIZARD** OFFERS ONE NIGHT STAYS 4 📶 🚗 🎧 🍎	

NAME	OTHER INFO		
Housel Bay Hotel The Lizard, TR12 7PG ☏ 01326 567500 ✉ stay@houselbay.com 🌐 www.houselbay.com	**GR:** SW708121	**DP:**	0 miles
	N: LIZARD		
	OFFERS ONE NIGHT STAYS		
	[20] 🐾 ⑪ 🤟 🛜 🚗		
The Paris Hotel The Cove, Helston, TR126SX ☏ 01326 280 258 ✉ info@pariscoverack.com 🌐 www.pariscoverack.com	**GR:**	**DP:**	0 miles
	N: COVERACK		
	OFFERS ONE NIGHT STAYS		
	[4] 🐾 ⑪ 🛜 🚗 🍎		
The Sail Loft B&B The Sail Loft, Point, Helford, Nr Helston, TR12 6JY ☏ 01326 231083 ✉ pamroyall@btinternet.com 🌐 www.southwestcoastpath.org.uk/sail-loft-point-helford	**GR:** SW758263	**DP:**	0 miles
	N: HELFORD		
	OFFERS ONE NIGHT STAYS		
	[1] 🛜 🚗		
Hotel Meudon Meudon Vean Ltd, Mawnan Smith, TR11 5HT ☏ 01326 250541 ✉ wecare@hotelmeudon.co.uk 🌐 www.meudon.co.uk	**GR:** SW785286	**DP:**	0 miles
	N: MAWNAN SMITH		
	OFFERS ONE NIGHT STAYS		
	[29] 🐾 ⑪ 🛜 🚗 🍴		
Chelsea House 2 Emslie Road, Falmouth, TR11 4BG ☏ 01326 212230 ✉ info@chelseahousefalmouth.com 🌐 www.chelseahousefalmouth.com	**GR:** SW812319	**DP:**	0 miles
	N: FALMOUTH		
	OFFERS ONE NIGHT STAYS		
	[9] 🐾 🛜 🍴		

Self Catering and Hostels

NAME	OTHER INFO		
Rosehill Lodges Rosehill, Porthtowan, TR4 8AR ☏ 01209 891920 ✉ reception@rosehilllodges.com 🌐 www.rosehilllodges.com	**GR:** SW693473	**DP:**	0.3 miles
	N: PORTHTOWAN		
	[20] 🐾 🛜 🚗		
Una St Ives Kingfisher Una Resort Ltd, Una St Ives, Carbis Bay, TR26 3HW ☏ 01736 257 000 ✉ hello@unastives.co.uk 🌐 www.unastives.co.uk	**GR:** SW526378	**DP:**	0.5 miles
	N: CARBIS BAY		
	[31] 🛜 🚗		
Trevalgan Farm Holidays Little Trevalgan, Trevalgan Farm, St Ives, TR26 3BJ ☏ 01736 796529 ✉ holidays@trevalgan.co.uk 🌐 www.trevalgan.co.uk	**GR:** SW489400	**DP:**	1 mile
	N: ST IVES		
	[3] 🐾 🛜 🚗 🍴		

NAME	OTHER INFO	
The Old Chapel 2 The Old Chapel, Newbridge, TR20 8QH ☎ 01841 533331 ✉ malc.g.irons@gmail.com 🌐 www.cornishhorizons.co.uk/west-coast-cottages/ penzance/p00869-the-old-chapel	**GR:** SW424316 **DP:** 3 miles **N: ST JUST** 3 🛜 🚗 🖥	
Land's End Hostel, Trevescan Mill Barn, Trevescan, Sennen, Penzance, TR19 7AQ ☎ 07585 625774 ✉ hello@landsendholidays.co.uk 🌐 www.landsendholidays.co.uk	**GR:** SW355248 **DP:** 0.7 miles **N: LAND'S END** OFFERS ONE NIGHT STAYS 4 🐕 🛜 🚗 🛒 🍽	
Sunnyside 10 Park Road, Penzance, TR18 5DZ ☎ 07929 616274 ✉ sunnysidenewlyn@gmail.com 🌐	**GR:** SW461284 **DP:** 0 miles **N: NEWLYN** OFFERS ONE NIGHT STAYS 2 🛜 ☕	
Porthgwarra Holiday Cottages Estate Office, Marazion, TR17 0EL ☎ 01736 888515 ✉ info@staubynestatescottages.co.uk 🌐 www.staubynestatescottages.co.uk	**GR:** SW371217 **DP:** 0.1 miles **N: PENZANCE** 🐕 🛜 🚗	
YHA Penzance (camping available) Castle Horneck Lodge, Penzance, TR20 8TF ☎ 0345 371 9653 ✉ penzance@yha.org.uk 🌐 www.yha.org.uk/hostel/yha-penzance	**GR:** SW457302 **DP:** miles **N: PENZANCE** OFFERS ONE NIGHT STAYS 🐕 🍴 🛜 🖥 £	
Guest Lodge Promenade, Penzance, TR18 4NW ☎ 07724310426 ✉ reservations@guestlodgepenzance.co.uk 🌐 www.guestlodgepenzance.co.uk	**GR:** SW469296 **DP:** 0.9 miles **N: PENZANCE** OFFERS ONE NIGHT STAYS 10 🛜	
Berepper Barns Gunwalloe, Helston, TR12 7PZ ☎ 07443522064 ✉ berepperbarns@gmail.com 🌐 www.berepperbarns.co.uk	**GR:** S SW656228 **DP:** 0 miles **N: HELSTON** 2 🐕 🛜 🚗	
Tresooth Cottages Penwarne Road, Falmouth, TR11 5PF ☎ 01326 618010 ✉ hayley@tresoothcottages.com 🌐 www.tresoothcottages.com	**GR:** SW767314 **DP:** 4 miles **N: MAWNAN SMITH** 33 🐕 🛜 🚗 🖥	

Campsites and Holiday Parks

NAME	OTHER INFO		
Perran View Holiday Park Trevellas, St Agnes, TR5 0XH ☎ 01872 552623 ✉ perran-gm@jfhols.co.uk 🌐 www.johnfowlerholidays.com/cornwall-holiday-park/perran-view-holiday-park	**GR:** SW738515	**DP:**	1 mile
	N: ST AGNES		
	[113] 🐾 🍴 🛜 🛒		
Cambrose Touring Park Cambrose, Redruth, TR16 4HT ☎ 01209 890747 ✉ cambrosetouringpark@gmail.com 🌐 www.cambrosetouringpark.co.uk	**GR:** SW686453	**DP:**	2 miles
	N: PORTREATH		
	OFFERS ONE NIGHT STAYS		
	[60] 🐾 🛜 🛒 🔲		
Camp Kovva Bridge, TR16 4QP ☎ 07856017675 ✉ stay@campkovva.co.uk 🌐 www.campkovva.co.uk	**GR:**	**DP:**	1 miles
	N: PORTREATH		
	OFFERS ONE NIGHT STAYS		
	🚗		
Hope Farm Holidays Hope Farm, 14 Gwithian Road, Connor Downs, TR27 5EA ☎ 01736 272011 ✉ hello@hopefarmholidays.co.uk 🌐 www.hopefarmholidays.co.uk	**GR:** SW602394	**DP:**	1 miles
	N: GWITHIAN		
	OFFERS ONE NIGHT STAYS		
	🐾 🚗		
Tolroy Manor Holiday Park Tolroy Road, Hayle, TR27 6HG ☎ 01736 753 082 ✉ tolroy-gm@jfhols.co.uk 🌐 www.johnfowlerholidays.com/cornwall-holiday-park/tolroy-manor-holiday-park	**GR:** SW565358	**DP:**	1 mile
	N: HAYLE		
	[202] 🐾 🍴 🛜 🚗 🛒		
St Ives Holiday Village Lelant, St Ives, TR26 3HX ☎ 01736 752000 ✉ stives-gm@jfhols.co.uk 🌐 www.johnfowlerholidays.com/cornwall-holiday-park/st-ives-holiday-village	**GR:** SW527362	**DP:**	3 miles
	N: CARBIS BAY		
	[292] 🐾 🍴 🛜 🚗 🛒		
Trevalgan Touring Park Trevalgan, St Ives, TR26 3BJ ☎ 01736 791892 ✉ reception@trevalgantouringpark.co.uk 🌐 www.trevalgantouringpark.co.uk	**GR:** SW490401	**DP:** 0.25 miles	
	N: ST IVES		
	OFFERS ONE NIGHT STAYS		
	🐾 🛜 🚗 🛒 🔲		
Ayr Holiday Park Alexandra Road, St Ives, TR26 1EJ ☎ 01736 795855 ✉ recept@ayrholidaypark.co.uk 🌐 www.ayrholidaypark.co.uk	**GR:** SW510405	**DP:**	0.5 miles
	N: ST IVES		
	OFFERS ONE NIGHT STAYS		
	🐾 🛜 🚗		
Trevellas Manor Farm Campsite Crosscombe, St Agnes, TR5 0XP ☎ 01872552238 ✉ contact@tmfcampsite.co.uk 🌐 www.trevellasmanorfarmcampsite.co.uk	**GR:** SW732516	**DP:**	0 miles
	N: ST AGNES		
	OFFERS ONE NIGHT STAYS		
	[60] 🐾 🔲		

NAME	OTHER INFO
Wheal Rodney Holiday Park Ltd Gwallon, Marazion, TR17 0HL 🕾 01736710605 ✉ reception@whealrodney.co.uk 🌐 www.whealrodney.co.uk	**GR:** SW524314 **DP:** 1 miles **N: MARAZION** OFFERS ONE NIGHT STAYS 43 🐕 📶 🚗 🛒 📷
Dropped Anchor Sea View Campsite Trewavas Lane, Breage, Helston, TR13 9QB 🕾 07706832152 ✉ droppedanchor1@gmail.com 🌐 www.seaviewcampingatdroppedanchor.co.uk	**GR:** SW598268 **DP:** 1 miles **N: PORTHLEVEN** OFFERS ONE NIGHT STAYS 🐕 🚗
Mill Lane Campsite Mill Lane, Porthleven, TR13 9LQ 🕾 01326 573881 ✉ enquiries@pitchup.com 🌐 www.pitchup.com/campsites/England/South_West/ Cornwall/porthleven/mill-lane-campsite	**GR:** SW628262 **DP:** 0.5 miles **N: PORTHLEVEN** OFFERS ONE NIGHT STAYS 🐕 📶 £
Teneriffe Farm Campsite Predannack, Mullion, Helston, TR12 7EZ 🕾 01326 240293 ✉ teneriffefarmcampsite@nationaltrust.org.uk 🌐 www.nationaltrust.org.uk/holidays/teneriffe-farm-campsite	**GR:** SW672167 **DP:** 1 mile **N: MULLION COVE** OFFERS ONE NIGHT STAYS 🐕 🚗 🛒 £
Trerise Farm Campsite Ruan Major, Helston, TR12 7NA 🕾 07966 186206 ✉ enquiries@pitchup.com 🌐 www.pitchup.com/campsites/England/South_West/ Cornwall/Helston/trerise_farm_campsite	**GR:** SW710167 **DP:** 0.5 miles **N: HELSTON** OFFERS ONE NIGHT STAYS 🐕 £
Silversands Holiday Park Gwendreath, Ruan Minor, Lizard, TR12 7LZ 🕾 01326 290631 ✉ info@silversandsholidaypark.co.uk 🌐 www.silversandsholidaypark.co.uk	**GR:** SW729169 **DP:** 0.62 miles **N: LIZARD** 15 🐕 📶 🚗
Little Trevothan Camping & Caravan Park Coverack, Helston, TR12 6SD 🕾 01326 280260 ✉ sales@littletrevothan.co.uk 🌐 www.littletrevothan.co.uk	**GR:** SW770178 **DP:** 0.5 miles **N: COVERACK** OFFERS ONE NIGHT STAYS 3 🐕 📶 🚗 🛒 📷
Tregedna Farm Touring Caravan and Camping Park Maenporth, Falmouth, TR11 5HL 🕾 01326 250529 ✉ tregednafarmcamping@gmail.com 🌐 tregednafarmholidays.co.uk/camping-touring	**GR:** SW791303 **DP:** 0.5 miles **N: MAWNAN SMITH** OFFERS ONE NIGHT STAYS 📶 🚗 🛒 📷 £

Eat and Drink

NAME	OTHER INFO		
Fort Inn 63 Fore Street, Newquay, TR7 1HA ☎ 01637 875700 ✉ fortinn@staustellbrewery.co.uk ⊕ fortinnnewquay.co.uk	**GR:** SW807619	**DP:** 0 miles	
	N: NEWQUAY		
Bowgie Inn Ltd West Pentire, Crantock, Newquay, TR8 5SE ☎ 01637 830363 ✉ enquiries@bowgie.com ⊕ www.bowgie.com	**GR:** SW776606	**DP:** 0 miles	
	N: CRANTOCK		
Breakers Beach Cafe Ltd The Quay, St Agnes, TR5 0RU ☎ 01872 552166 ✉ info@breakersbeachcafe.co.uk ⊕ www.breakersbeachcafe.co.uk	**GR:** SW721515	**DP:** 0 miles	
	N: ST AGNES		
The Unicorn on the Beach Beach Road, Truro, TR4 8AD ☎ 01209 890381 ✉ hello@theunicornonthebeach.com ⊕ www.theunicornonthebeach.com	**GR:** SW693478	**DP:** 0 miles	
	N: PORTHTOWAN		
Tideline Cafe 2 The Square, Portreath, TR16 4LA ☎ 01209 844882 ✉ hello@tidelinecafe.com ⊕ www.tidelinecafe.com	**GR:** SW657453	**DP:** 0.5 miles	
	N: PORTREATH		
Portreath Arms The Square, Portreath, TR16 4LA ☎ 01209 842259 ✉ djilett@aol.com ⊕ www.theportreatharms.co.uk	**GR:** SW657453	**DP:** 0 miles	
	N: PORTREATH		
	OFFERS ONE NIGHT STAYS		
Lifeboat Inn Wharf Road, St Ives, TR26 1LF ☎ 01736 794123 ✉ lifeboat@staustellbrewery.co.uk ⊕ lifeboatinnstives.co.uk	**GR:** SW518406	**DP:** 0 miles	
	N: ST IVES		
	OFFERS ONE NIGHT STAYS		
Count House Cafe Geevor Tin Mine, Boscaswell, Penzance, TR19 7EW ☎ 01736788864 ✉ counthousecafe@hotmail.co.uk ⊕ www.counthousecafe.com	**GR:** SW374344	**DP:** 1.3 miles	
	N: PENDEEN		
The Commercial 13 Market Square, St Just, TR19 7HE ☎ 01736 788455 ✉ enquiries@commercial-hotel.co.uk ⊕ www.commercial-hotel.co.uk	**GR:** SW370313	**DP:** 1 mile	
	N: BOTALLACK		
	OFFERS ONE NIGHT STAYS		

NAME	OTHER INFO		
Old Success Inn Sennen Cove, TR19 7DG ☎ 01736 871232 ✉ oldsuccess@staustellbrewery.co.uk ⊕ oldsuccess.co.uk	**GR:** SW354263 **DP:** 0 miles **N: SENNEN COVE** OFFERS ONE NIGHT STAYS		
Ship Inn South Cliff, Penzance, TR19 6QX ☎ 01736 731234 ✉ shipmousehole@staustellbrewery.co.uk ⊕ shipinnmousehole.co.uk	**GR:** SW468263 **DP:** 0 miles **N: MOUSEHOLE** OFFERS ONE NIGHT STAYS		
The Godolphin The Godolphin, West End, Marazion, TR17 0EN ☎ 01736 888510 ✉ hello@thegodolphin.com ⊕ www.thegodolphin.com	**GR:** SW517305 **DP:** 0.1 miles **N: MARAZION**		
Twisted Currant Tea Room 10 Fore Street, Porthleven, TR13 9HJ ☎ 01326565999 ✉ info@twistedcurrant.co.uk ⊕ www.twistedcurrant.co.uk	**GR:** SW629258 **DP:** 0 miles **N: PORTHLEVEN**		
Harbour Inn Commercial Road, Porthleven, TR13 9JB ☎ 01326 573876 ✉ harbourinn@staustellbrewery.co.uk ⊕ harbourinnporthleven.co.uk	**GR:** SW628257 **DP:** 0 miles **N: PORTHLEVEN** OFFERS ONE NIGHT STAYS		
Wavecrest Café - Lizard Point The Lizard, Helston, TR12 7NU ☎ 01326 290898 ✉ hello@wavecrestcornwall.co.uk ⊕ www.wavecrestcornwall.co.uk	**GR:** SW701115 **DP:** 0 miles **N: LIZARD**		
Housel Bay Hotel Restaurant The Lizard, TR12 7PG ☎ 01326 567500 ✉ eat@houselbay.com ⊕ www.houselbay.com	**GR:** SW708121 **DP:** 0 miles **N: LIZARD**		
Life's A Beach Cafe Meanporth Road, Falmouth, TR11 5HN ☎ 01326 251176 ✉ maenporthbeachcafe@gmail.com ⊕ www.lifesabeachcafe.co.uk	**GR:** SW789296 **DP:** 0 miles **N: FALMOUTH**		

Activities

NAME	OTHER INFO		
SUP in a Bag 25 Tregease Road, St Agnes, Truro, TR5 0SL ☎ 07949196011 ✉ paddle@supinabag.co.uk 🌐 www.supinabag.co.uk	**GR:** SX015439	**DP:**	0 miles
	N: ST AGNES		
PK Porthcurno - Museum of Global Communications Eastern House, St. Levan, TR19 6JX ☎ 01736 810966 ✉ info@pkporthcurno.com 🌐 www.pkporthcurno.com	**GR:** SW384227	**DP:**	0 miles
	N: PORTHCURNO		
The Minack Theatre Porthcurno, Churchdown, St Levan, Penzance, TR19 6JU ☎ 01736 818181 ✉ info@minack.com 🌐 www.minack.com	**GR:** SW384 2220	**DP:**	0 miles
	N: PORTHCURNO		
Jubilee Pool & Cafe Battery Road, Penzance, TR18 4FF ☎ 01736 369224 ✉ contact@jubileepool.co.uk 🌐 www.jubileepool.co.uk	**GR:** 476 272	**DP:**	0 miles
	N: PENZANCE		
St Michael's Mount TR17 0EL ☎ 01736 710265 ✉ enquiries@stmichaelsmount.co.uk 🌐 www.stmichaelsmount.co.uk	**GR:** SW514300	**DP:**	0.1 miles
	N: MARAZION		
Cornish Seal Sanctuary Gweek, Helston, TR12 6UG ☎ 01326 221361 ✉ slcgweek@sealifetrust.com 🌐 www.sealsanctuary.sealifetrust.org	**GR:** SW708266	**DP:**	0 miles
	N: HELSTON		

Getting Around

NAME	OTHER INFO		
Meneage Taxis Goonhilly Downs, Helston, TR12 6LQ ☎ 01326 560530 ✉ meneagetaxis@yahoo.com 🌐 www.helstontaxis.com	**GR:** SW663281	**DP:**	0 miles
	N: PORTHLEVEN		
Telstar Taxi & Private Hire Goonhilly Downs, Helston, TR12 6LQ ☎ 01326 221007 ✉ telstarlizardtaxis@yahoo.com 🌐 www.telstartravel.co.uk	**GR:** SW720222	**DP:**	4 miles
	N: COVERACK		
Helford River Boats The Kiosk, Helford PasSage, TR11 5LB ☎ 01326 250770 ✉ helfordriverboats@yahoo.com 🌐 www.helford-river-boats.co.uk	**GR:**	**DP:**	0 miles
	N: HELFORD		

Information

NAME	OTHER INFO		
Visit Newquay Tourist Information Centre Marcus Hill, Newquay, TR7 1BD ☎ 01637838516 ✉ newquay.tic@newquay.town ⊕ www.visitnewquay.org	**GR:** SW811615	**DP:**	0 miles
	N: NEWQUAY 		
St Ives Information Centre St Ives Library, Gabriel Street, St Ives, TR26 2LX ☎ 01736 796297 ✉ info@visitstives.org.uk ⊕ www.stives-cornwall.co.uk	**GR:** SW517404	**DP:**	0 miles
	N: ST IVES		
Land's End Visitor Centre & Attraction Land's End, Sennen, Penzance, TR19 7AA ☎ 01736 871501 ✉ visitorscentre@landsend-landmark.co.uk ⊕ landsend-landmark.co.uk	**GR:** SW343250	**DP:**	0 miles
	N: LAND'S END		
Penzance Welcome Centre Station Approach, Penzance, TR18 2NF ☎ 01736335530 ✉ west.cornwall@nationaltrust.org.uk ⊕ www.facebook.com/welcometowestcornwall	**GR:** SW476305	**DP:**	0 miles
	N: PENZANCE		

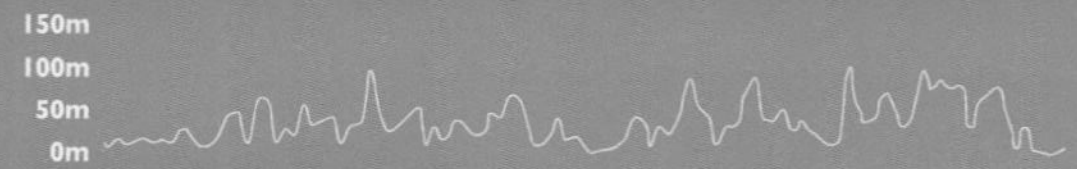

CORNWALL

150m
100m
50m
0m

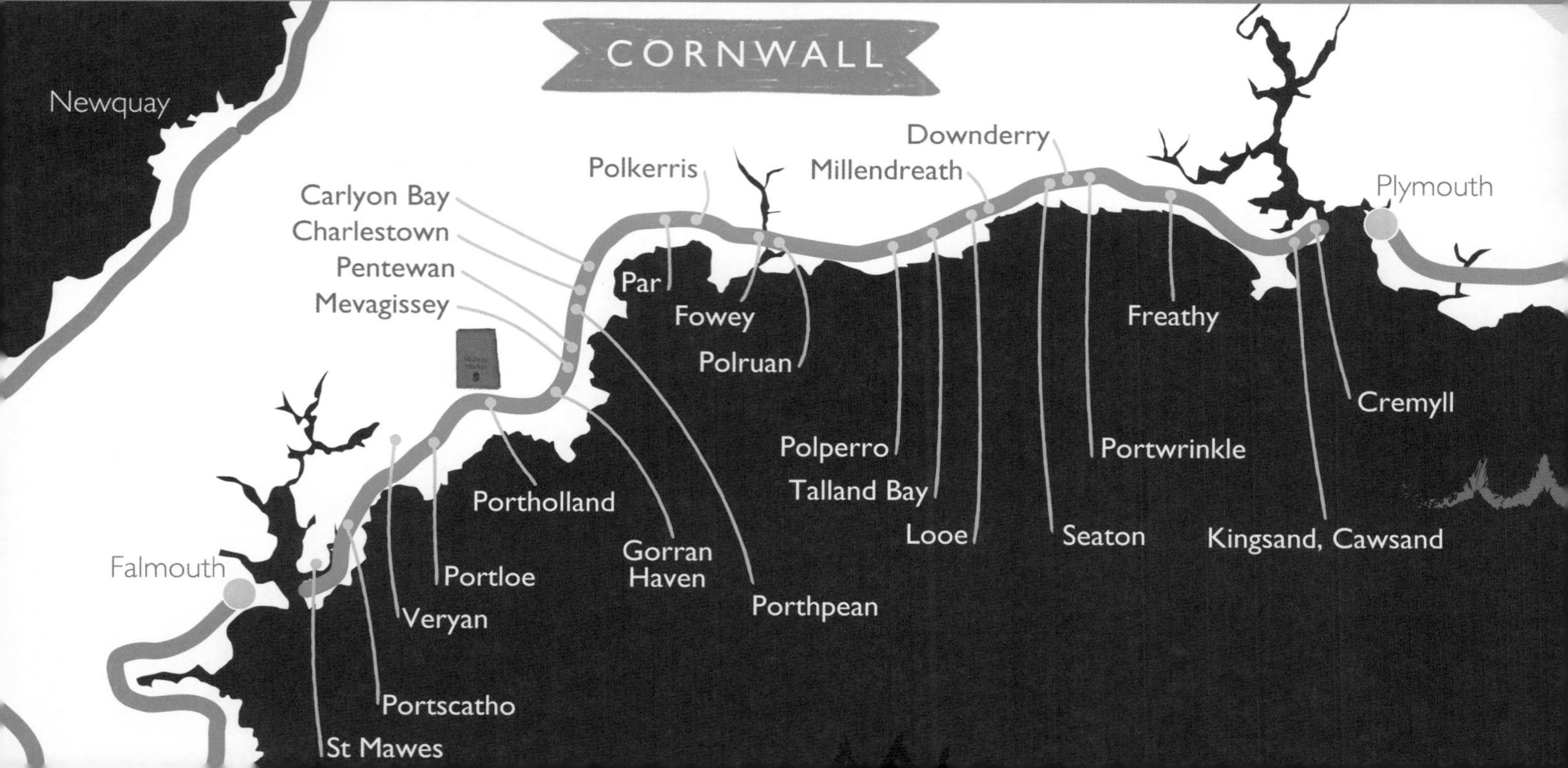

Plymouth

Cremyll

Kingsand, Cawsand

Freathy

Portwrinkle

Seaton

Downderry

Millendreath

Looe

Polperro

Talland Bay

Porthpean

Polkerris

Par

Fowey

Polruan

Gorran Haven

Portholland

Portloe

Veryan

Portscatho

St Mawes

Carlyon Bay

Charlestown

Pentewan

Mevagissey

Newquay

Falmouth

The South Cornwall stretch of coast is relatively sheltered, being either south-east or south-facing with much of it in the lee of the large peninsula of the Lizard. Cliffs of moderate height are found along most of the length, and there are numerous intimate little bays and some quite prominent headlands. In the west the main feature is the superb estuary of the River Fal. Also known as Carrick Roads, this forms one of the largest natural harbours in the world. Walkers will need to take two ferries to cross this superb estuary, which contains the maritime centre of Falmouth. St Austell Bay comprises the central part of this length, the only stretch that lacks the otherwise ubiquitous cliffs. The bay also has the only major length of coastal development on the south coast of Cornwall, based around the town of St Austell. It includes the wonderfully preserved Georgian port of Charlestown, as well as the picturesque traditional fishing town of Mevagissey. To the east, there are attractive estuaries at Fowey and Looe, drowned mouths of river valleys. The great sweep of Whitsand Bay, again backed by cliffs, then leads to the mouth of Plymouth Sound.

> All of the locations on the map illustration to the left, have at least 1 facility including toilets, a cafe/restaurant, shop or pub.

Mevagissey. Photographer Jonathan Warren

OS Maps: Landranger 204; Explorer 105

	This Walk	Cumulative	This Walk	Cumulative	Grading	Timing
Ascent	974ft	63,998ft	297m	19,507m	Easy	2.75 hours
Distance	6.2mi	340.3mi	10.0km	547.7km		

For detailed directions see our Walking Guide no. 38, St Mawes (Ferry) to Portscatho.

This Section includes a trip on the ferry across the mouth of the River Fal, a treat of scenery and interest in its own right. Beyond, the walk round St Anthony Head is one of superb estuarine and coastal views, followed by an easy but charming Path on low cliffs, sheltered from the westerlies, while passing some fine sandy beaches and giving excellent views up the South Cornwall coast.

Directions

A regular bus route serves Portscatho and St Mawes from Truro, which is also linked to Falmouth by bus and train. There is also a very popular circular walk using the Coast Path in the St Anthony Head area and another from Portscatho.

Two ferries are required to cross between Falmouth and the Coast Path at Place, east of the large estuary. The first goes between Falmouth and St Mawes, across the mouth of the main Fal Estuary, sometimes referred to as Carrick Roads. The ferry operates from Prince of Wales Pier (year round) and Custom House Quay (summer only). For ferry details see page 27.

The second leg of the crossing is the ferry between St Mawes and Place, crossing the mouth of the Fal's tributary, the Percuil River. For ferry and alternative water taxi services, see page 27.

The water taxi service ordinarily operates between Falmouth and St Mawes or Place. It is advisable to call 2 or 3 days prior to travel.

Information is also available from the Fal River Visitor Information Centre at Prince of Wales Pier, or visit www.falriver.co.uk.

If arriving at St Mawes and wishing to proceed to Place when the Place ferry is not operating, it is possible to take the regular bus service from St Mawes to Gerrans, walking from here to Place (2.5 miles/4 kilometres). For this option, go to Gerrans Church and pick up the walking route described below. Local taxi firms will carry walkers around the peninsula.

Walk between St Mawes and Place

A walking route also exists between St Mawes and Place, via Gerrans. This adds 9 miles/14 kilometres to the overall route, effectively an extra day to the itinerary. Leaving the ferry point in St Mawes, turn left along the road. Approaching the castle, take the minor lane left, which leads to a footpath at the end. This becomes a scenic Path alongside the Carrick Roads – the Fal Estuary. At the minor road go right, then bear left in front of the boatyard and then on a bank above the shore. This leads to the churchyard of St Just in Roseland, a beautiful spot. Pass the church and keep to the Path next to the shore. Follow the Path as it bears right up the hill, signed St Just Lane, to emerge on a road. Turn left, ignoring the first footpath on the right, but take the second a little afterwards. Follow the Path alongside field boundaries, first to the right, then to the left, then to the right again. Go down to the road at the end of the fourth field and turn right to the A3078 at Trethem Mill. Turn left and immediately right after the bridge, up some steps and through a small wood. Out of the wood, cross the field diagonally right (bearing 110°) then in the next field bear diagonally right again (bearing 140°), leaving it by a wooded track. Cross the stile at the top and bear diagonally right again (bearing 137°) to meet a hedge, which is followed to a road. Turn right on the road. At the next junction, follow the road curving to the right past Polhendra Cottage, then turn left through the second gate. Descend towards the bottom of the hedge visible on the opposite side of the valley (bearing 123°). Cross the bridge and climb as close as possible with the hedge to the left. Cross the stone steps behind the gorse at the top and bear slightly left across the next two fields (bearing 125°) to emerge on a road. Turn right to arrive at Gerrans Church. (Those who have taken the bus from St Mawes will join here – see above.)

At the church, fork left into Treloan Lane, keeping ahead past the buildings. Go through the gate at the end of the lane, crossing an open field ahead into another enclosed track, which leads to Porth Farm. At the road turn right then go left at the sign indicating "Footpath to Place by Percuil River". Follow this very scenic Path which leads to the ferry landing point, then on to Place itself.

Coast Path, Place – Portscatho

At Place, walk up the lane past the gates to the grand house. Turn right into the churchyard of St Anthony Church, passing behind the church and up into a wooded area. Turn right at the track, then at the creek look for the sign on the left taking the Path alongside the plantation. The Path now gives superb views over Carrick Roads to Falmouth. Approaching St Anthony Head, keep to the Coast Path to the right until passing through the gate towards the lighthouse. Just after the gate, climb the steps to the left to the car parking area. There are also toilets here. Leave the car park next to the coast and the superb and easy Path then leads to Portscatho, which has a shop, toilets and pubs, as well as a bus service to St Mawes and Truro.

Portscatho. Photographer Gemma De Cet

OS Maps: Landranger 204: Explorer 105

	This Walk	Cumulative	This Walk	Cumulative	Grading	Timing
Ascent	1,674ft	65,672ft	510m	20,017m	Strenuous	3.75 hours
Distance	7.4mi	347.7mi	11.9km	559.6km		

For detailed directions see our Walking Guide no. 39, Portscatho to Portloe.

This is a very quiet Section for the most part. Cliffs are relatively low at first, but increase in height as the great promontory of Nare Head, with its superb views, is approached. The long sandy beaches below the cliffs passed west of Nare Head are replaced by tiny isolated and inaccessible coves east of the headland. This length has a wonderfully remote atmosphere.

Directions

Portscatho and Portloe are both served by regular, but different, bus services, both linking with Truro. There are some local circular walks using the Coast Path around Nare Head, based on the inland village of Veryan.

Portscatho has a shop, pubs, toilets and bus service. The Coast Path leaves past the Harbour Club; keep right just after leaving the village at the footpath junction.
The Path goes round the back of Porthcurnick Beach, then up the road on the far side, turning right along the coastal edge. The Path continues to undulate along the coast, until it turns inland to reach a road. Turn right, past Pendower Court and down the road to its end at Pendower Beach. Cross the rear of the beach and head for the public toilets, going up the hill and turning right. The Path soon diverts around the rear of the Nare Hotel to a road, descending to Carne Beach. Follow the road round the bend and up the hill for a short way, turning right to return to the cliffs. The Path now heads for Nare Head, via a steep descent and ascent at Tregagle's Hole and past an old fisherman's cottage. A short diversion at the top of Nare Head reveals some stunning coastal views.

The Path now goes round the seaward edge of Rosen Cliff and over the valley behind Kiberick Cove to Blouth Point. At this point, enter a field and keep left for a short way before bearing right, downhill, towards some trees. The Path zigzags upward to pass Broom Parc and then goes through a field to round Manare Point. After this it is downhill, going over a short uneven section before joining a tarmac Path which descends into Portloe. The village is very picturesque and has pubs and toilets as well as a bus service.

Portloe. Photographer Tim Jepson

OS Maps: Landranger 204; Explorer 105

	This Walk	Cumulative	This Walk	Cumulative	Grading	Timing
Ascent	2,841ft	68,513ft	866m	20,883m	Strenuous then easy	5.75 hours
Distance	12.2mi	359.9mi	19.6km	579.2km		

For detailed directions see our Walking Guide no. 40, Portloe to Mevagissey.

This is a quiet Section of mostly high cliffs, often covered in lush vegetation. Towards Gorran Haven these cliffs reduce in height. The section includes the great headland of Dodman Point, from where there are views to the Lizard in one direction and Devon in the other on a clear day. Below the cliffs are some sandy beaches, often all but inaccessible. This is a coastline for those preferring remoteness.

Directions

There are some excellent circular walks using the Coast Path at Dodman Point and linking to Gorran Haven, giving a variety of options here.

The scenic little harbour village of Portloe has toilets, pubs and a bus service. The Coast Path leaves behind the Lugger Hotel, leaving the road to reach a prominent converted chapel. Pass this then climb steeply to the cliffs. After a quite strenuous length the Path arrives at West Portholland. Follow the road above the shore to a junction, then turn right to East Portholland. There are toilets here and a seasonal cafe and shop. Pass the cottages at the far end and climb behind them on a clear path to a field, turning right down the field edge. The Path leads to a road which descends to Porthluney Cove. Here are toilets and seasonal refreshments, and the picturesque setting is enhanced by the presence of Caerhays Castle just inland. Walk behind the beach and turn right into parkland. Climb behind the field-edge trees then go to the right and follow the field edge to the woods. After crossing the rocky ridge at Greeb Point, the Path descends to a road behind Hemmick Beach. Cross the bridge and go right, climbing to the headland of Dodman Point ("The Dodman"), with its memorial cross and superb views. The Path stays clear above the lovely sands of Bow or Vault Beach, then rounds the headland of Pen-a-maen to enter Gorran Haven. This little harbour village has a shop, pub and toilets. There is a Gorran community bus that runs 4 days a week (**www.gorranbus.org**), which walkers have recommended and can be hailed anywhere along its route.

Leave Gorran Haven up Church Street, turning right into Cliff Road. At the top of the hill, follow to the end of the road and a small wooden bridge will lead to a stile into the field, which leads to the cliffs. The clear Path leads to Chapel Point, where it crosses the tarmac access road to follow the Path along the coast into Portmellon. Follow the road uphill and go down through the park on the right on entering Mevagissey. Steps descend to the harbour. Mevagissey is the archetypal Cornish fishing village and has all facilities.

OS Maps: Landranger 204; Explorer 105 (western half); Explorer 107 (eastern half)

	This Walk	Cumulative	This Walk	Cumulative	Grading	Timing
Ascent	2,434ft	70,947ft	742m	21,625m	Strenuous then easy	5 hours
Distance	10.7mi	370.6mi	17.2km	596.4km		

For detailed directions see our Walking Guide no. 41, Mevagissey to Par.

The western half of this Section has a relatively remote feel, enhanced by some quite strenuous climbs and some attractive cliffs and headlands. To the east the coastline is more urbanised, but with beaches and the lovely Georgian docks of Charlestown found among the houses, golf courses and clay industry. The cliff-top Path between Porthpean and Charlestown was reinstated in late 2022, avoiding two miles of road diversion.

Directions

There are bus routes from St Austell to Charlestown and Par, one of these routes also serving Mevagissey, making a range of bus-walks possible.

The attractive fishing village of Mevagissey has all facilities. The Coast Path goes along the back of the harbour and then turns right along its eastern side before forking left steeply uphill. After crossing some playing fields, pass seaward of the houses, then continue along the undulating cliffs to descend behind the ruined fish cellars at Portgiskey Cove. Continue uphill along the seaward and far field boundaries to a fenced path at the top. Turn right here, parallel to the road. At the entrance to Pentewan Sands Holiday Park, follow the B3273 road pavement and turn first right before the petrol station, signposted to Pentewan. There are a few shops, toilets, pub and café in the village. The official route then follows the road through Pentewan and up the hill for about 100 yards/90 metres, taking the first turn sharp right along The Terrace and along a narrow Path at the end to arrive at the cliffs. An interesting alternative turns right, away from the road into the harbour area just after the public toilets then, immediately after the last cottage, goes left steeply uphill, through gardens, to arrive at the official route on the cliffs.

After some 1.25 miles/2 kilometres the Path descends through a wood and reaches a track. Turn right here to arrive at another track just behind the remote Hallane Mill Beach. Turn left here then quickly right, climbing back up the cliffs to arrive at Black Head. A diversion from the memorial stone goes to the tip of this atmospheric location. Continuing from Black Head the Path enters Ropehaven Woods with some confusing paths – it is important to follow the waymarking. Entering the wood turn right down a rocky and sometimes slippery path, then left. Go left again onto a walled path, ignoring descending paths on the right, to arrive beside a cottage and emerge onto a track. Go right here, then leave the road to the right just after a parking area and follow the cliff-top Path down, up and down again to Porthpean. Walk along the promenade to the far end and climb the steps to rejoin the newly reinstated cliff-top Path all the way to Charlestown.

Charlestown has a fascinating Georgian harbour, the home of a group of tall ships, and has refreshments, toilets, pubs and buses. Note that the official Coast Path does not cross the dock gate at the mouth of the harbour, though many people use that route. On the east side, climb the Path and on to reach a suburban road for a short way, soon forking off right over a long grassy area. Arriving at a large car park above

Carlyon Bay Beach, keep seaward then cross the beach access road where a new resort is being developed and continue ahead on the low cliffs. Keep seaward of the golf course to approach the old china clay works at Par Docks. At the little beach at Spit Point, turn inland and follow the narrow Path past the works and then turn right alongside a railway line to emerge on a road. Turn right along the pavement past the docks entrance and under a railway bridge. Turn right at the junction, signposted to Fowey, over a level crossing and then under another railway bridge before forking right on the road, Par Green.

To continue beyond Par on the Coast Path, walk along Par Green, looking for house no.52 and follow the Path signed on the right. Par has all facilities, including a mainline railway station; for the station turn left at the far end of Par Green along Eastcliffe Road.

Near Mevagissey. Photographer Lisa Dorne MacLeod

OS Maps: Landranger 200 or 204; Explorer 107

	This Walk	Cumulative	This Walk	Cumulative	Grading	Timing
Ascent	1,132ft	72,079ft	345m	21,970m	Moderate	3 hours
Distance	6.8mi	377.4mi	10.9km	607.4km		

For detailed directions see our Walking Guide no. 42, Par to Fowey.

This Section goes out to the prominent Gribbin Head. The west side of the headland is relatively exposed, mostly on high cliffs, with views west over St Austell Bay. The east side is more indented and sheltered, the cliffs lower, and the Path passes numerous scenic little sandy coves. At its eastern end the Path enters the lovely part-wooded estuary of the River Fowey, culminating in the atmospheric little town of Fowey.

Directions

Par and Fowey are linked by two bus routes giving a half-hourly service, making this a bus-walk option. In addition, a popular local circular walk from Fowey takes in Gribbin Head, using the waymarked Saints' Way path with the Coast Path.

Par has all facilities, including a mainline railway station. For the Coast Path, walk along the road called Par Green and follow the Path which leaves the road next to no.52. After crossing the private clay haul road, fork right along a grassy Path immediately before the chalet park. Follow this Path, before turning left then quickly right along the road to a small car park at the western end of the sands of Par Beach. Walk along the back of the beach to another car park at the far, eastern end. This is Polmear; a pub and buses are to be found on the road outside the car park.

The Coast Path crosses the car park to a footbridge and then up the cliffs and continues on to the little harbour village of Polkerris. Here are a pub, toilets and restaurant. The Path continues from the back of the beach, up a ramp to join a zigzag Path through woods to the top. The Path now continues to the Daymark on Gribbin Head (or "The Gribbin"). The tower is open to visitors on some summer Sundays. From the Daymark follow the Path downhill to the scenic cove at Polridmouth ("Pridmouth"), said to have inspired the setting for Daphne du Maurier's "Rebecca". Cross behind the beach on the stepping stones and turn right into the woods, then on over cliff-top fields and past a couple of small coves to arrive at another woodland. Look out for the Path on the right, which goes past St Catherine's Castle and gives superb views upriver to Fowey. Now follow the Path down the woodland track and behind Readymoney Cove, before following the road into Fowey.

Note that it is possible to walk Coast to Coast across Cornwall between Fowey and Padstow on the north coast using the Saints' Way. A guidebook is available from Pelican Studio by post.

OS Maps: Landranger 200 or 204 (Fowey); Landranger 201 (remainder); Explorer 107

	This Walk	Cumulative	This Walk	Cumulative	Grading	Timing
Ascent	1,939ft	74,018ft	591m	22,561m	Strenuous	3.5 hours
Distance	7.1mi	384.5mi	11.4km	618.8km		

For detailed directions see our Walking Guide no. 43, Fowey to Polperro.

This is a connoisseur's Section – it is quiet and remote; it is scenic, with beautiful large sandy bays and smaller coves plus impressive headlands; it is started and finished at superbly picturesque locations, the Fowey estuary at one end and Polperro at the other; and it is quite hard work, emphasising that nothing this good should come too easily.

Directions

Polruan and Polperro are linked by a bus service, giving a bus-walk option, though unfortunately it does not operate at weekends. There is a popular scenic circular walk (the Hall Walk) taking in Fowey and Polruan and using two ferries, an estuary tributary valley and an optional section of the Coast Path.

Fowey is a charming little town, well worth exploring, with all facilities. The crossing of the river to Polruan on the opposite bank is by foot ferry. In summer it usually operates from Whitehouse Quay, below the Esplanade opposite Fowey Hotel, while in winter and in summer early mornings and evenings it operates from Town Quay (centre of Fowey). See pages 27 and 28 for further details.

At Polruan, a picturesque little place, go up the steps next to The Lugger. Turn right at the top in West Street, then turn left up Battery Lane. At the grassy area keep left by the wall, then through the car park parallel to the coast to a signed Path on the right. After around 2 miles/3 kilometres the Path passes above and behind the impressive Lantic Bay, climbing steeply at the far end. There is a higher Path here, going to the top of the hill and turning right, or a lower one, turning off right 30 yards/28 metres before the top, dropping then climbing again to meet the higher Path (ignore beach turnings to the right). The Path goes out around Pencarrow Head, then behind an old watch house to descend and pass behind two charming and remote coves at Lansallos West and East Coombes. After climbing past a marker warning shipping of an offshore rock, more ups and downs follow until the Path approaches the almost hidden inlet of Polperro. Follow the waymarked Path to arrive at a rocky outlook point – go left here then fork right to descend to the harbour. Polperro, an impossibly picturesque harbour village which figures justifiably in most picture books and calendars of Cornwall, has all facilities.

OS Maps: Landranger 201; Explorer 107

	This Walk	Cumulative	This Walk	Cumulative	Grading	Timing
Ascent	774ft	74,792ft	236m	22,797m	Moderate	2.25 hours
Distance	5.0mi	389.5mi	8.0km	626.8km		

For detailed directions see our Walking Guide no. 44, Polperro to Looe.

The cliffs on this Section, never really lofty, tend to decrease in height towards the east. This is a relatively sheltered length passing around lush bays, while offshore, Looe Island is a seaward focal point from the eastern end. Here, also, extensive rocky platforms are exposed at low tide. These factors, and the popularity of Polperro and Looe, have made this a justifiably popular length of coast.

Directions

There is a bus route between Polperro and Looe, making a bus-walk a popular option here.

Polperro is a popular visitors' destination with all facilities. The Coast Path crosses the stone bridge behind the harbour then turns right along The Warren. Climb out of the village, keeping left at the first fork, and right at the second, which leads to the war memorial on its headland. Continue along the Path towards Talland Bay. The Talland Bay Hotel, a short walk up the hill, is open all the year round. Cafes by the beaches are open here from Easter to the end of October. Pass behind the first beach, going left then right along the narrow road, and behind a second beach to a small car parking area. The Path climbs back to the cliffs from here – keep well back from the crumbling edge. It then continues very clearly (ignore all turnings towards the beach) eventually arriving at the end of a suburban road at Hannafore, the western end of Looe. Continue along the road, or the lower promenade; there are toilets and seasonal refreshments along here. At the end, a short stretch of road with no pavement turns alongside the mouth of the Looe River. Take steps down on the right to the riverside of West Looe. There is a seasonal and tidal ferry from here to East Looe, the main part of the town, as an option. Otherwise continue along the West Looe riverside and over the bridge, turning right into East Looe's main street. Looe has buses to Plymouth and a branch to the mainline railway at Liskeard – for the station turn left after the bridge. Between them, East and West Looe have all necessary facilities.

Polperro. Photographer Marcin Jankowski

OS Maps: Landranger 201; Explorer 107 (western half); Explorer 108 (eastern half)

	This Walk	Cumulative	This Walk	Cumulative	Grading	Timing
Ascent	1,965ft	76,757ft	599m	23,396m	Strenuous, moderate in places	4.5 hours
Distance	7.7mi	397.2mi	12.4km	639.2km		

For detailed directions see our Walking Guide no. 45, Looe to Portwrinkle.

Quiet and relatively remote cliff lengths in the western and eastern parts of this Section are separated by a low-level, suburban length, or by an optional route via sea wall and beach between Seaton and Downderry. The western cliffs are covered in lush vegetation, scrub and woodland, and there are stretches where the sea is only glimpsed through the trees. The eastern cliffs are more open and give some superb views along the coast in both directions, with the distinctive Rame Head a focal point.

Directions

A bus service connects Seaton, Downderry and Portwrinkle, making a bus-walk option possible over the eastern end of this section. Further bus-walk options may be possible with a change of bus from Looe at Hessenford (inland of Seaton).

From East Looe's town centre, turn up Castle Street (Ship Inn on the corner) and keep climbing until it becomes a footpath above the sea. Continue, then at a road turn right, passing Plaidy Beach, and continue until just after the road veers left inland. Here go right, up a steep tarmac path, then ahead at the top until the road turns left. The Coast Path descends steps between houses to Millendreath Beach. Café with toilets open all year here. On the far side, go up the cul-de-sac road and climb the sunken lane to reach another road. After 50 yards/45 metres turn right and take the signed route left through twin gates across a drive. Follow the Path ahead through woods to rejoin the road. Turn right on the road and keep ahead past the Monkey Sanctuary onto a narrow lane. At the crest of this lane turn right and cross the field, going left on the far side to follow the Path until it arrives at the lane again. Turn right to descend to Seaton beach.

Turn right, where there are cafés, Pub and public toilets. Although the official Path follows the narrow and busy road up the hill to Downderry, if the tide is not high it is preferable to walk along the top of the sea wall from Seaton and then the beach, taking one of the choice of footpath links into Downderry, where there are pubs, café, shops and public toilets.

Follow the road to the eastern end of Downderry, where it turns inland, and take the signed Path right, which zigzags steeply upward. A superbly scenic cliff-top Path, with several ups and downs, continues until it arrives at a road just above Portwrinkle. Turn right to descend to the village and the quiet sea-front road. The Jolly Roger Cafe and Bistro is open all year in Portwrinkle or other facilities are at Crafthole, a 10 minute walk uphill inland.

OS Maps: Landranger 201; Explorer 108

	This Walk	Cumulative	This Walk	Cumulative	Grading	Timing
Ascent	2,169ft	78,926ft	661m	24,057m	Moderate	5.75 hours
Distance	13.2mi	410.4mi	21.2km	660.5km		

For detailed directions see our Walking Guide no. 46, Portwrinkle to Cawsand and Cawsand to Cremyll (Plymouth Ferry).

This is a Section of great interest rather than spectacular drama. There is a golf course, a gunnery range, a cliff face of wooden chalets and an historic Country Park. It also includes the magnificent and atmospheric Rame Head, which is a significant landmark for many miles along the coast in both directions, the charming twin villages of Cawsand and Kingsand and some superb views, including Plymouth Sound and, indeed, the city itself.

Directions

A bus route links Cawsand to Cremyll, part-way along the section, and also runs along the coast road adjacent to the Coast Path between Tregantle and Rame Head, giving various bus-walk options. There are a number of popular circular walks using the Coast Path based on Mount Edgcumbe Country Park, next to Cremyll, and also around Rame Head.

From Portwrinkle walk up the road, past the first footpath, which leads to the beach, then turn right on the signed Path opposite the golf club. After climbing, the Path goes along the seaward side of the golf course. After leaving the golf course the Path begins to rise towards the Tregantle Firing Ranges. When firing is not taking place it is possible to walk an excellent, well-signed permissive Path through the ranges. Please note that live firing may still take place on weekends if operational requirements demand. In addition, there is no live firing on Bank Holiday weekends nor on any day in August. Other non-firing days are known up to two weeks in advance - telephone The Ranges on 01752 822516 during office hours to check. If live firing is in progress red flags will be raised and the access gates locked – do not proceed into the range. If open, keep closely to the marked Path and, at the far end of the range Path, emerge through another security gate onto the National Trust's cliff-top Path.

If the range Path is closed, continue on the official Coast Path through a field to a road, where the Path initially continues inside the hedge before joining the road further along. The road is usually quite busy so take care. There is the compensation of a magnificent view up the Tamar to Plymouth from the car parking area here, where there is often a refreshment van. Follow the road (past Tregantle Fort entrance) then turn right at the first road junction and continue along the road to the cliffs (passing where the range Path emerges).

The Coast Path is then off-road, along National Trust land, before it rejoins the road for about 1.25 miles/2 kilometres. The signed Path then leaves the road again just past The View Restaurant. The Path undulates quite steeply and meanders unexpectedly among chalets and gardens – keep alert for the waymarking – climbing back to the road. The route then descends gently across the cliff slope to Polhawn Cove at the base of Rame Head. After crossing a private access road for Polhawn Fort, the Path climbs to reach the headland.

The official Coast Path route omits the very end, with its medieval chapel, but the easy climb is worthwhile for the views and the atmosphere. Just inland is a public toilet and car park adjacent to the Coastwatch lookout.

A good cliff Path then goes to Penlee Point, where there are the first views of Plymouth Sound. Bear left to reach a road, then fork off to the right on the signed Path through woods to descend to the charming little village of Cawsand, with pubs, toilets, shops and refreshments. Go through the village square to Garrett Street and continue, turning right in front of the Post Office having, imperceptibly, crossed into Kingsand. At The Cleave turn left then first right up Heavitree Road, which leads to a gate on the right into Mount Edgcumbe Country Park. Continue through the park to a road, turning right then almost immediately left, forking uphill through woods. After a woodland drive there is a waymarked diversion to avoid a cliff fall, the route climbing left to a higher level Path before continuing parallel to the coast. Once around the fallen cliff, the Path descends to the foreshore of Plymouth Sound. Keep on the signed Path up and through a deer gate then back down towards the shore to follow into an Italian Ornate garden, past the Orangery of Mount Edgcumbe House (refreshments), and out through the park gates to the ferry point. Cremyll has a pub and toilets, but most will use it as the staging point for the ferry across the Tamar to Plymouth, an interesting excursion in its own right.

Portwrinkle. Photograph Kaytie Thomas

The businesses listed here are our 'Way Makers'. They make the great South West Coast Path experience possible, and give back to the Trail. Please support them if you can. **More info at www.southwestcoastpath.org.uk/waymaker**

> **If you enjoy staying, eating, drinking or doing an activity with a business along the Path, please let them know about our Way Maker scheme so we can share their brilliance!**

GR Grid Reference	[!] Evening Meal Available	[] Laundry Facilities
DP Distance from the Path	[?] Wifi	[] Caters to Specific Dietary Needs
N Nearest Town/Village with facilities	[] Parking	[] Early Breakfast Available
[3] Number of Rooms	[] Grocery Shop On Site	[] Packed Lunch Offered
[] Dogs Welcome	[] Private Transport to the Path	[£] Budget

Bed & Breakfast and Hotels

NAME	OTHER INFO	
Braganza B&B 4 Grove Hill, St Mawes, TR2 5BJ ☎ 01326 270281 ✉ braganzak@googlemail.com ⊕ www.braganza-stmawes.co.uk	**GR:** SW846331	**DP:** 0.25 miles
	N: ST MAWES	
	OFFERS ONE NIGHT STAYS	
	[5] [] [?] []	
Trenona Farm Holidays Ruan High Lanes, Truro, TR2 5JS ☎ 01872 501339 ✉ info@trenonafarmholidays.co.uk ⊕ www.trenonafarmholidays.co.uk	**GR:** SW915411	**DP:** 3 miles
	N: VERYAN	
	OFFERS ONE NIGHT STAYS	
	[5] [] [?] []	
Landaviddy Farm B&B Landaviddy Lane, Polperro, PL13 2RT ☎ 01503 273302 ✉ enquiries@landaviddyfarm.co.uk ⊕ www.landaviddyfarm.co.uk	**GR:** SX205510	**DP:** 0.25 miles
	N: POLPERRO	
	OFFERS ONE NIGHT STAYS	
	[2] [?] [] [] []	
Talland Bay Hotel Porthallow, PL13 2JB ☎ 01503 272667 ✉ info@tallandbayhotel.com ⊕	**GR:** SX225518	**DP:**
	N: PORTHALLOW	
	OFFERS ONE NIGHT STAYS	
	[20] [] [!] [?] [] [] [] []	
Bridgeside Guest House Fore Street, East Looe, PL13 1HH ☎ 01503 263113 ✉ bridgesideguesthouse@googlemail.com ⊕ www.bridgeside-guesthouse-looe.co.uk	**GR:** SX254535	**DP:** 0.5 miles
	N: LOOE	
	OFFERS ONE NIGHT STAYS	
	[8] [] [?]	

Self Catering and Hostels

NAME	OTHER INFO	
Coastal Gems Maenlay, Foxhole Lane, St Austell, Pl26 6JP ☎ 07880206964 ✉ lisa@coastalgems.co.uk ⊕ www.coastalgems.co.uk	**GR:** SX012415	**DP:** 0 miles
	N: GORRAN HAVEN	
	[3] [?] [] []	

NAME	OTHER INFO		
The Milking Parlour Cornwall	**GR:** SW994486	**DP:** 3 miles	
Tregenna Farm Barns, London Apprentice, PL26 7AW	**N: PENTEWAN**		
📞 07793009405			
✉ ca.allen@outlook.com			
🌐 www.themilkingparlourcornwall.co.uk	③ 🐕 📶 🚗 🔲		
Little Sea View, Duporth	**GR:** SX031512	**DP:** 0 miles	
10 Pavilion Rise, Duporth, St Austell, PL26 6DH	**N: CHARLESTOWN**		
📞 01726 337849			
✉ info@littleseaview.co.uk			
🌐 www.littleseaview.co.uk	③ 📶 🚗 🔲		
The Crow's Nest 38	**GR:** NW503047	**DP:** 0.4 miles	
38 Par Green, Par, PL24 2AF	**N: PAR**		
📞 07570295264			
✉ sconnibeer@yahoo.co.uk			
🌐 airbnb.com/h/thecrowsnest38	① 📶 🚗 ☕		
Retreat to Fowey	**GR:** SX122515	**DP:** 0.4 miles	
No. 1 Claremont House, Hanson Drive, Fowey, PL23 1ET	**N: FOWEY**		
📞 01726 253015			
✉ info@retreattofowey.co.uk			
🌐 www.retreattofowey.co.uk	③ 📶 🚗 🔲		
Eden's Yard Backpackers	**GR:** SX042541	**DP:** 2 miles	
17 Tregrehan Mills, St Austell, PL25 3TL	**N: FOWEY**		
📞 01726 814907	OFFERS ONE NIGHT STAYS		
✉ info@edensyard.uk			
🌐 www.edensyard.uk	⑭ 🍴 📶 🚗		
Seascape Escape at Windsworth	**GR:** SX279547	**DP:** 0.4 miles	
Windsworth, St Martin, Looe, PL13 1NZ	**N: LOOE**		
📞 01503 262671			
✉ stay@windsworth.org.uk			
🌐 www.windsworth.org.uk	③ 🐕 🍴 🚗 ☕ 🍷		
East Trenean Farm Luxury Holiday Cottages	**GR:** SX283574	**DP:** 3.1 miles	
Widegates, Looe, PL13 1QN	**N: MILLENDREATH**		
📞 01503240938			
✉ easttreneanfarm@icloud.com			
🌐 www.easttreneanfarm.co.uk	⑩ 📶 🚗		
Freathy Retreat	**GR:** SX399520	**DP:** 0 miles	
Dragon's Hold, 83, Field 3, Millbrook, Pl10 1JP	**N: FREATHY**		
📞 07837 370680	OFFERS ONE NIGHT STAYS		
✉ phillipajane83@gmail.com			
🌐 www.southwestcoastpath.org.uk/freathy-retreat	① 🍴 📶 🚗		

Campsites and Holiday Parks

NAME	OTHER INFO		
Portholland Escapes	**GR:** SW960413	**DP:** 0.3 miles	
Rocky Close, East Portholland, St Austell, PL26 6NA	**N: PORTLOE**		
📞 07788373673	OFFERS ONE NIGHT STAYS		
✉ porthollandescapes@gmail.com			
🌐 www.porthollandescapes.co.uk	① 🍴		

NAME	OTHER INFO		
Treveague Campsite Treveague Farm Campsite, Gorran, St Austell, PL26 6NY 01726844027 info@treveaguecampsite.co.uk www.treveaguecampsite.co.uk	**GR:** SX002410	**DP:** 1.7 miles	
	N: GORRAN HAVEN		
	OFFERS ONE NIGHT STAYS		
Menagwins Farm Pentewan Road, St Austell, PL26 7AN 07887 424662 enquiries@pitchup.com www.pitchup.com/campsites/England/South_West/ Cornwall/St_Austell/menagwins-farm	**GR:** SX013505	**DP:** 3 miles	
	PORTHPEAN		
	OFFERS ONE NIGHT STAYS		
Great Kellow Farm Caravan & Campsite Lansallos, Polperro, PL13 2QL 01503 272387 enquiries@greatkellowfarm.co.uk www.greatkellowfarm.co.uk	**GR:** SX203520	**DP:** 1 mile	
	N: POLPERRO		
	OFFERS ONE NIGHT STAYS		
Highertown Farm Campsite Lansallos, Looe, PL13 2PX 01208 265211 highertownfarmcampsite@nationaltrust.org.uk www.nationaltrust.org.uk/holidays/highertown-farm-campsite	**GR:** SX173517	**DP:** 1 mile	
	N: POLPERRO		
	OFFERS ONE NIGHT STAYS		
Killigarth Manor Holiday Park Polperro, PL13 2JQ 01503 272216/01503 272213 killigarth-gm@jfhols.co.uk www.johnfowlerholidays.com/cornwall-holiday-park/ killigarth-manor-holiday-park	**GR:** SX214519	**DP:** 1.5 mile	
	N: POLPERRO		
	OFFERS ONE NIGHT STAYS		
Trelawne Manor Holiday Park Looe, PL13 2NA 01503 272151 trelawne-gm@jfhols.co.uk www.johnfowlerholidays.com/cornwall-holiday-park/ trelawne-manor-holiday-park	**GR:** SX220539	**DP:** 0 miles	
	N: LOOE		
Maker Camp The Nissen Huts, Maker Heights, Torpoint, PL10 1LA 01752 822618 makercamp@makerheights.co.uk www.makercamp.org.uk	**GR:** SX434504	**DP:** 0.25 miles	
	N: KINGSAND/CAWSAND		
	OFFERS ONE NIGHT STAYS		

Eat and Drink

NAME	OTHER INFO		
Chain Locker Quay Street, Falmouth, TR11 3HH 01326 311085 chainlocker@staustellbrewery.co.uk chainlockerfalmouth.co.uk	**GR:** SW810325	**DP:** 0.6 miles	
	N: FALMOUTH		
	OFFERS ONE NIGHT STAYS		
Coast Path Cafe Gorran Haven, St Austell, PL26 6JN 07512 543735 geoff.cooke@icloud.com www.facebook.com/Coast-Path-Cafe-287587094719036	**GR:** SX014416	**DP:** 0 miles	
	N: GORRAN HAVEN		

NAME	OTHER INFO	
Pier House	GR: SX038516	DP: 0 miles
Charlestown, Saint Austell, PL25 3NJ	N: **CHARLESTOWN**	
01726 67955 pierhouse@stausellbrewery.co.uk		
pierhousehotel.com		
Encounter Cornwall	GR: SX123546	DP: 1 mile
The Boatshed, Golant, Fowey, PL23 1LW	N: **FOWEY**	
07792062471 paddlecornwallsup@outlook.com		
www.encountercornwall.com		
Readymoney Beach Shop	GR: SX117511	DP: 0 miles
Readymoney Beach Shop, St Catherine's Cove, Fowey, PL23 1JH	N: **FOWEY**	
07980311646 hello@readymoneybeachshop.com		
www.readymoneybeachshop.com		

Activities

NAME	OTHER INFO	
National Maritime Museum Cornwall	GR: SW813 3240	DP: 0 miles
Discovery Quay, Falmouth, TR11 3QY	N: **FALMOUTH**	
01326 313388 enquiries@nmmc.co.ukm		
www.nmmc.co.uk		
Glendurgan Garden, National Trust	GR: SW768276	DP: 1.2 miles
Mawnan Smith, Falmouth, TR11 5JZ	N: **FALMOUTH**	
01326252020 glendurgan@nationaltrust.org.uk		
www.nationaltrust.org.uk/glendurgan-garden		
Talland Church	GR: SX228516	DP: 0 miles
Talland Bay, PL13 2JB	N: **POLPERRO**	
07527 002884 admin@tallandchurch.co.uk		
www.tallandchurch.co.uk		

Getting Around

NAME	OTHER INFO	
Barries Taxis	GR: SX254536	DP: 0 miles
Taxi Rank, Looe, PL13 1HL	N: **POLPERRO**	
07792 722549 barrie48@icloud.com		
barries-taxis-looe.business.site		

Information

NAME	OTHER INFO	
Fal River Visitor Information Centre	GR: SW807329	DP: 0 miles
11 Market Strand, Prince of Wales Pier, Falmouth, TR11 3DB	N: **FALMOUTH**	
01326 741194 info@falriver.co.uk		
wwwfalriver.co.uk		
Mevagissey Tourist Information Centre	GR: SX014448	DP: 0.7 miles
Hurley Books, 3 Jetty Street, St Austell, PL26 6UH	N: **MEVAGISSEY**	
01726 842200 enquiries@hurleybooks.co.uk		
mevagissey.net		
Looe Tourist Information	GR: SX252536	DP: 1.2 miles
Millpool Centre, The Millpool, Looe, PL13 2AF	N: **LOOE**	
01503 262255 welcome@looetowncouncil.gov.uk		
www.visitlooe.co.uk		

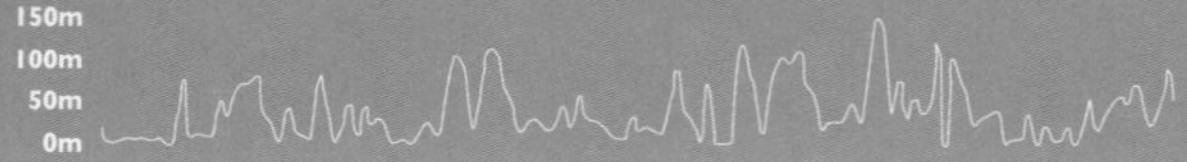

150m
100m
50m
0m

South Devon Plymouth to Starcross – 104 miles

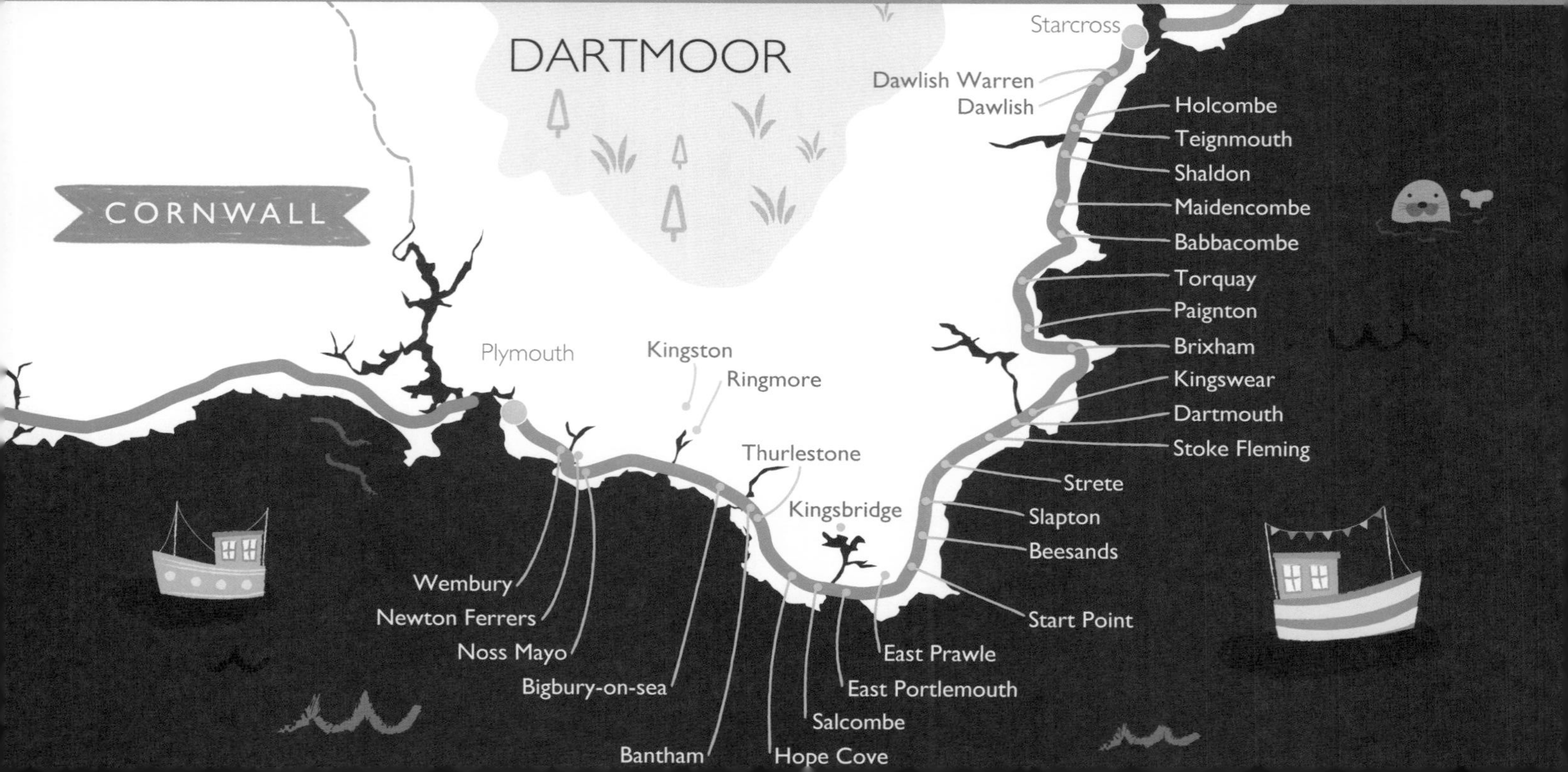

DARTMOOR

CORNWALL

Starcross

Dawlish Warren
Dawlish

Holcombe
Teignmouth
Shaldon
Maidencombe
Babbacombe
Torquay
Paignton
Brixham
Kingswear
Dartmouth
Stoke Fleming

Strete
Slapton
Beesands
Start Point

East Prawle
East Portlemouth
Salcombe
Hope Cove

Kingsbridge

Thurlestone

Kingston
Ringmore

Plymouth

Wembury
Newton Ferrers
Noss Mayo
Bigbury-on-sea

Bantham

At the west of this length is the estuary of the River Tamar with the major naval port of Plymouth, the biggest urban area on the South West Coast Path that is full of historic interest. East of Plymouth the coast is largely characterised by cliff scenery cut by attractive estuaries, the drowned mouths of wooded river valleys – the Yealm, Erme, Avon, Kingsbridge and Dart estuaries. As well as the ups and downs of the cliffs these estuaries present the walker with a number of ferry crossings (some seasonal and with limited timetables) and one (low-tide only) ford. This southernmost part of Devon forms the area known as the South Hams and includes the attractive and historic town of Dartmouth. Following the dramatic cliffs that lead to to the limestone headland of Berry Head, the coast becomes an area of low, mostly red sandstone cliffs. This length, the "Riviera", is largely occupied by towns based on tourism such as Paignton, Torquay, Teignmouth and Dawlish. The major estuary of the River Exe forms the eastern boundary of this length.

> All of the locations on the map illustration to the left, have at least 1 facility including toilets, a cafe/restaurant, shop or pub.

Paignton Pier. Photographer Rob Davey

OS Maps: Landranger 201; Explorer 108

	This Walk	Cumulative	This Walk	Cumulative	Grading	Timing
Ascent	463ft	79,389ft	141m	24,198m	Easy	3.5 hours
Distance	7.5mi	417.9mi	12.1km	672.5km		

For detailed directions see our Walking Guide no. 47, Admiral's Hard (Plymouth) to The Barbican and The Barbican to Mount Batten.

This is an urban walk along the waterfront of one of the country's prime historical maritime cities. It is therefore quite different to the vast majority of the Coast Path, but is nevertheless well worth doing. The view over Plymouth Sound, flanked on both sides by cliffs, is inspiring, and often referred to as the finest urban vista in the country. Elsewhere are lengths of waterside industry, historic quays and modern marinas, making this a fascinating excursion.

Directions

A range of urban bus services run throughout Plymouth, including to and from Admiral's Hard, the ferry point for Cremyll, and Mount Batten. Though not on the same route, they link in the city centre. There is also a ferry link across the mouth of the River Plym between the historic Sutton Harbour and Mount Batten. These links make a range of public transport-walks possible.

The Coast Path from Cremyll uses the ferry across the Tamar. The ferry operates all year, weather, tide and other circumstances permitting, generally at 30 minute intervals. For ferry details see page 28.

Plymouth's Waterfront Walk is enhanced by a variety of information plaques and pieces of artwork relating to the city's history. A companion guidebook "Plymouth's Waterfront Walkway" is available free of charge from the Association with a small fee to cover postage.

The route through Plymouth is marked in a range of ways. In addition to many acorns on lamp posts, white arrows and South West Coast Path white on black stickers, there are red metal diamond signs, red South West Coast Path signs, waymarks set in the pavement and even some Coast Path engraved stones along the route. From the ferry walk up the road and turn right, going round the car park into Cremyll Street and on to the gates of the Royal William Yard. Enter the Yard via the walkway to the right of the main entrance and go through the Yard following the sea wall. (There is a ferry from the Royal William Yard to the Barbican that will also stop at Mount Batten on request for those who want a short cut). At the far corner of the Yard's sea wall climb the Eric Wallis Memorial Steps to Devil's Point Park. Follow the Path around the Park, overlooking Drake's Island and Plymouth Sound to reach the Artillery Tower, now a restaurant. At this point bear inland into Durnford Street and continue past the Royal Marines Barracks, turning right immediately after them. Continue along Millbay Road and a few metres after passing the entrance to Millbay Docks and Brittany Ferries turn right along Brunel Way to a waterside path along the north-eastern side of Millbay Docks. At the time of writing, due to work in progress, after about 300 metres you will need to leave this path and head ENE between new apartments for 30 metres, and up steps to join West Hoe Road just before turning into Great Western Road. Take the right fork into Great Western Road and continue for 250 metres, then bear off right, just beyond a bus stop, down a narrow path along the shoreline. The Path returns to the road; here turn right to walk along the Hoe promenade all the way to The Barbican and

Sutton Harbour, Plymouth's original harbour. Above on the left, away from the Coast Path but worth a visit, are the lighthouse of Smeaton's Tower, Drake's statue and other points of interest.

At The Barbican on the right are the Mayflower Steps, marking the site of the Pilgrim Fathers embarkation. The large pontoon on nearby Commercial Wharf is the ferry point for Mount Batten, a short cut direct to the end of the Section.

The ferry operates all year. For ferry details see page 28.

Continuing on the Coast Path Waterfront Walk, walk across the lock gates at the entrance to Sutton Harbour, past the Marine Aquarium and then along Teat's Hill Road past the entrance to Queen Anne's Battery. At Breakwater Road, just after the entrance to Victoria Wharves, turn right up a narrow hill and footpath and down to the industrial Cattedown Wharf area. Continue past warehouses, then turn right into Neptune Park. Keep to the right of the car parks and exit left just beyond the TR2 building up a slope and right onto Finnigan Road to Laira Bridge. (However if you keep well right of the car parks there is a better path skirting the waterside edge of Neptune Park with good views up and down the Cattewater.) Turn right to cross the River Plym then, at the first roundabout, turn right (at the rhinoceros!). Go right into Breakwater Road, and continue for about 500 yards/450 metres, then turn left, still in Breakwater Road, to the entrance to Yacht Haven Quay Boatyard. To the left of a mesh fence is a path, signed as the Coast Path, which is followed to Oreston Quay. At the quay, walk past the grassy area into Marine Road then left into Park Lane. Turn left at the top of the hill, and this Path descends to Radford Lake. From here a Coast-to-Coast walk goes to Lynmouth on the north coast, following the Erme-Plym Trail and the Two Moors Way. Guidebooks are available at Ivybridge Tourist Information Centre (TIC).

Go across the causeway with its old mini castle folly and turn right. Follow the Path along, then turn left and at a junction turn right down Hexton Hill Road to Hooe Lake. Skirt the lake, going along Barton Road skirting Hooe Lake and Turnchapel Wharf to Turnchapel. Go through the village, bearing left at the Clovelly Bay Inn, up the hill then turn right down steps to the marina. Due to a landslip, which is being looked at for repairs, there could be a temporary diversion around Yacht Haven Quay Boatyard; follow diversion signage over the slipway and along the shoreline to Mount Batten and the Sutton Harbour ferry. There are toilets, refreshments and a pub here. The short walk along the breakwater is very popular, although not part of the Coast Path.

Saltash Passage, Plymouth. Photographer Kaytie Thomas

OS Maps: Landranger 201; Explorer OL20

	This Walk	Cumulative	This Walk	Cumulative	Grading	Timing
Ascent	1,260ft	80,649ft	384m	24,582m	Easy	3 hours
Distance	7.5mi	425.4mi	12.1km	684.6km		

For detailed directions see our Walking Guide no. 48, Mount Batten to Warren Point (Yealm Ferry).

This is a Section of low cliffs, much of it overlooking Plymouth Sound. Below the cliffs are extensive areas of rock platform and offshore the Great Mew Stone becomes a focal point. Caravan and chalet sites and suburban villages are never far away. Towards its eastern end, as the cliffs rise somewhat, is the picturesque mouth of the River Yealm, forming a dramatic wooded gap in the cliffs.

Directions

Separate bus routes serve Mount Batten and Wembury village, and also Heybrook Bay (midway along this section), all from Plymouth city centre, allowing bus-walk options. There is a popular circular walk using the Coast Path between Wembury and Warren Point and a longer, full-day circular using the Erme-Plym Trail between Wembury and Mount Batten, plus the Coast Path.

Mount Batten has toilets and refreshments, as well as a direct ferry link to and from Plymouth's Sutton Harbour. From Mount Batten the Coast Path heads over the little hill and past the old fort tower to the grassy area at Jennycliff, where there are more toilets and refreshments. Stay to the lower side of the field and at the end of the grass, from the stone "doormat" to Plymouth, use the renovated steps down and stairs up again to access woodland. The Path then undulates and emerges above Fort Bovisand; there are refreshments here. Cross the carpark and follow the Path down to Bovisand beach, then up to the chalet park road; follow round to the right to pass seaward of the chalets, past a cafe and toilets and on round the point and so to Heybrook Bay. There is a pub a little way up the road here, as well as a bus stop. Keep right and follow the Path above the shore around Wembury Point and on to Wembury Beach. Yet more toilets and refreshments await here, and the bus stop, together with pub and shop, are in the village a little way inland.

From Wembury Beach a Coast-to-Coast walk goes to Lynmouth on the north coast, following the Erme-Plym Trail and the Two Moors Way. Guidebooks are available from Ivybridge Tourist Information Centre (TIC).

Continuing on the Coast Path, climb seaward of the church and along the now higher cliffs to a junction of paths at the Rocket House. The Path going inland from here leads to Wembury village and its facilities. For the Coast Path, bear right, downhill, to reach the ferry point. Please note that this ferry crossing is seasonal only – see page 28 and Walk 49.

OS Maps: Landranger 201 (western end); Landranger 202 (remainder); Explorer OL20

	This Walk	Cumulative	This Walk	Cumulative	Grading	Timing
Ascent	1,466ft	82,115ft	447m	25,029m	Easy then strenuous	4 hours
Distance	10.3mi	435.7mi	16.6km	701.2km		

For detailed directions see our Walking Guide no. 49, Wembury to River Erme.

This is a fine Section of high-level coastal cliffs, cut mid-way by the substantial and extremely picturesque estuary of the River Erme. The western end is a particularly good length, since the superb cliff coastline is easily accessed by a scenic former carriage route. Beyond that a series of descents and ascents, some quite steep, accentuate the dramatic landscape of the coastline. At the eastern extremity is the tidally insular Burgh Island, a focal point on this part of the coast. Because of its remoteness and strenuous nature, much of this section has a quiet character, which will specially appeal to those in search of a remote coastline.

Directions

A once-daily bus service links Noss Mayo, near the western end of this length, with Battisborough cross, a little way inland from the eastern end, making a bus-walk feasible. There is a very popular local walk using the Coast Path on the carriage drive from Noss Mayo.

The ferry at Wembury's Warren Point operates three ways over the River Yealm and its tributary Newton Creek. Warren Point is thus linked with both Newton Ferrers and Noss Mayo, and these two points with each other. For the Coast Path the link between Warren Point and Noss Mayo is needed. The ferry operates seasonally and at limited times. For ferry details see page 28.

There is a signal board to summon the ferryman by the steps at Warren Point or the slipway at Noss Mayo. Alternatively, telephone beforehand.

Because of the somewhat limited nature of the ferry, it may be necessary to make alternative arrangements to reach Noss Mayo. Both Wembury and Noss Mayo have a regular bus service to and from Plymouth, so it is possible to use these services as a link, perhaps combining with an overnight stop in Plymouth. Alternatively, local taxi companies are available.

It is also possible to walk round the Yealm Estuary from ferry point to ferry point. This is a distance of some 9 miles/14.5 kilometres, effectively adding an extra day or half day to the itinerary.

Walk around the Yealm Estuary

Walk uphill inland from the ferry steps to the house at the top, the Rocket House. Continue inland along the track, which in turn becomes a road. Where the road bears sharp right go ahead along a public footpath into a field, then keep ahead alongside a high wall. At the end of the wall, after two gates, bear left (bearing 330°) across fields, then go down a few steps. The now enclosed Path goes left then right to arrive at a road. This is Knighton, on the outskirts of Wembury. The bus stop for Plymouth is a little way to the left, just before the pub.

To continue the walking route around the estuary, cross the road at Knighton to a minor lane, following it left to another junction. Turn right here and continue until the road meets another, more major, road. Cross this road, going ahead and left for a short way then turn right on a signed footpath. This is part of a waymarked route, the Erme-Plym Trail, and is shown on the OS Explorer OL20 map. Follow the waymarked route across fields, over Cofflete Creek, next to a lane and on to the village of Brixton. Turn right and follow the road through the village to Brixton Church then back on the Erme-Plym Trail up Old Road, along a suburban road, over fields, along a minor lane then over more fields to arrive at Yealmpton village. On reaching the A379 road at Yealmpton, leave the Erme-Plym trail and turn right along the A379 then quickly left, into Stray Park. At the bottom bear right along a tarmac Path then, when it arrives at a road, turn left along a stony track. At the footpath sign continue ahead, eventually emerging at a road by a car park. Turn left along the road to cross Puslinch Bridge then follow the road up the hill. Take the footpath on the right near the top of the hill, crossing a couple of fields to a road. Turn right and continue to meet a more major road, which is followed ahead to Newton Ferrers. At the edge of the village turn left down the road signed to Bridgend and Noss Mayo, and at the junction at the head of the creek keep to the right. Follow the riverside road, forking right into Noss Mayo. Keep on the road round Noss Creek, and continue on the creekside road out of the village until this becomes a track. A signed Path on the right leaves the track for the ferry point.

Coast Path, Noss Mayo-River Erme

From the ferry point, follow the Path westward through the woods as it climbs to meet a track, an old carriage drive. (NB if refreshments are needed here, turn left and continue for about a mile to Noss Mayo village, where there are two pubs and seasonal toilets). The drive continues through woods, past a row of former coastguard cottages, into more woods, then on a superb cliff-face shelf round Mouthstone Point. Further on, keep right where the more obvious Path bears left inland to a car park, the drive continuing round Stoke Point and on to Beacon Hill. A series of ups and downs now ensues as the Path approaches the estuary of the River Erme, which has been fairly described as England's most unspoiled river estuary, and is possibly the most attractive. The Path crosses the top of a small beach, then passes through a short woodland stretch to arrive at Mothecombe slipway on the Erme. There are seasonal refreshments a little way inland.

There is no ferry at the River Erme. It is usually possible to wade the river 1 hour either side of low water along the old ford and, under normal conditions, at low tide the water is about knee deep and the river bed is of sand with pebbles. The crossing is between grid references 614 476 and 620 478, ie the road by the row of coastguard cottages at Mothecombe and the end of the inland road to Wonwell Beach. However, great care should be taken as heavy rains or high seas can make conditions dangerous. Low water is approximately at the same time as at Devonport; see tide tables from page 30.

Alternatively, it is possible to walk round the estuary. There are no riverside rights of way, and for the most part minor roads must be used. The distance is approximately 8 miles/13 kilometres, adding extra time to the itinerary.

Walk round the Erme Estuary

From the slipway follow the road inland, following signs to Holbeton. Go through the village and leave on the minor lane to Ford and then Hole Farm. At the sharp bend after this farm, follow the waymarked Erme-Plym Trail to the A379 and across the River Erme at Sequer's Bridge. Then leave the waymarked Trail, continuing very carefully along the A379 for a couple of hundred yards/metres, before turning right on the lane signed to Orcheton. Follow this for about 2 miles/3 kilometres then turn right, following signs for Wonwell Beach. Follow the lane downhill to arrive at the estuary.

OS Maps: Landranger 202; Explorer OL20

	This Walk	Cumulative	This Walk	Cumulative	Grading	Timing
Ascent	1,860ft	83,975ft	567m	25,596m	Moderate	4 hours
Distance	9.3mi	445.0mi	15.0km	716.2km		

For detailed directions see our Walking Guide no. 50, River Erme to Hope Cove.

While the western end of this Section is relatively remote, in the east it is a well-used and popular Section, never far from residential and holiday accommodation. It is a length of low cliffs and sandy beaches, the coastline providing some interesting seascapes. These include views of the tidal Burgh Island, the estuary of the River Avon, the distinctive holed Thurlestone Rock and the headland of Bolt Tail. At the end of the Section, Hope Cove is a charming little settlement with a picturesque harbour and an old centre of historic cottages.

Directions

A regular, if infrequent, bus service links Thurlestone and Hope Cove, making a bus-walk option possible on the eastern part of this Section. There are popular short circular walks using the Coast Path between Bantham and Thurlestone.

For details of crossing the River Erme, see Section 49. On the eastern side, just inland of Wonwell slipway, a Path leaves the lane into the woods then continues above the shore, emerging on cliffs which rollercoaster up and down to the holiday park at Challaborough and then Bigbury-on-Sea. There are toilets here and also the year-round café. There is a pub offshore on Burgh Island, reached by walking across the sands or by unusual sea tractor.

From the main facilities at Bigbury-on-Sea, the Coast Path goes along the road, turning right immediately after the car park entrance to follow a short cliff-top length which re-joins the road further up. Cross the road and follow the Path along the field edge next to the road, climbing Folly Hill. Leave the field where signed and cross the road, passing through Folly Farm and down the cliffs to the flat open area of Cockleridge Ham. At the edge is the ferry point for the crossing of the mouth of the River Avon.

In 2022 the ferry operated from 8th April until 2nd October between the hours of 10.00 to 12.00 and 14.00 to 16.00. Operating times are not available at the time of going to print so check the Bantham Estate website at **banthamestate.co.uk/getting-here/ferry** or phone the estate office on **01548 560897**. Alternatively, there is a waymarked walk round the estuary between Bigbury-on-Sea and Bantham. This route, the Avon Estuary Walk, is signed with blue waymarks and adds about 8 miles/13 kilometres to the route, or another half day to a day to the itinerary. The route is shown on OS Explorer map OL20 and can be followed from the top of Folly Hill.

Avon Estuary Walk

Continue up the road, without turning into Folly Farm, for a further 60 yards/55 metres and then turn right. The Path reaches the golf course, turning left on a track then off this to the right, down another track past Hexdown Farm. Follow this track to the bottom, then go left along a drive which eventually arrives at a road. There is a permissive Path alongside the road and at the end of this a Path goes right over a field, through the top of a wood then downhill over another field to a road alongside the estuary. This tidal road is then followed to Aveton Gifford on the A379.

At high tide there is a waymarked diversion which provides a route around the tidal road to rejoin the trail at the next village. From Aveton Gifford cross the Avon on the A379 then take the first lane on the right, which becomes a track and continues to Stadbury Farm. Bear left approaching the farm onto a footpath, following field edges towards the valley bottom to cross Stiddicombe Creek. Enter the wood on the right and climb to leave at the far top corner. Follow the top edge of fields, then cross a farm track and a stream to a junction of paths. Turn right and continue to Bantham village, where there is a pub, shop, toilets and seasonal refreshments.

Coast Path, Bantham-Hope Cove

From the ferry point, go through the car park and round the edge of the dunes of Bantham Ham. Follow the shore, leaving the dunes to climb the hill and reach the undulating track around Thurlestone Golf Club, passing the small Leas Foot Sand beach, and continuing on to Thurlestone Sands. Cross a long footbridge at an inland lagoon (South Milton Ley), pass public toilets and seasonal refreshments, then join a road for a short stretch before turning back to the shoreline and over low cliffs to Outer Hope, where there are all facilities in season. Follow the Path behind the little harbour and down to the old lifeboat station at Inner Hope, where the bus stop is situated. Buses to Kingsbridge leave from here. A little inland is the old village centre of Inner Hope, at The Square, a picture-postcard location worth seeing before leaving.

Hope Cove. Photographer James Loveridge

OS Maps: Landranger 202; Explorer OL20

	This Walk	Cumulative	This Walk	Cumulative	Grading	Timing
Ascent	1,506ft	85,481ft	459m	26,055m	Moderate	4 hours
Distance	8.1mi	453.1mi	13.0km	729.2km		

For detailed directions see our Walking Guide no. 51, Hope Cove to Salcombe.

This is a very scenic Section of the coast, largely comprising quite spectacular high cliffs soaring above tiny, mostly inaccessible coves. Near both ends are dramatic headlands, Bolt Tail in the west and Bolt Head in the east, offering superb coastal views in their respective directions. At the eastern end this Section turns into the mouth of the estuary of Salcombe Harbour, and there is the contrast of softer, sandy bays. This is a length which is not really remote but never exceptionally busy.

Directions

Separate bus routes serve Hope Cove and Salcombe from Kingsbridge and Malborough, a few miles inland, making a bus-walk feasible from there. There are numerous local circuits using the Coast Path based on Hope Cove and Salcombe, as well as Bolberry and Soar.

Leave Hope Cove from the old lifeboat station at Inner Hope, up the signed Coast Path and out to the magnificent viewpoint of Bolt Tail, where the ramparts of an Iron Age cliff fort are crossed to reach the end. The Path doubles back along the cliff top over Bolberry Down (seasonal refreshments), and then down to the splendid Soar Mill Cove (there are seasonal refreshments inland from here). Climbing steeply from the Cove, a long level stretch of easy walking follows. Keep along the cliff top, and as the Path approaches Bolt Head pass through a couple of gates, staying on the closest path to the cliff top as possible. A steep descent will then lead to the headland, where a sharp turn to the north leads to the cliff-face Path round Starehole Bay and then on to the Courtenay Walk below rocky pinnacles. Passing into woodland at the National Trust's Overbecks property, the Path joins a road which is followed past South Sands and North Sands – toilets and seasonal refreshments at both – and then on into Salcombe town centre. For a variation, there is a summer ferry service between South Sands and Salcombe. The town is a renowned yachting centre and has all facilities.

Blackpool Sands. Photographer Nick Shepherd

OS Maps: Landranger 202; Explorer OL20

	This Walk	Cumulative	This Walk	Cumulative	Grading	Timing
Ascent	2,251ft	87,732ft	686m	26,741m	Moderate, strenuous in places	6.75 hours
Distance	12.6mi	465.7mi	20.3km	749.5km		

For detailed directions see our Walking Guide no. 52, Salcombe to Torcross.

This is a superb section of walking. Part of it is on exposed cliff faces, the sometimes stark cliffs contrasting with numerous tiny sandy coves below. A significant length in the middle is on an old "raised beach", a low shelf a little above the sea giving an easy passage. In the east the Path crosses the rocky spine of Start Point, behind its lighthouse, a dramatic stretch with views across Start Bay, before following a lush, sheltered length into Torcross.

Directions

Salcombe and Torcross are both on regular bus routes to and from Kingsbridge, a little inland, making a bus-walk possible. There is also a popular local circuit using the Coast Path from the Salcombe Ferry.

Salcombe has all necessary facilities. The ferry across the estuary leaves from steps next to the Ferry Inn, a little way downstream from the town centre. The ferry operates all year. For ferry details see page 28.

From the ferry point on the eastern side, where there are toilets and seasonal refreshments, the Coast Path follows the road down the estuary side then, after crossing the rear of the beach at Mill Bay (toilets), the Path passes Gara Rock where refreshments are available, then on past a number of sandy coves before reaching Prawle Point. The Path goes to the Coastwatch lookout at the very end, then descends to follow the "raised beach" shelf just above the waves, before a short inland length to avoid a cliff fall leads to Lannacombe Beach. Beyond here a dramatic length goes along and up to the rocky ridge leading to Start Point, the Path dropping to the lighthouse access road. From the car park at the top, the Path bears off right down the cliff face to Hallsands, passing above the old ruined village. The Path continues over low cliffs to Beesands, where there is a pub, toilets and seasonal refreshments. Continue along the shingle ridge then behind an old quarry to descend into Torcross, with a panoramic view of Slapton Ley. Pass down some steep steps before returning to the promenade in front of the houses. Torcross has a pub, refreshments and toilet facilities, plus buses to Kingsbridge, Plymouth and Dartmouth.

Start Point Lighthouse. Photographer Rob Davey

OS Maps: Landranger 202; Explorer OL20

	This Walk	Cumulative	This Walk	Cumulative	Grading	Timing
Ascent	1,493ft	89,225ft	455m	27,196m	Easy then strenuous	4.75 hours
Distance	10.3mi	476.0mi	16.6km	766.0km		

For detailed directions see our Walking Guide no. 53, Torcross to Dartmouth.

Something like a quarter of this Section consists of the low shingle ridge known locally as the Slapton Line, cutting off the freshwater lake of Slapton Ley from the sea. Most of the remainder of the Section is cliffs and coves, partly looking to the sea and partly to the outer reaches of the picturesque wooded Dart Estuary.

Directions

A regular bus service runs along the coast road which is, for much of the Section, adjacent to the Coast Path. With stops at most obvious locations this gives numerous bus-walk options. There is also a very popular and scenic circular walk using the Coast Path between Dartmouth and the mouth of the Dart Estuary.

From Torcross, with limited facilities, the Coast Path runs along the shingle ridge. The official route is on the landward side of the road. After the Strete Gate car park, look out for the fingerpost signing the section of Coast Path which was opened in Summer 2015. Follow the Path along the cliff top and through the woods to the A379. It is now necessary to walk along this for the next 400 yards/365 metres.

Follow the main road through Strete village (pub and shop), then just after the village ends, take the Path to the right which passes over fields, and a footbridge to reach a high point above the sea. Continuing parallel to the coast for a while, it then heads inland over a deep valley, crossing the main road and over more fields to a lane. Descend the lane, then leave it across more fields until, after crossing the main road again, the picturesque cove of Blackpool Sands is reached. There are toilets and seasonal refreshments here. Follow the Path uphill through the woods, then the route enters and meanders along various paths in the village of Stoke Fleming (pub, shop and toilets), arriving at the village hall. Cross the main road again and follow a lane to a National Trust car park at Little Dartmouth. From here a scenic cliff Path proceeds, latterly through woods, to reach the Dart Estuary and arrive at Dartmouth Castle (toilets and seasonal refreshments). An estuary-side Path passes the adjacent church and joins the road, which is followed into the town. Look out for some steps on the right just after the public toilets before reaching the centre; the steps lead down to Bayards Cove through its little castle and on to the Embankment at the town centre. Dartmouth, of course, has all facilities.

OS Maps: Landranger 202; Explorer OL20

	This Walk	Cumulative	This Walk	Cumulative	Grading	Timing
Ascent	2,992ft	92,217ft	912m	28,108m	Strenuous	5.75 hours
Distance	10.9mi	486.9mi	17.5km	783.6km		

For detailed directions see our Walking Guide no. 54, Dartmouth (Kingswear) to Brixham.

This is a Section of superb cliff scenery, tough going in places and often quite remote. In the west, near the mouth of the Dart, are substantial wooded areas, but further along the cliffs become higher and more open. This makes for a dramatic, steeply undulating landscape ending at the sea in steep cliff faces.

Directions

A regular bus service links Brixham and Kingswear, on the east side of the Dartmouth Ferry, making a bus-walk possible. There is also a bus service from Paignton to Kingswear. A popular circuit using the Coast Path exists based around Kingswear.

Walkers have two ferry options from Dartmouth town centre to cross the river, the Lower Car Ferry, which also carries foot passengers, and the Dartmouth Passenger Ferry. The Lower Car Ferry operates all year on a continuous service. The Dartmouth Passenger Ferry also operates all year on a continuous service. For ferry details see pages 28 and 29. The Lower Ferry is the easiest option for the Coast Path.

From either ferry landing point in Kingswear, follow the Coast Path signposts, turning left along Beacon Road then right up Church Hill and down Beacon Lane. Continue out of the village. After some 1.25 miles/2 kilometres turn right down some steps. The route then undulates, sometimes steeply, into and through woodland to the old Battery buildings at Froward Point. Here the Path descends steeply to the right from the corner of an old lookout building, passing World War II searchlight and gun positions before continuing along the cliffs. Pass Pudcombe Cove, by the National Trust Coleton Fishacre Gardens, and then on over Scabbacombe Head and past Scabbacombe Sands and Mansands and over Southdown Cliff to Sharkham Point – this is a particularly strenuous length. If it is difficult to cross Mansands beach because of the flow of water from the lake behind, follow the signs for the alternative route behind the lake which re-joins the Path at the end of the beach. Passing holiday accommodation the Path arrives at Berry Head, a Napoleonic fortified area. Divert to the end of the headland to see the unusually squat lighthouse. Berry Head has toilets and year round refreshments available at the Guardhouse Café. From here descend past an old quarry to a road, where there are further refreshment facilities. Turn right then go right again through the Shoalstone car park and along above the shoreline, returning to the road before descending steps to Brixham Breakwater. Follow the promenade to the harbour. Brixham has all facilities.

OS Maps: Landranger 202: Explorer OL20 (western half); Explorer 110 (eastern half)

	This Walk	Cumulative	This Walk	Cumulative	Grading	Timing
Ascent	1,972ft	94,189ft	601m	28,709m	Moderate	6 hours
Distance	13.2mi	500.1mi	21.2km	804.8km		

For detailed directions see our Walking Guide no. 55, Brixham to Paignton and Paignton to Babbacombe.

This is mostly an urban Section, passing along the shoreline of the "English Riviera", or Tor Bay. There is a mixture of grand terraces, open green parkland, amusement parks and the elegant white buildings overlooking the sea at Torquay. At the western end there is also the old fishing town of Brixham and at the other end the almost rural wooded cliffs around Babbacombe. All in all, this is a surprisingly diverse Section.

Directions

A range of bus routes runs throughout the Torbay area, including one which follows the coast road between Brixham and Torquay, and another linking Torquay to Babbacombe. As a result, a wide variety of bus-walks is possible. A pleasant alternative is the Torquay to Brixham ferry which runs regularly.

Leaving Brixham by the fish market, the Coast Path initially passes a car park and gardens, before passing two small coves and climbing into woodland which takes the Path to Elberry Cove. From here it passes behind the sweep of Broadsands, climbing by the railway viaduct at the far end to proceed alongside the steam railway line to the promenade at Goodrington. At the far end, climb through ornamental gardens and go down a road to Paignton Harbour and along the promenade. Paignton's railway station is inland of the pier. Turn inland at Hollicombe, at the far end of Preston Sands, going through a park to the main sea-front road which is followed to Torquay Harbour. Torquay Station is inland a little before the harbour.

Cross the pedestrian bridge across the harbour (if the bridge is out of commission, follow the brass floor plaques around the inner harbour) and climb the hill, turning right at the Imperial Hotel on the signed Path, which leads to the open area at Daddyhole Plain. Descend to the sea-front road at Meadfoot Beach, climbing again at Ilsham Marine Drive. Take the cliff path round Thatcher Point to Hope's Nose. A cul-de-sac path goes to the end of this low headland.

From Hope's Nose follow the Path inland of the road, crossing the road to the Bishop's Walk, which in turn arrives at a car park above Anstey's Cove. The Path now goes up and round the edge of the grassy downs on Walls Hill, with excellent views across Lyme Bay, bearing off right to descend to Babbacombe Beach. Cross a wooden footbridge to Oddicombe Beach, then climb by the cliff railway to reach Babbacombe's facilities at the top.

OS Maps: Landranger 202; Explorer 110

	This Walk	Cumulative	This Walk	Cumulative	Grading	Timing
Ascent	2,090ft	96,279ft	637m	29,346m	Strenuous	3.75 hours
Distance	6.4mi	506.5mi	10.3km	815.1km		

For detailed directions see our Walking Guide no. 56, Babbacombe to Teignmouth.

This is a tough Section of almost constant ups and downs. The characteristic red cliffs of this part of Devon are often quite high and quite sheer, though unfortunately the terrain is such that sea and cliff views are perhaps less frequent than would be hoped for as you pass through some attractive woods. Its strenuous nature makes it a relatively quiet Section, except for the two ends, although it is never far from roads or housing.

Directions

A regular bus service links Babbacombe and Teignmouth, making a bus-walk option.

From Babbacombe, a pleasant suburb of Torquay with all facilities, the Coast Path descends next to the cliff railway and then soon climbs again to avoid a cliff fall. The Path goes up a grassy area to a main road where it turns right, then right again into Petitor Road. At the bottom turn left on the Coast Path again, which soon descends onto a cliff face before reaching the wooded valley at Watcombe. Cross the track running down the valley and on through a wooded length to a short rocky stretch, turning right at a junction before reaching the car park at Maidencombe. There is a pub and toilets here. Turn right after the car park and keep on the rollercoaster Path, which eventually climbs to go alongside the coast road, then quickly leaves it to pass alongside fields to a track. Turn right and go round the wooded Ness headland, with super views ahead, descending to the promenade at Shaldon, on the estuary of the River Teign. The ferry service across the River Teign operates throughout the year, weather permitting. For ferry details see page 29.

Walk, Shaldon-Teignmouth

If the ferry is not operating, continue inland along the riverside roads to Shaldon Bridge and cross the Teign. On the Teignmouth side turn right into Milford Park, through Bitton Sports Ground into Park Hill, cross into Bitton Avenue then into Clay Lane and right into Willow Street. At the end bear left then right into Quay Road, then right to go along the Strand and right to the Harbour Beach and the ferry point. Teignmouth has all facilities, including a mainline rail station and buses to Exeter.

Teignmouth. Photographer Kavita Solder

OS Maps: Landranger 192; Explorer 110

	This Walk	Cumulative	This Walk	Cumulative	Grading	Timing
Ascent	488ft	96,767ft	149m	29,495m	Easy	3 hours
Distance	8.0mi	514.5mi	12.9km	828.0km		

For detailed directions see our Walking Guide no. 57, Teignmouth to Exmouth.

This Section primarily comprises two fairly large seaside towns, flanked by a coastline of high red cliffs at one end and marshes and a sand bar at the other. Running through it, often next to the Coast Path, is possibly the most scenic part of Brunel's GWR railway line, the embankment of which forms the sea wall for much of this length. This is a busy, largely urban and much used Section of historic importance to the tourist trade. Please note, temporary diversions will apply as and when sections of the sea wall are closed to allow Network Rail to carry out planned works.

Directions

A regular bus service links Teignmouth and Starcross, the ferry point for Exmouth, and also passes through Dawlish and Dawlish Warren. There are also stations on the railway line at these places so bus or train-walks are options here.

From the ferry point at Teignmouth, or from the town centre, go to the car park at The Point, jutting out into the Teign Estuary, and begin by walking along the promenade. Leaving the town the Coast Path continues between railway and sea below the red cliffs to the end, where it descends steps to pass under the railway and then up Smugglers Lane to the A379 road at the top.

High water route, Teignmouth-Smugglers Lane

With a high sea and an onshore wind the far end of the promenade can become very wet, and at exceptionally high tides the steps at Smugglers Lane may become impassable. In these cases, immediately after leaving the town, fork left and cross the railway on a footbridge on Eastcliff Walk. Follow this lane around the outside of Eastcliff Park and then along a lane to Cliff Walk, eventually reaching the A379, which is then followed ahead to meet the official Path at the top of Smugglers Lane.

Coast Path, Smugglers Lane-Dawlish Warren

Use the footway on the inland side of the A379, and walk for about 150 yards/135 metres before turning right into Windward Lane, going immediately left on a path which skirts fields before returning to the A379. Bear right into Old Teignmouth Road, which in turn returns to the A379, then very soon, turn right into a park through some railings and follow the Path around its edge, which then zigzags down to the shoreline. Follow the sea wall through Dawlish, past the station – all facilities are found beyond the railway here. The Coast Path then continues on the sea wall between railway and sea, again below the red cliffs, to Dawlish Warren. Just before the amusement area at Dawlish Warren, cross the obvious railway footbridge to a car park, turn right and follow to the main road. Part of the Path from Dawlish Station along the sea wall may be re-routed in the short term as Network Rail carry out construction work for the railway line. The alternative route is signposted.

High water route, Dawlish-Dawlish Warren

Occasionally, at the highest tides, it becomes impossible to proceed along the sea wall for a short stretch just beyond the station. In this case, from the sea wall, cross the footbridge immediately after the end of station platform and follow the Path up to the A379.

Turn right and continue alongside the road until the Path reaches a path on the right between properties. Follow this Path, passing though a small park and up steps to a Path locally known as Lady's Mile. This Path follows the line of coast above the sea wall. Continue to follow this Path until you reach the main road in Dawlish Warren to pick up the Coast Path here.

Coast Path, Dawlish Warren-Starcross

The Coast Path does not go around the large sand spit at Dawlish Warren itself, jutting out into the mouth of the River Exe, or the marshes behind it, but if there is time this can be an exhilarating experience. Otherwise continue along Warren Road on the pavement, then opposite the entrance to Dawlish Warren Sandy Park join the cycleway and footpath to Cockwood Harbour. After following the road around the harbour join the A379. Cross the road and follow the footpath and cycleway to Starcross, and the ferry point to Exmouth. Starcross has all facilities.

For ferry details see page 29. If there is no ferry operating on arrival at Starcross, there are several options to reach Exmouth.

Option 1: Exeplorer Water Taxi – this runs daily from April until October. Check their website before travelling as times vary: **www.watertaxi.squarespace.com**.

Option 2: Bus or train from Starcross to Exeter, bus or train from Exeter to Exmouth.

Option 3: Walk from Starcross to Turf Lock following the waymarked Exe Estuary Trail on the riverside road and footpath (3 miles/5 kilometres), then ferry Turf Lock-Topsham and bus or train from Topsham to Exmouth. For ferry details see page 29.

Option 4: Walk from Starcross to Topsham Lock following the waymarked Exe Estuary Trail on the riverside road and footpath and Exeter Canal towpath (4.5 miles/7 kilometres), then ferry Topsham Lock-Topsham and bus or train from Topsham to Exmouth. For ferry details see page 29.

Start Point. Photographer James Loveridge

If you enjoy staying, eating, drinking or doing an activity with a business along the Path, please let them know about our Way Maker scheme so we can share their brilliance!

The businesses listed here are our 'Way Makers'. They make the great South West Coast Path experience possible, and give back to the Trail. Please support them if you can. More info at www.southwestcoastpath.org.uk/waymaker

- **GR** Grid Reference
- **DP** Distance from the Path
- **N** Nearest Town/Village with facilities
- **3** Number of Rooms
- Dogs Welcome
- Evening Meal Available
- Wifi
- Parking
- Grocery Shop On Site
- Private Transport to the Path
- Laundry Facilities
- Caters to Specific Dietary Needs
- Early Breakfast Available
- Packed Lunch Offered
- **£** Budget

Bed & Breakfast and Hotels

NAME	OTHER INFO
Whitemoor Farm B&B Holbeton, Plymouth, PL8 1JJ 07903366403 vicjoywhitemoor@gmail.com	GR: SX607494 DP: 1.5 miles N: PLYMOUTH OFFERS ONE NIGHT STAYS
Edgcumbe Guesthouse 50 Pier Street, West Hoe, Plymouth, PL1 3BT 01752 660675 enquiries@edgcumbeguesthouse.co.uk www.edgcumbeguesthouse.co.uk	GR: SX473537 DP: 0 miles N: PLYMOUTH OFFERS ONE NIGHT STAYS
Mariners Guest House 11 Pier Street, West Hoe, Plymouth, PL1 3BS 01752 261778 marinersguesthouse@blueyonder.co.uk www.marinersguesthouse.co.uk	GR: SX472538 DP: 0.02 miles N: PLYMOUTH OFFERS ONE NIGHT STAYS
First Fruits, Bigbury on Sea Avon Court, Bigbury on Sea, TQ7 4AR +441548811179 bexwells2002@yahoo.com www.airbnb.com/h/firstfruitsbigbury	GR: SX660446 DP: 0 miles N: BIGBURY ON SEA OFFERS ONE NIGHT STAYS
Wembury Bay B&B 2 Warren Close, Wembury, PL9 0AF 01752 863392 pwgreenwood59@gmail.com wemburybaybedandbreakfast.yolasite.com	GR: SX523488 DP: 0.1 miles N: WEMBURY OFFERS ONE NIGHT STAYS
Waverley B&B Waverley, Devon Road, Salcombe, TQ8 8HL 01548 842633 pauline@waverleybandb.co.uk www.waverleybandb.co.uk	GR: SX738388 DP: 0.1 miles N: SALCOMBE OFFERS ONE NIGHT STAYS
Rocarno B&B Rocarno, Grenville Road, Salcombe, TQ8 8BJ 01548 842732 rocarno@aol.com www.rocarno.co.uk	GR: SX736388 DP: 0.25 miles N: SALCOMBE OFFERS ONE NIGHT STAYS

NAME	OTHER INFO		
Brightham House Boutique B&B Higher Town, Kingsbridge, TQ7 3RN 🕿 01548 560111 ✉ hello@brighthamhouse.co.uk 🌐 www.brighthamhouse.co.uk	GR: SX708398 DP: 1 mile N: **SALCOMBE** OFFERS ONE NIGHT STAYS [8] 🐕 📶 🚗 🍴 ☕		
Shute Farm South Milton, Kingsbridge, TQ7 3JL 🕿 01548 560680 ✉ shutefarmdevon@gmail.com 🌐 www.shutefarm.co.uk	GR: SX699432 DP: 1.25 miles N: **SALCOMBE** OFFERS ONE NIGHT STAYS [3] 📶 🚗 🥾 🍴 ☕		
The Cricket Inn Beesands, Kingsbridge, TQ7 2EN 🕿 01548 580215 ✉ enquiries@thecricketinn.com 🌐 www.thecricketinn.com	GR: SX819403 DP: 0 miles N: **BEESANDS** OFFERS ONE NIGHT STAYS [7] 🍴 📶 🚗		
Eight Bells B&B South Embankment, Dartmouth, TQ6 9BB 🕿 07813 803472 ✉ lizheyler20@gmail.com 🌐 www.dartmouthbandb.com	GR: SX878511 DP: 0.15 miles N: **DARTMOUTH** OFFERS ONE NIGHT STAYS [2] 📶 🍴 ☕ 🍴		
Brixham House 130 New Road, Brixham, TQ5 8DA 🕿 01803 853954 ✉ stay@brixhamhouse.co.uk 🌐 www.brixhamhouse.co.uk	GR: SX916555 DP: 0.5 miles N: **BRIXHAM** OFFERS ONE NIGHT STAYS [6] 🐕 📶 🚗		
The Clifton at Paignton 9-10 Kernou Road, Paignton, TQ4 6BA 🕿 01803 556545 ✉ enquiries@thecliftonatpaignton.co.uk 🌐 www.cliftonhotelpaignton.co.uk	GR: SX891607 DP: 0.01 miles N: **PAIGNTON** [12] 🍴 📶 🍴 ☕ 🍴		
Earlston House Hotel 31 St Andrews Rd, Paignton, TQ4 6HA 🕿 01803 558355 ✉ stay@earlstonhouse.co.uk 🌐 www.earlstonhouse.co.uk	GR: SX890601 DP: 0 miles N: **PAIGNTON** [9]		
The Millbrook B&B Old Mill Road, Torquay, TQ2 6AP 🕿 01803 297394 ✉ stay@themillbrook.co.uk 🌐 www.themillbrook.co.uk	GR: SX904642 DP: 0.5 miles N: **TORQUAY** [8] 📶 🚗		
Garway Lodge Guest House 79 Avenue Road, Torquay, TQ2 5LL 🕿 01803 293126 ✉ info@garwaylodge.co.uk 🌐 www.garwaylodge.co.uk	GR: SX904645 DP: 1.5 miles N: **TORQUAY** OFFERS ONE NIGHT STAYS [6] 🐕 📶 🚗 🍴 ☕		

NAME	OTHER INFO		
The 25 Boutique B&B	GR: SX905642	DP:	0 miles
25 Avenue Road, Torquay, TQ2 5LB	N: **TORQUAY**		
01803 297517			
stay@the25.uk			
www.the25.uk	5 📶 🚗 ☕ ☕		
The Cleveland Bed and Breakfast	GR: SX906644	DP:	1 miles
7 Cleveland Road, Torquay, TQ2 5BD	N: **TORQUAY**		
01803 297522	OFFERS ONE NIGHT STAYS		
info@clevelandbandbtorquay.co.uk			
www.clevelandbandbtorquay.co.uk	6 📶 🚗		
Haytor Hotel	GR: SX922 633	DP:	0 miles
Meadfoot Road, Torquay, TQ1 2JP	N: **TORQUAY**		
01803 294708	OFFERS ONE NIGHT STAYS		
enquiries@haytorhotel.com			
www.haytorhotel.com	📶 🚗 🖥 ☕ ☕		
Coastguard Cottage	GR: SX927653	DP:	0.3 miles
84 Babbacombe Downs, Babbacombe, Torquay, TQ1 3LU	N: **BABBACOMBE**		
01803 311634	OFFERS ONE NIGHT STAYS		
sheila.besidethesea@gmail.com			
www.babbacombebandb.co.uk	3 📶 ☕ ☕		
The Cary Arms Hotel & Spa	GR: 930 653	DP:	0 miles
Babbacombe Beach, Torquay, TQ1 3LX	N: **BABBACOMBE**		
01803 327110	OFFERS ONE NIGHT STAYS		
dany@caryarms.co.uk			
www.caryarms.co.uk	10 🐕 🍴 📶 🚗		
The Laurels	GR: SX650456	DP:	0.4 miles
Ringmore, Kingsbridge, TQ7 4HR	N: **RINGMORE**		
01548 811104	OFFERS ONE NIGHT STAYS		
eamonn.byrnes@gmail.com			
bit.ly/swcp-thelaurels	1 🐕 📶 🚗 ☕		
Farthings B&B	GR: SX924722	DP:	1.1 miles
102 Ringmore Road, Shaldon, Teignmouth, TQ14 0ET	N: **SHALDON**		
01626 872860	OFFERS ONE NIGHT STAYS		
farthings_bb@btinternet.com			
www.farthings-shaldon.co.uk	3 📶 ☕ ☕		
The Thornhill	GR: SX944730	DP:	0 miles
Mere Lane, Seafront, Teignmouth, TQ14 8TA	N: **TEIGNMOUTH**		
01626 773460	OFFERS ONE NIGHT STAYS		
stay@thethornhill.co.uk			
www.thethornhill.co.uk	10 🐕 📶 ☕		
Brunswick House	GR: SX940727	DP:	0.3 miles
5 Brunswick Street, Teignmouth, TQ14 8AE	N: **TEIGNMOUTH**		
01626 774102	OFFERS ONE NIGHT STAYS		
hello@brunswickhouseteignmouth.co.uk			
www.brunswickhouseteignmouth.co.uk	4 📶 ☕ ☕		

NAME	OTHER INFO	
The Blenheim 1 Marine Parade, Dawlish, EX7 9DJ 📞 01626 862372 ✉ blenheimholidays@btconnect.com 🌐 www.theblenheim.uk.net	**GR:** SX962765 **DP:** 0 miles **N: DAWLISH** OFFERS ONE NIGHT STAYS 🔢II 🐕 📶	

Self Catering and Hostels

NAME	OTHER INFO	
Carswell Cottages Holbeton, Plymouth, PL8 1HH 📞 01752 830020 ✉ enquiries@carswellcottages.com 🌐 www.carswellcottages.com	**GR:** SX589477 **DP:** 0.3 miles **N: NOSS MAYO** 6 🐕 📶 🚗	
Anchor Cottage 7 Malthouse, Bridgend, Noss Mayo, PL8 1DX 📞 07969415551 ✉ hello@holidaycottagesnossmayo.co.uk 🌐 holidaycottagesnossmayo.co.uk	**GR:** SX554 479 **DP:** 0.4 miles **N: NOSS MAYO** 4 🐕 📶 🚗 📷	
Compass Quay Coastal Holidays 3 North Upton Barns, Bantham, TQ7 3AB 📞 01548 560910 ✉ nicky@cqch.co.uk 🌐 www.compassquaycoastalholidays.com	**GR:** **DP:** **N: BANTHAM**	
Bolberry Farm Cottages Malborough, Kingsbridge, TQ7 3DZ 📞 07718 187469 ✉ info@bolberryfarmcottages.co.uk 🌐 www.bolberryfarmcottages.co.uk	**GR:** SX689673 **DP:** 0 miles **N: HOPE COVE** 7 🐕 📶 🚗	
Ocean Reach Holiday Homes Bolberry Down, Salcombe, TQ7 3DY 📞 07718 187469 ✉ info@oceanreachholidays.co.uk 🌐 www.oceanreachholidays.co.uk	**GR:** SX688385 **DP:** 0 miles **N: HOPE COVE** 4 🐕 🍴 📶 🚗 📷	
Guest Suite in Salcombe 9 Kingsale Road, Salcombe, TQ8 8AS 📞 07790056460 ✉ katiebessant@hotmail.com 🌐 bit.ly/swcp-salcombeguestsuite	**GR:** SX735387 **DP:** 0 miles **N: SALCOMBE** OFFERS ONE NIGHT STAYS 1 📶	
Kittiwake Cottage East Prawle, TQ7 2BY 📞 07980310696 ✉ admin@kittiwakecottage.com 🌐 www.kittiwakecottage.com	**GR:** SX781364 **DP:** 0.5 miles **N: EAST PRAWLE** 2 🐕 📶 🚗 🛒	
The Old Forge Bickerton Farm, Bickerton, Kingsbridge, TQ7 2EU 📞 01548 511804 / 07522360138 ✉ elizabethhigginson@hotmail.com 🌐 abnb.me/z06ld5RPhrb	**GR:** SX812389 **DP:** 0 miles **N: HALLSANDS** OFFERS ONE NIGHT STAYS 1 🐕 📶 🚗 📷	

NAME	OTHER INFO		
Dittisham Hideaway Dittisham, Dartmouth, TQ6 0JB © 01803 925034 ✉ reservations@dittishamhideaway.co.uk ⊕ www.dittishamhideaway.co.uk	GR: SX849537	DP:	2 miles
	N: DARTMOUTH		
	15 🐕 🛜 🚗 🔄 🍴		
Rose Court Holiday Apartments York Road, Torquay, TQ1 3SG © 01803 327203 ✉ holidays@rosecourttorquay.co.uk ⊕ www.rosecourttorquay.co.uk	GR: SX923655	DP:	0.6 miles
	N: BABBACOMBE		
	8 🐕 🛜 🚗 🔄		
Deckchair And Dreams 11 The Green, Shaldon, TQ14 0DW © 07734056272 ✉ deckchairanddreams@gmail.com ⊕ www.deckchairanddreams.co.uk	GR: SX933723	DP:	0 miles
	N: SHALDON		
	3 🐕 🛜		
Jubilee Cottage 21 King St, Dawlish, EX7 9LG © 07854022594 ✉ scottshomes2020@gmail.com ⊕ jubileecottage.promotemyplace.com	GR: SX958767	DP:	0 miles
	N: DAWLISH		
	2 🐕 🛜 🚗		

Campsites and Holiday Parks

NAME	OTHER INFO		
Drakes View The White House, Staddon Lane, Plymouth, PL9 9SP © 07831 225440 ✉ enquiries@pitchup.com ⊕ www.pitchup.com/campsites/England/South_West/ Devon/Plymouth/drakes-view	GR: SX495517	DP:	0.25 miles
	N: PLYMOUTH		
	OFFERS ONE NIGHT STAYS		
	🐕 £		
Mount Folly Farm Bigbury on Sea, TQ7 4AR © 01548 810267 ✉ info@bigburyholidays.co.uk ⊕ www.bigburyholidays.co.uk	GR: SX660446	DP:	0.1 miles
	N: BIGBURY ON SEA		
	OFFERS ONE NIGHT STAYS		
	🐕 🚗 £		
East Prawle Farm Holidays Higher House Farm, East Prawle, Kingsbridge, TQ7 2BU © 01548 511422 ✉ eastprawlecamping@btinternet.com ⊕ www.eastprawlefarmholidays.co.uk	GR: SX779358	DP:	0 miles
	N: EAST PRAWLE		
	OFFERS ONE NIGHT STAYS		
	🐕 🚗 £		
Quarry Lake Camping Quarry Lake, Dartmouth, TQ6 0LS © 07969791127 ✉ enquiries@pitchup.com ⊕ www.pitchup.com/campsites/England/South_West/ Devon/Dartmouth/quarry-lake-camping	GR: SX836505	DP:	1.5 miles
	N: DARTMOUTH		
	OFFERS ONE NIGHT STAYS		
	£		
South Bay Holiday Park St Mary's Road, Brixham, TQ5 9QW © 01803 853004 ✉ southbay-gm@jfhols.co.uk ⊕ www.johnfowlerholidays.com/devon-holiday-park/ south-bay-holiday-park	GR: SX926548	DP:	0.5 miles
	N: BRIXHAM		
	OFFERS ONE NIGHT STAYS		
	333 🐕 🍴 🛜 🚗 🛒		

NAME	OTHER INFO		
Holidayhomes4rent	**GR:** SX926548	**DP:**	0.5 miles
South Bay Holiday Park, Brixham, TQ5 9QW	**N: BRIXHAM**		
02920 670134/07875043020			
info@holidayhomes4rent.co.uk			
www.holidayhomes4rent.co.uk	15 📶 🚗 🛒		
Longmeadow Farm Campsite & Self Catering Accommodation	**GR:** SX922721	**DP:**	1 mile
Coombe Road, Ringmore, Shaldon, TQ14 0EX	**N: SHALDON**		
07800795532	OFFERS ONE NIGHT STAYS		
anne@longmeadowfarm.co.uk			
www.longmeadowfarm.co.uk	🐕 📶 🚗		
The Hen's Dens at Orchard Organic Farm	**GR:** SX921692	**DP:**	0 miles
Gabwell Hill, Stokeinteignhead, TQ12 4QP	**N: SHALDON**		
07805 894522	OFFERS ONE NIGHT STAYS		
jerry@orchardorganicfarm.co.uk			
www.orchardorganicfarm.co.uk/camping	🐕 🚗 📷 £		

Eat and Drink

NAME	OTHER INFO		
The Ship	**GR:** SX482541	**DP:**	0 miles
The Barbican, Plymouth, PL1 2JZ	**N: PLYMOUTH**		
01752 667604			
theship@staustellbrewery.co.uk			
theshipplymouth.co.uk	🐕 📶		
Salcombe Dairy Shop & Café, Salcombe	**GR:** SX738392	**DP:**	0.5 miles
Shadycombe Road, Salcombe, TQ8 8DX	**N: SALCOMBE**		
01548 843228			
jack.wibberley@salcombedairy.co.uk			
www.salcombedairy.co.uk	🐕 📷		
The Pigs Nose Inn	**GR:** SX781363	**DP:**	0.3 miles
East Prawle, Kingsbridge, TQ7 2BY	**N: EAST PRAWLE**		
01548 511209			
contact@pigsnoseinn.co.uk			
www.pigsnoseinn.co.uk	🐕 🍴 📶 🛏 📷 📷 👟		
Salcombe Dairy Shop & Café, Dartmouth	**GR:** SX878513	**DP:**	0.5 miles
Taylors Restaurant, 8 The Quay, Dartmouth, TQ6 9PS	**N: DARTMOUTH**		
01548 843228			
hayley.rutherford@salcombedairy.co.uk			
www.salcombedairy.co.uk	🐕 📶 📷		
The Guardhouse Café	**GR:** SX943564	**DP:**	0 miles
Berry Head Nature Reserve, Brixham, TQ5 9AW	**N: BRIXHAM**		
01803 855778			
info@guardhousecafe.com			
www.guardhousecafe.com	🐕 📶 📷 👟		
Old Market House	**GR:** SX925563	**DP:**	0 miles
The Quay, Brixham, TQ5 8AW	**N: BRIXHAM**		
01803 856891			
oldmarkethouse@staustellbrewery.co.uk			
oldmarkethousebrixham.co.uk	🐕 📶		

NAME	OTHER INFO		
Cafe Rio SUP & Kayak Hire	GR: SX927684	DP:	0 miles
Maidencombe Beach, Maidencombe, TQ1 4TS	N: **MAIDENCOMBE**		
01803 317737			
linzi.conday@me.com			
www.caferio-maidencombe.co.uk	🐕 🍽 🍵 🍎		
Salty Dog Kiosk	GR: SX957747	DP:	0 miles
Smugglers Lane, Holcombe, EX7 0JL	N: **TEIGNMOUTH**		
07850 243 292			
tq14@icloud.com			
saltydogkiosks.business.site	🐕 🚗		
Le Cygnerie	GR: SX961767	DP:	0 miles
12 The Strand, Dawlish, EX79PS	N: **DAWLISH**		
07534 144745			
lecygnerie12@hotmail.com			
www.facebook.com/lecygnedawlish	🐕		

Information

NAME	OTHER INFO	
Discover Dartmouth at the Flavel Cafe	GR: SX877514	DP:
Flavel Place, Dartmouth, TQ6 9ND	N: **KINGSBRIDGE**	
01803 839530		
discoverdartmouth.com		

Activities

NAME	OTHER INFO		
South West SUP	GR: SX462535	DP:	0 miles
Firestone Arch, Royal William Yard, Plymouth, PL1 3RP	N: **PLYMOUTH**		
07898 984497			
info@southwestsup.co.uk			
www.southwestsup.co.uk			
The Rockpool Project (Plymouth)	GR: SX463539	DP:	0 miles
50 Admiralty Street, Plymouth, PL1 3RY	N: **PLYMOUTH**		
07813 469350 info@therockpoolproject.co.uk			
www.therockpoolproject.co.uk			
Mount Batten Watersports and Activities Centre	GR: SX487532	DP:	0 miles
70 Lawrence Road, Plymouth, PL9 9SJ	N: **PLYMOUTH**		
01752 404567			
enquiries@mount-batten-centre.com			
www.mount-batten-centre.com	26 📶 🚗 🍽 🍎		
Patricia Rose Charters Ltd	GR: SX485533	DP:	0 miles
Mountbatten Ferry Landing Stage, 90 Lawrence Road, Plymouth, PL9 9SJ	N: **PLYMOUTH**		
07967 002445 mail@patriciarosecharters.com			
www.patriciarosecharters.com	🚗		
Shoalstone Seawater Pool	GR: SX935567	DP:	0 miles
Berry Head Road, Brixham, TQ5 9FT	N: **BRIXHAM**		
01803 302024 info@shoalstonepool.com			
www.shoalstonepool.com	🐕 🍴 🚗 🍽		

Jurassic Coast Exmouth to South Haven Point – 115 miles

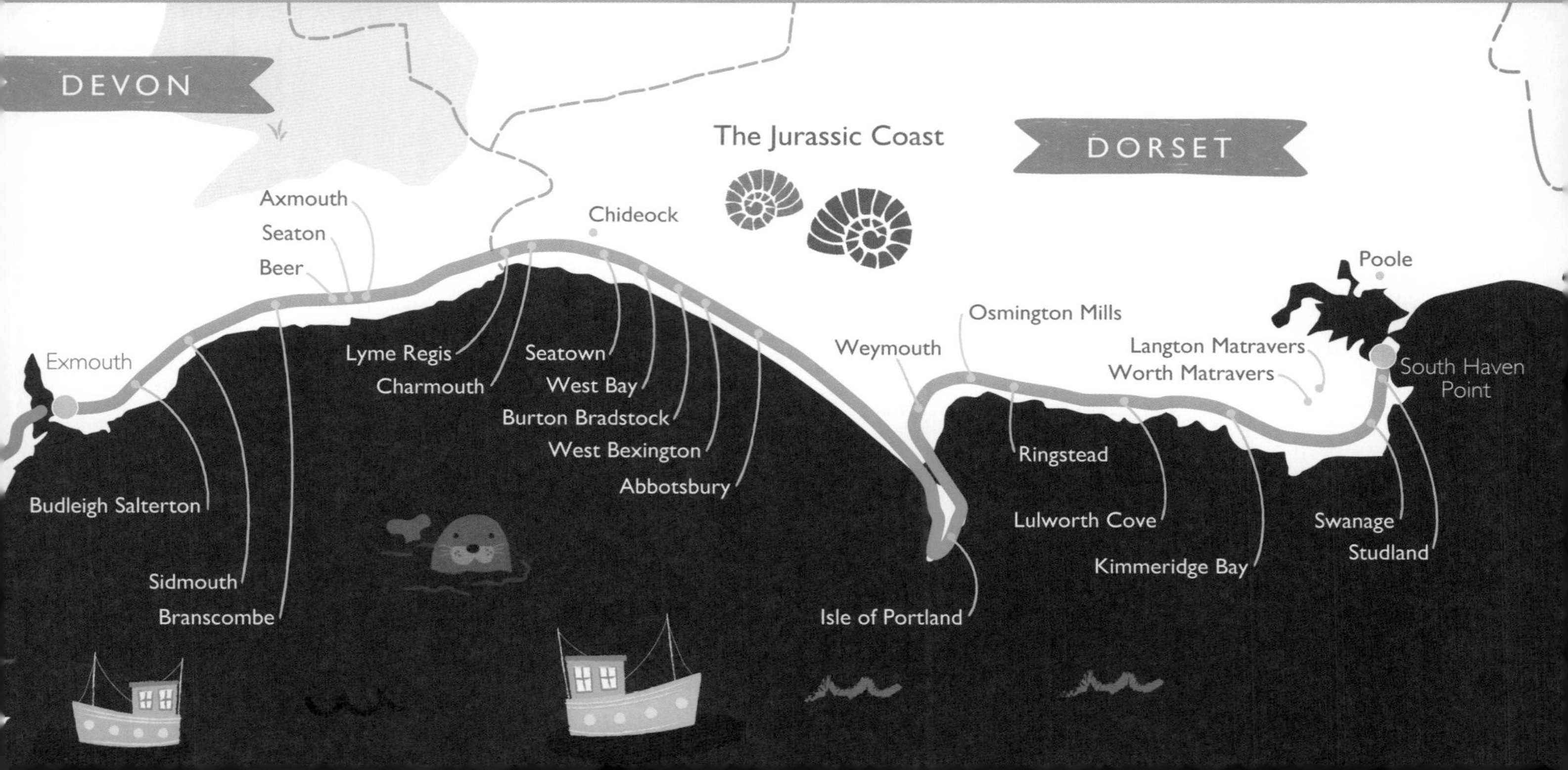

The Jurassic Coast

DEVON

DORSET

Exmouth
Budleigh Salterton
Sidmouth
Branscombe
Beer
Seaton
Axmouth
Lyme Regis
Charmouth
Seatown
West Bay
Burton Bradstock
West Bexington
Abbotsbury
Chideock

Weymouth
Osmington Mills
Ringstead
Lulworth Cove
Kimmeridge Bay
Langton Matravers
Worth Matravers
Swanage
Studland
Isle of Portland

Poole
South Haven Point

200m
150m
100m
50m
0m

Geology is both the curse and the boon of this part of the South West Coast Path. As a curse, the geology means the cliffs are vulnerable to slippage, especially in the Sidmouth area, in the Undercliffs and in West Dorset. This has meant that several diversions, necessary but hardly ideal, have had to be put in place for the Coast Path. However, as a boon, the Jurassic Coast's exposed and accessible layers of geological history have made it a textbook example for a wide range of coastal features. These features are also landscape highlights – the classic red cliffs of East Devon; the undisturbed nature reserve of the Axmouth to Lyme Regis Undercliffs; the great shingle bar of Chesil Beach backed by the semi-freshwater lagoon of the Fleet; the fortress-like monolith of the Isle of Portland, jutting into the English Channel; the familiar arch of Durdle Door; the erosion of soft rock once the harder limestone has been broken through forming hollowed-out bays, as at Lulworth Cove; the offshore Purbeck stone stacks at Handfast Point. In addition, the Jurassic Coast contains a number of classic holiday towns; Exmouth, Sidmouth, Lyme Regis, Weymouth and Swanage. This length also contains some taxing gradients for walkers including the climb to the highest point on the south coast of England, Golden Cap, as well as the challenge of the military firing ranges east of Lulworth Cove with its frequent closures.

All of the locations on the map illustration to the left, have at least 1 facility including toilets, a cafe/restaurant, shop or pub.

West Bay. Photographer Daryl David

OS Maps: Landranger 192; Explorer 115

	This Walk	Cumulative	This Walk	Cumulative	Grading	Timing
Ascent	722ft	97,489ft	220m	29,715m	Moderate	3 hours
Distance	5.4mi	519.9mi	8.7km	836.7km		

For detailed directions see our Walking Guide no. 58, Exmouth to Budleigh Salterton.

This is a well-used and popular Section, never far from houses and passing a large caravan site and golf course on the way. Most of this length is on relatively low cliffs, and in the west these give excellent views over the mouth of the Exe and the great sandy bar of Dawlish Warren. Further east, the high point of West Down Beacon gives exceptionally fine panoramic views, while beyond the Beacon the Path becomes more enclosed. It is an easy-going Section of some variety, ideal for those not wishing to explore remote or strenuous lengths.

Directions

A regular bus service links Exmouth and Budleigh Salterton, making this a good bus-walk option. In addition, a summer service links Exmouth with Sandy Bay, approximately mid-way along the section, giving another, shorter bus-walk.

Exmouth has all the usual facilities and a railway station connecting to Exeter. The Coast Path follows the promenade from the redeveloped docks area at the mouth of the Exe, which is also the ferry landing point. Continue to the cliffs at Orcombe Point, then climb the steps and continue on the cliff top, passing the Jurassic Coast marker and on to the caravan site at Sandy Bay. Follow the fence line inland of the Straight Point rifle range, then climb to the high point at West Down Beacon. The Path then descends, seaward of the golf course, though offering relatively few sea views on this stretch. Approaching Budleigh Salterton, a charming and traditional small town, the Path turns inland then almost immediately, at a junction, goes right to descend to the end of the promenade. The shops, pubs and other facilities are immediately inland of the Path, which continues towards the distinctive line of pine trees to the east of the town.

Burton Bradstock. Photographer James Loveridge

OS Maps: Landranger 192; Explorer 115

	This Walk	Cumulative	This Walk	Cumulative	Grading	Timing
Ascent	1,037ft	98,526ft	316m	30,031m	Moderate then strenuous	3.5 hours
Distance	7.1mi	527.0mi	11.4km	848.1km		

For detailed directions see our Walking Guide no. 59, Budleigh Salterton to Sidmouth.

Most of this pleasant Section is on relatively low red cliffs, with attractive views inland over an undulating pastoral countryside as well as seaward. However, there are contrasts at both ends. The western end skirts the narrow, marsh-fringed estuary of the River Otter, while the eastern end includes a wooded cliff top and high cliffs on the appropriately named High Peak and Peak Hill. This is a pleasant and pleasingly quiet Section.

Directions

A regular bus service links Budleigh Salterton and Sidmouth, making a bus-walk a possible.

Budleigh Salterton, a town with something of an attractive feel of yesteryear, has all the usual facilities. The Coast Path goes along the promenade to the car park at the eastern end. Progress east seems tantalisingly close, but the River Otter, with no bridge at its mouth, bars the way. The Path passes through a gate at the rear riverside corner of the car park and follows the riverside Path, passing through the wetland creation project by the Environment Agency, until it meets a road. Turn right and cross the River Otter on the road bridge, then bear right to follow the Path back downriver to the sea.

The Path is clear to the caravan site at Ladram Bay, where there are toilets and seasonal refreshments. Here, descend across a field to the beach access track, going left then immediately right, past a pub and on to climb into woodland at High Peak. Here, the Path goes behind the very top, emerging onto a track. Turn right and follow the Path that emerges onto open land at Peak Hill then turn right again and climb up Peak Hill. Follow the Path down the cliff through woodland to a road, turn right then keep right along an old road, then onto a large grassy area down to a zigzag Path next to the white Jacob's Ladder steps. At the bottom, follow the seafront Path to reach the main esplanade. Sidmouth is an elegant Regency town and has all facilities.

Budleigh Salterton. Photographer Mike Kukuczka

OS Maps: Landranger 192; Explorer 115 (most); Explorer 116 (eastern end)

	This Walk	Cumulative	This Walk	Cumulative	Grading	Timing
Ascent	2,408ft	100,934ft	734m	30,765m	Severe then strenuous	5.5 hours
Distance	10.3mi	537.3mi	16.6km	864.7km		

For detailed directions see our Walking Guide no. 60, Sidmouth to Branscombe and Branscombe to Seaton.

This is a Section of lofty cliffs cut by deep and narrow valleys, making for a magnificent coastal landscape but a testing one to walk. In the west the cliffs are characteristically red, but this changes quite abruptly along the length as the Section reaches the most westerly chalk cliffs in England, appropriately bright white. Add an elegant Regency town, a charming picture-postcard village, a quaint fishing town and a Victorian town and the result is a length of great attraction.

Directions

A regular bus service links Sidmouth with Seaton, making a bus-walk possible. There are also regular, if less frequent, bus links to Branscombe and Beer along the length giving further options.

The Coast Path passes along the elegant esplanade at Sidmouth to the footbridge over the mouth of the River Sid at the eastern end. Some dramatic cliff falls have occurred just east of Sidmouth and a well-signed diversion is necessary past housing until, at the top of Laskeys Lane, it turns back to the cliff top. A steep climb up Salcombe Hill is soon followed by an equally steep descent and climb through the Salcombe Regis valley. The Path skirts behind the hollow of Lincombe, then descends to the beach at Weston Mouth. A short way along the beach, the Path leaves to climb steeply back to the cliffs and a good level stretch, which eventually turns inland to meet a track. This descends to Branscombe Mouth, where there are refreshments and toilets. Beyond Branscombe the official Path passes among some holiday chalets, then along an undercliff Path, with imposing cliffs rising above, before climbing to the cliff top at Beer Head. These are the most westerly chalk cliffs in England. An alternative route from Branscombe Mouth climbs up the valley side and proceeds directly along the cliff top to Beer Head.

Follow the signed Path from Beer Head, past a caravan site and into the village behind the beach. Beer, an attractive fishing village, has all the usual facilities. Climb the Path on the east side of the beach to the cliff top, descending to a road and down to Seaton Hole, where there are refreshments. Only if the tide is low, walk along the beach to the end of the promenade at Seaton. If not, an inland diversion must now be taken. A cliff fall caused by the extreme wet weather in 2012 necessitated permanent closure of the previous Coast Path route. At Seaton Hole turn left on to Old Beer Road and walk approximately 220 yards/200 metres inland towards Beer. Turn right on a Path through woodland to arrive at the B3172 Beer Road and turn right here. After approximately 875 yards/800 metres, leave Beer Road and take the Path on the right through the Chine, where there are refreshments, and on to the promenade and into Seaton, which has all facilities, including bus services to Exeter and Lyme Regis.

OS Maps: Landranger 193; Explorer 116

	This Walk	Cumulative	This Walk	Cumulative	Grading	Timing
Ascent	1,401ft	102,335ft	427m	31,192m	Moderate then strenuous	3.5 hours
Distance	7.1mi	544.4mi	11.4km	876.1km		

For detailed directions see our Walking Guide no. 61, Seaton to Lyme Regis.

Changes have occurred to part of this length following landslides. After crossing a golf course then cliff land, the route now climbs to a superb viewpoint known as Goat Island, part of the old cliff top which was subject to a massive cliff fall in 1839. From here the Path descends into the Axmouth-Lyme Regis Undercliff. This length, a National Nature Reserve, has been undisturbed since that cliff fall and is effectively a wilderness area of virtually virgin woodland and dense scrub, often with an almost eerie character. For most of this part the sea will not be visible. It is an odd and impressive experience, delighting some, but frustrating others.

Directions

Leave Seaton at the east end, using the old concrete bridge to cross the River Axe. Follow the road for a short while and then turn right up the steep golf course access road, past the club house then across the fairway to the end of a lane. Follow this for a short while, then turn right off the lane onto a path across farmland, eventually reaching the cliffs. Leaving the farmland, the Path then rises to the open vantage point of Goat Island, with its magnificent views. Keep to the top of grassy area, then follow the Path as it descends through woodland to enter the strange world of the Undercliff. This old landslip is a National Nature Reserve, being an area of wildlife wilderness. The Path through the Undercliff rarely offers sea views and can feel almost claustrophobic in places. There are no escape routes inland nor safe paths to the sea shore. However, the route is well waymarked and the maps on the Natural England display boards show walkers their exact location; no one should ever feel lost and many find it an exhilarating experience.

Eventually the Path emerges on cliffs, and is then waymarked down through woods to arrive adjacent to Lyme Regis's scenic harbour, the Cobb. Lyme Regis is a charming and attractive town and has all the usual facilities.

Lyme Regis. Photographer James Loveridge

OS Maps: Landranger 193; Explorer 116

	This Walk	Cumulative	This Walk	Cumulative	Grading	Timing
Ascent	3,097ft	105,432ft	944m	32,136m	Moderate then strenuous	5.5 hours
Distance	10.0mi	554.4mi	16.1km	892.2km		

For detailed directions see our Walking Guide no. 62, Lyme Regis to West Bay.

A major feature of this Section is the large number of cliff slippages caused by a combination of wet weather and geology. This means that the route between Lyme Regis and Charmouth (approximately 3 miles/4.5km) relies on a footpath diversion. However, the remainder of this Section is a superb coastal experience, climbing as it does over the top of Golden Cap, the highest point on the entire south coast of England, with views to match, as well as a challenging steep climb!

Directions

A regular bus service between Lyme Regis, Charmouth, Chideock (which is about 0.75 mile/1.25km inland of Seatown) and West Bay makes a variety of bus walks possible.

Lyme Regis to Charmouth

Between Lyme Regis and Charmouth major diversions have had to be put in place, to avoid the cliff falls that have occurred. Improvements to this part of the route have been made. For up-to-date details on diversions and route changes, check the Association's website **southwestcoastpath.org.uk**.

Lyme Regis is a charming and attractive town with all facilities. From the Cobb harbour proceed along the esplanade to the small car park at Cobb Gate and the Millennium Clock Tower: the town centre is on your left. Continue along the sea wall, passing seaward of the Millennium Theatre for approximately 550 yards/500 metres, turn up the large flight of steps on the left that lead to Charmouth Road car park. Cross the car park to the main road (A3052), then turn right uphill past the Football Club beyond. Opposite the cemetery, go through a pedestrian gate to follow the Path across fields to a lane on the edge of the woodland. Turn left and after 100 yards/90 metres turn right at a sign before the wooden gate, climbing through woods to emerge onto the road at Timber Hill.

On the route from the woodland on Timber Hill to the outskirts of Charmouth there are several public footpaths shown on the Ordnance Survey map seaward of the current Coast Path. These cross The Spittles, Black Ven and the edge of the golf course, but are all impassable and closed due to active landslips, which had made this a hazardous area.

Since the major cliff falls of 2001, this part of the walk has been shown as a 'diversion' in the expectation that the Path could be reinstated along the cliff top. However, the ongoing instability of the cliffs has meant that this has not been possible, and so the Path has been routed inland and across the golf course. In 2022 a route was established with the permission of the golf course which allows walkers to follow a stone surfaced waymarked route avoiding the main A3052 road.

Once you have re-joined the road, turn right and follow the road uphill for 600 yards/550 metres past the entrance to the Golf Club, until you reach a fingerpost pointing the route across the golf course. Follow the Path and white stones marking the route of the Trail across the golf course to the woods on the far side. This is an active Golf Course area and so please be mindful of golf course users and golf balls.

The new route of the Coast Path turns right at the fingerpost around 20 metres into the woods and follows a stone surfaced path through the woods and along the edge of the golf course.

At the end of the woods continue along the Path, which now has a tall fence on the right-hand side. Continue along the path following the edge of the golf course and then following the hedge-line. When the path reaches a viewpoint on the cliff top, turn left at the fingerpost and follow the path downhill onto the Old Lyme Hill Track, which then joins into Old Lyme Hill Road.

Go left along Old Lyme Hill road which then meets Old Lyme Road. Turn right down The Street and then right into higher Sea Lane and continue ahead, ignoring various signs pointing off the lane, continuing round the bend to the west in the lane that rises for some 130 yards/120 metres to an oak signpost on the left. Here leave the lane through a metal gate to re-join the Coast Path, descending over grassy slopes to Charmouth Beach, with its toilets and refreshments.

Beach route, Lyme Regis to Charmouth

It is possible to walk along the beach between Lyme Regis and Charmouth, but this is not recommended. Mudslides midway along mean that the route is very narrow and only passable at low tide. As such *it should only be attempted after checking tide tables and on a falling tide.* Many people are cut off or get stuck trying to cross one of the innocuous looking mud flows and have to be rescued.

Coast Path, Charmouth East to Seatown (Chideock)

Refreshments are available near the seafront car park. From the Jurassic Coast Heritage Centre on the seafront at Charmouth (well worth a visit), head for a footbridge across the River Char. After crossing the footbridge, follow the Path up the grassy slope to Stonebarrow Hill. After a couple of moderate hills, and passing the remains of St Gabriel's church and its old village, the route starts the long, steep climb to Golden Cap, the highest point on England's south coast, but the climb is rewarding as the views from the top are spectacular. At the top, go slightly left to the trig point which then leads to the long and steep descent. Approaching Seatown, the Coast Path detours slightly inland before it emerges at Seatown, which has toilets and a pub. A shop and other facilities are at Chideock, 0.75 mile/1.25 kilometres inland.

From Seatown, the Coast Path climbs the cliff slope on its way to the high point of Thorncombe Beacon. There is a descent to the little beach at Eype, then a further climb and descent to the harbour at West Bay, which has most facilities.

East of Golden Cap. Photographer Terry Dean

OS Maps: Landranger 193 (western half); Explorer 116 (western half)
Landranger 194 (eastern half); Explorer OL15 (eastern half)

	This Walk	Cumulative	This Walk	Cumulative	Grading	Timing
Ascent	275ft	105,707ft	84m	32,220m	Strenuous then moderate	6 hours
Distance	9.3mi	563.7mi	15.0km	907.2km		

For detailed directions see our Walking Guide no. 63, West Bay to Abbotsbury.

From West Bay a sheer red sandstone cliff rises from the sea, looking almost artificial in its straight lines. Then the coastline takes on a low level profile and the Coast Path loses its ups and downs. It can still be hard work here though, as the shingle of at the far western end of Chesil Beach tests the legs.

Directions

A regular bus service links West Bay with Abbotsbury, and also calls at Burton Bradstock along the length of this Section, giving various bus-walk options. A popular circular walk based on Abbotsbury uses the Coast Path as well as the South Dorset Ridgeway.

At West Bay go round the back of the harbour, pass to the right of the church and ahead to the West Bay public house, opposite which is the Coast Path sign pointing to the surprisingly steep cliff. Arriving at Burton Freshwater, the Path runs between the caravan park and the beach and is well signed. There is a short inland diversion around the hotel leading to Burton Beach where there are refreshments and toilets. Further on, the Path passes inland of Burton Mere (which can flood in wet weather), before coming to West Bexington, where there are toilets and seasonal refreshments.

See Section 71 for details of the alternative Inland Coast Path (South Dorset Ridgeway) between West Bexington and Osmington Mills.

The Coast Path continues along the back of the beach, later passing another car park with toilets and seasonal refreshments, and some 200 yards/185 metres beyond this it turns inland to Abbotsbury. There are alternative routes either going into the village, or going south and east of Chapel Hill and missing the village. A permissive Path alternative leaves the Coast Path and leads directly to the famous Swannery. Abbotsbury is a beautiful stone-built village with much of historic interest and most facilities.

The Milky Way over West Bay cliffs. Photographer James Loveridge

OS Maps: Landranger 194; Explorer OL15

	This Walk	Cumulative	This Walk	Cumulative	Grading	Timing
Ascent	955ft	106,662ft	291m	32,511m	Easy. Chesil Beach route strenuous	4 hours official route
Distance	10.9mi	574.6mi	17.5km	924.7km		

For detailed directions see our Walking Guide no. 64, Abbotsbury to Weymouth.

Just after Abbotsbury there is a high, far-reaching view of the sea, the Fleet lagoon and Chesil Beach, followed by an inland, field route. The Fleet and Chesil Beach become visible again in the descent alongside Wyke Wood to Rodden Hive. From Rodden Hive to Ferry Bridge, Weymouth, the Path follows the edge of the Fleet with views of the unusual shingle bank of Chesil Beach.

Directions

For a bus/walk there is a bus between Abbotsbury and Weymouth.

From Abbotsbury follow signs to the Swannery down Grove Lane. Go past the car park to a sharp right-hand bend in the road, just past a barn, where Walk 64 starts at some steps and a stile. Follow the boundary wall on the left, over a stone stile and up a steep 40m climb aiming for marker posts on the hillside. Continue straight, go past Clayhanger Farm (75m away on the right) across fields to a gate, through a copse, over a stone stile, down some steps and the hill to a finger post and turn left. Cross fields, a footbridge, a narrow road and another field to a finger post and turn right towards Wyke Wood. At the wood turn left over a stile, skirt round the wood, going downhill to a gravel track. 20m or so along the track turn left at a finger post, cross some fields to the remains of a gate at a bridge over a stream. Cross the bridge, through a kissing gate and turn right along a field boundary. Continue through fields, over a stile and turn right to the Fleet at Rodden Hive. The Path then follows the edge of the Fleet passing Langton Hive, Herbury promontory, Gore Cove, Moonfleet Manor Hotel (refreshments available), the gallops of Sea Barn Farm stables, over a wooden bridge near East Fleet, to Chickerell Hive point and then to Chickerell Firing Range. If the red flag is flying, turn left and walk inland around the range. If there is no flag turn right. After the range these routes join. Next is Littlesea Holiday Park from where the Path climbs a little, levels out and drops to the Wyke Regis Training Area and Bridging Camp. Follow the fence around the camp to a road. Turn right, down the road to the bend and left into the field along a permissive Path to the Fleet. At the next cove descend steps, cross the sand (at low tide), and take the Path up the hill which is to the right of a five-bar metal gate. Continue walking alongside The Fleet and you will pass the Chesil Vista Holiday Park where you will note that a new walk way has been constructed. At Ferry Bridge Road (the causeway to Portland), bear slight right and cross over to continue the path via Weymouth or turn right for the Portland section.

Alternatively, it is possible to walk along Chesil Beach to Ferry Bridge, starting at the beach where Walk 63 turns inland to Abbotsbury. However please note; 1) it is extremely hard, slow walking and there is no way off before Ferry Bridge; 2) it is closed from 1 May to 31 August for the bird nesting season; and 3) it is necessary to check the Chickerell Range website to ensure firing is not scheduled; **www.gov.uk/government/publications/chickerell-firing-times** or telephone the Commandant on **01305 831930**.

OS Maps: Landranger 194; Explorer OL15

	This Walk	Cumulative	This Walk	Cumulative	Grading	Timing
Ascent	1,112ft	107,774ft	339m	32,850m	Moderate	7 hours
Distance	13.0mi	587.6mi	20.9km	945.6km		

For detailed directions see our Walking Guide no. 65, The Isle of Portland.

Portland is unique. An almost-island jutting out into the English Channel, joined to the mainland only by the end of Chesil Beach, it has an isolated air. Formed of limestone, it has been extensively quarried and these workings, some still operational, characterise much of the landscape. Elsewhere, former military buildings and those of Verne Prison and the Young Offenders' Institution are prominent. Portland has a rugged beauty and is well worth exploring with superb views and a rich natural and historic heritage.

Directions

Bus routes run the length of Portland in the summer season (June-September), making a variety of bus-walks possible. There is also a regular bus from Weymouth to Portland throughout the year. This Section is, in any event, a circular walk. Check on local bus information.

Note that signage can be confusing as the circular route now brings together the Coast Path and the new English Coastal path. Signage and routings are currently being reviewed.

From Ferrybridge cross the causeway onto Portland; this is done by simply following the shared footway/cycleway alongside the A354 road or alternatively by crossing the bridge on the A354 to beyond the boatyard. Then walking along the raised bed of the old Easton to Weymouth railway on the eastern bank, to near the end of the causeway at the roundabout for the access road to Osprey Quay and here returning to the footway/cycleway. At the southern of the two roundabouts, at Victoria Square, take the main road south and shortly turn right into Pebble Lane, then left just before the disused public toilet block. Continue and bear right up onto the promenade at Chesil Cove. About half way along, at the floodgates, cut back sharp left then right, following Coast Path signs up a steep tarmac Path, past the new housing frontage and up the steep Path in the grass incline (known locally as 'Lankridge') to the stone steps up to the Path that was once the old road. Bear off right onto the signed Path running between quarry banks and the cliff face, leading to 3 miles/5 km of airy cliff-top walking to Portland Bill. Due to cliff movements above West Wears the path diverts into Tout (sculpture Park) and Bowers Quarries. Follow the signed diversions. When you have stepped back on to the West Cliffs' old quarrymen's tramway, proceed south towards Portland Bill. At Portland Bill there are refreshments, toilets, the famous Portland Bill Lighthouse and bus stops.

Continue around the end of the low headland then start northwards, seaward of the wooden chalets, to follow a winding path along the top of low cliffs to join a road above Freshwater Bay after about 1.5 miles/2.5 kilometres. Turn right on the road (use the footway on the west side of the road) for 600 yards/550 metres, past Cheyne Weares car park to a signpost on the right. Follow the zigzag path into the undercliff area and follow the waymarking through disused quarry workings to Church Ope Cove.

Ascend the stepped and signed Path up to Rufus Castle viewing area. Here, the South West Coast Path also becomes the England Coast Path.

After Rufus Castle, the Coast Path soon joins the track bed of the former Weymouth to Easton railway line. This is then followed northwards for some 1,585 yards/1,450 metres to a pair of signposts. Here, turn left to follow a rocky path that climbs up the cliffs to what appears to be an isolated chimney seen on the skyline above (a Victorian Sewerage Vent). At the top, turn sharp right along the prison road northwards and through a gap in a high wall. On the right is the Old Engine Shed. From GR 703.723 with remnants of old diversions and signage following the current trail can be difficult. On reaching a narrow road there are two walking options, the official route is signed across the road and takes a route across open ground, passing disused quarries to reach the perimeter fence of the Verne prison. Alternatively, at the road turn right and just over the brow of a hill turn left on an access track to compounds. Continue ahead on a grassy path towards a large pinnacle of rock (Nichodemus Knob), after which, at the "rock falls" sign, bear left steeply up onto the higher escarpment, heading for a large communications mast. At the high wire perimeter fence, turn left and follow it along then round to the right, to reach the south entrance to the Verne Prison.

Take a path through a little gap to the left of the entrance, passing beside railings and down steep steps. Bear left to join the Path below, which traverses under the grassy banks.

The Path drops downhill towards houses to a waymark post. Ignore the left fork and continue on the right-hand path, which then passes through an underpass below a road. Descend steeply towards Castletown down the Merchant's Incline (a former quarry tramway), crossing two footpaths and a road. Pass under a footbridge and through another underpass to reach an access road, and turn left to a roundabout.

Continue ahead for some 30 yards/27 metres and then cross to turn right down Liberty Road, signposted to Portland Castle. Go past the castle entrance to the car park and turn right towards the harbour, heading for five black posts. Here join the footway/cycleway to follow the harbour-side to the Sailing Academy, the venue of the sailing events at the 2012 Olympics. Continue on the footway/cycleway to reach the roundabout on the A354 road. From here, follow the former railway trackbed to the boatyard before the bridge over the mouth of the Fleet, and follow the footway alongside the road to Ferry Bridge.

Portland Bill. Photographer Colin Foster

OS Maps: Landranger 194; Explorer OL15

	This Walk	Cumulative	This Walk	Cumulative	Grading	Timing
Ascent	2,385ft	110,159ft	727m	33,577m	Easy to moderate to strenuous	6.25 hours
Distance	14.4mi	602.0mi	23.2km	968.8km		

For detailed directions see our Walking Guide no. 66, Weymouth to Lulworth Cove.

**The signposting throughout this section generally only refers to "Coast Path".
The western part of this Section is a well-trodden walk through the seaside town
of Weymouth with its working harbour, sandy beach and attractive Georgian sea
front. East of the town is a length of relatively low cliffs, but then at White Nothe,
two thirds of the way along the section, the coastal geology changes. East of here
is a rollercoaster of often sheer white cliffs, the length punctuated by the iconic
landmarks of Durdle Door and Lulworth Cove. Both ends of this Section are busy,
but in the centre is an often quiet and remote length.**

Directions

*A bus service from Weymouth to Osmington and Lulworth Cove (and on to Wool) enables access
to the Coast Path mid-way along the Section, allowing some bus-walk options.*

From Ferrybridge the Coast Path follows the foot/cycle Path on the route of the old
Weymouth to Portland railway (the Rodwell Trail), and passes inland of the sailing
centre. Shortly afterwards, follow the Coast Path signs and bear off right and then
left to walk up the road (Old Castle Road), passing Sandsfoot Gardens and café on
your right. Turn right into Belle Vue Road. At the end of Belle Vue Road turn right
into Redcliff View, then turn left onto the signed Path across a grassed area, passing
to the left of the Portland Stone monument erected in memory of Thomas Fowell
Buxton (1786-1845), Abolitionist & Social Reformer. Follow the Path to the right
of the housing estate, cross the pedestrian bridge over Newtons Road at Newtons
Cove, and follow the Path to and through Nothe Gardens towards Nothe Fort.
(Alternatively, for a route closer to the sea, turn right down the steps just beyond
the seasonal ice cream kiosk and follow the lower Path, Jubilee Walk.)

Before reaching the fort, take the signed Path left past the public conveniences. Cross
the fort access road to the footpath and follow the signed Path left, until you reach
steps on your right heading down to Weymouth harbourside. Turn left at the foot
of the steps. There is a seasonal ferry (rowing boat) which crosses the harbour by
Weymouth Sailing Club. If you don't take the ferry, walk along the harbour and cross
the Town Bridge (a lifting bridge which opens at set times of the day to give access
to Weymouth Marina). Take the steps at the end of the bridge down to the other side
of the harbour to walk towards the Pavilion Theatre. Before reaching the Pavilion,
turn off left to follow the Esplanade along Weymouth's sea front to reach Overcombe.
Here you leave the beach behind. Walk up the minor road towards Bowleaze Cove.
After passing the Spyglass Inn, the route bears right to cross the crest of the grassed
public open space to reach the Beachside Centre at Bowleaze Cove. Follow the signed
Path through the Beachside Leisure Centre. The Path passes to the right of the
Riviera Hotel and then on to Redcliff Point. The Path skirts around an education and
adventure centre at Osmington and then goes on to Osmington Mills.

See Section 71 for details of the alternative Coast Path (South Dorset Ridgeway) between West Bexington and Osmington Mills. At Osmington Mills turn right and walk down the road to the Smugglers Inn. The Path goes through the pub garden, across a bridge in front of the pub and then round to the back of the pub, where the Path crosses a field and passes through an area of scrub and then along the cliffs towards Ringstead. After walking through a wooded area, you reach Ringstead.

At Ringstead follow the track in front of some houses, then bear left on the tarmac road. Turn right just before the car park and café and toilets (both seasonal). Follow the Path towards White Nothe. Shortly after the church (St Catherine's By the Sea) at Holworth the official Path goes straight on, forming two sides of a triangle. (The former Path bears off to the right and is still useable, but it can become muddy in wet weather.) At the top of a short incline turn right to continue to follow the Coast Path, signed White Nothe.

Turn left through a kissing gate into a field. Follow the Path and bear right through scrub and up a series of steps. Continue on to White Nothe where you pass in front of the former coastguard cottages. From here follow the Path along the cliffs towards Durdle Door. The route is straightforward to follow but does involve some particularly severe gradients.

Just below the car park and caravan park at Durdle Door, turn right at the bridle gate and follow the Path to Lulworth Cove, descending a stone pitched Path into the car park. Lulworth Cove has toilets and refreshments, and most facilities are found here or at West Lulworth, a little way inland. At this point there are two options to following the coastal path mainly depending on tidal conditions with both options described in guide 67. To complete this section follow the option to the Cove.

Walk to the left of the Visitor Centre and then right to walk round the back of the Visitor Centre. At a junction of roads take the Path leading to Stair Hole, with its spectacular upturned rock formations, and then on to the Commemorative Stone marking the inauguration of the Jurassic Coast as a World Heritage Site. Walk down a series of steps, turning left at the Boat Shed Café, to the shore of the Cove itself.

Lulworth Cove to Durdle Door. Photographer Catherine Lawson

OS Maps: Landranger 194 (most); Landranger 195 (eastern end); Explorer OL15

	This Walk	Cumulative	This Walk	Cumulative	Grading	Timing
Ascent	2,002ft	112,161ft	610m	34,187m	Severe	4 hours
Distance	7.1mi	609.1mi	11.4km	980.2km		

For detailed directions see our Walking Guide no. 67, Lulworth to Kimmeridge.

This is part of the Jurassic Coast, a UNESCO World Heritage site, and is of great geological importance, largely formed by lines of relatively hard limestone having been breached at intervals to form coves and bays as the sea erodes the softer rocks behind. The result is a dramatic coastline of white cliffs and darker coloured coves, some prominent headlands, and a succession of extremely steep slopes to walk. Although there is some military hardware on the Ranges the landscape has been largely unchanged by farming for some eighty years. Although relatively short, this Section is severe because of several long, steep climbs.

Directions

For train-bus-walk options: A year-round bus service connects Bridport-Weymouth-Lulworth Cove-Wool-Wareham-Poole and a summer service connects Weymouth-Lulworth Cove-Swanage and Wool-Durdle Door-Lulworth Cove. There is no public transport on the Section apart from Lulworth Cove.

There are 4 large car parks giving access to the Section; Lulworth Cove, Tyneham, Whiteways on the hill above Tyneham for level access to Flowers Barrow, and Kimmeridge.

IMPORTANT: This Section passes through the Lulworth Army Firing Ranges so before deciding to walk check that the Ranges, including Tyneham Village, are open. As a rule-of-thumb the Ranges are closed on weekdays and open at weekends, open at Easter, Christmas, Bank Holidays and during August, but see the exceptions and exact times below. As opening times can change at the last minute, call **01929 404714** or visit **www.gov.uk/government/publications/lulworth-access-times** for the latest information.

LULWORTH RANGE WALKS AND TYNEHAM VILLAGE ACCESS TIMES 2023

The Lulworth Range walks and Tyneham Village are open every weekend excluding:
· 18 to 19 February 2023
· 11 to 12 March 2023
· 17 to 18 June 2023
· 23 to 24 September 2023
· 7 to 8 October 2023
· 18 to 19 November 2023

In addition, they are open on these days:
· Christmas: 17 December 2022 to 22 January 2023
· Easter: 1 to 16 April 2023
· Bank Holiday: 29 April to 1 May 2023
· Spring: 27 May to 4 Jun 2023
· Summer: 27 July to 3 September 2023
· Christmas: 16 Dec 2023 to 1 Jan 2024

During opening times:

The exhibitions in Tyneham School and Tyneham Church are open from 10am until 4pm. The vehicle gate into Tyneham Village and car park is opened at 9am and closed at dusk. The gates to the walks are opened as near as possible to 9am on the Saturday morning (or on the day of opening) and remain open until 8am on the Monday morning.

If the Ranges are closed, two inland diversions are suggested below; you are strongly advised to use OS 1:25,000 Explorer Map OL15 (Purbeck and South Dorset) as they are not signed as Coast Path.

Coast Path – Lulworth Cove to Kimmeridge Bay

There are two options for the first part of the walk from Lulworth Cove to the Army Ranges gate.

The easy option, at most states of the tide, is to walk from the Visitor Centre and car park down the road, or via Stair Hole to the Cove. Go around the Cove on the pebble beach and up the stone steps at the east end of the Cove. At the top of the steps turn right and follow the coast path.

The other option, longer and harder, is rewarded with high, panoramic views of the Cove; follow the road up to West Lulworth for about 500 yds/460m. 55yds/50m before the road forks left to Durdle Door turn right into Bindon Road, walk for 70 yds/65m and turn right through a metal gate. Bear left here and climb steps to another metal gate, then turn right to the hedge and follow it left in a long curve, along the cliff edge with views of Lulworth Cove on the right. Follow this path until it meets the firing range fence by a kissing gate, turn right and descend 330 steps to meet the path that comes up from the steps from the beach.

Go left here (right if coming up from the beach), immediately past a milestone, after 50m turn right at another milestone, go over a wooden bridge and a boardwalk and follow the path up to Pepler's Point. Turn left and follow the Coast Path to the gate to the Ranges; the Fossil Forest is just beyond the gate.

The route is now straightforward – just follow the yellow topped posts through the Ranges to the exit gate and then to Kimmeridge Bay where there is a car park (paid), toilets and seasonal refreshments, or all year refreshments in the village 0.6 mi/1km to the north. The Etches Museum in Kimmeridge is dedicated to fossils and is worth visiting **www.theetchescollection.org**.

If Ranges are Closed – Alternative Option 1 (13.5mi/22.0km)

This route is safer and quieter but more strenuous than Option 2; it uses mainly rights of way plus some permissive paths. An OS Map is needed as this route is not signed or waymarked as an alternative to the Coast Path. Leave Lulworth Cove for West Lulworth and follow the B3070, past the fork to Durdle Door, taking the next road on the left just after a bus shelter. In 100yds/90m turn right on to a footpath that heads uphill for 0.75mi/1.2km. At the second junction of paths turn right (east) and after 100yds/90m turn left (north) to pass Belhuish Coppice and Belhuish Farm. On reaching the B3070 at GR835 832, cross the road and take the track opposite. Ignore the first path junction to the north-east and continue downhill to the eastern boundary of Burngate Wood (GR 845 828). Turn north-east on a permissive path (blue) past Park Lodge and go across the road at GR 855 832 onto a bridleway. Continue along the bridleway for just over 2mi/3.4km to GR 866 856, to join a minor road from Highwood veering north and later north-east to meet an east-west road at

GR 871 861. Walk east along the road then fork right (signposted Stoborough) at GR 883 856. Go over the crossroads (seat) with the B3070 at GR 886 855 (*Route Option 2 joins this route here) and walk east for a further 1.5mi/2.5km along Holme Lane to GR 909 854 (about 330 yds/300m before railway underbridge), and turn southwards onto diverted Doreys Farm bridleway (see Option 1A below), which is followed for 1.25mi/2.1km before turning right onto Creech Road. Turn right and in 0.9mi/1.5km after Creech Grange, the road climbs steeply for 0.6 mi/1.0km to the Steeple Viewpoint car park. Just before the car park turn left at GR 905 817 on a bridleway that falls steeply southwards to re-join the same road. As the road levels out, at a left-hand bend at GR 907 812, take the bridleway/access road ahead that leads south through Steeple Leaze Farm. About 200 yds/185m south of the farm, take the narrow footpath that heads up steeply south through woods to a bridleway on the ridge. Turn left through a gate and look for a narrow path on the right raking steeply downhill and then across three fields towards the coast ahead and Kimmeridge Bay, where the Coast Path is joined at a T-junction.

Option 1A (to avoid 0.6 mi/1.0km of road walking)

On Doreys Farm bridleway (see above), after emerging from Bridewell Plantation (GR 914 839), (where a fine house comes into view through trees on the left), go through the first field gate on the right onto the east side of Grange Heath. Initially the route is indistinct and the ground can be wet during and after rain. However, head south-west across the heath and in some 160yds/146m a good gravel path winds its way across Grange Heath. Although this is described as a permissive path on some maps, legal access is as shown, as this area is designated as Access Land. Follow the path south-west across the heath to join a bridleway that runs south-east, passing a farm to join Creech Road by a telephone box. Turn right on the road and in 0.3mi/0.5km pass Creech Grange, and then follow the details set out in the final paragraph of Option 1 above.

If Ranges are Closed – Alternative Option 2 (12 miles/19km)

This option is mainly road walking, and care is needed on narrow bends. Leave the Cove to West Lulworth on the B3070, then turn right to East Lulworth and beyond, keeping to the B3070 for some 3mi/5km to GR 886 855. Here turn right along Holme Lane to GR 911 854. From here, follow the route described from (*) in Option 1 above.

Old Harry Rocks. Photographer Waveslider Photography

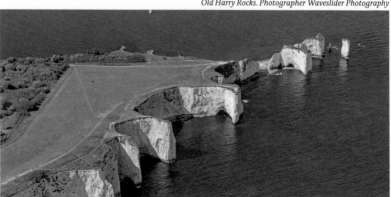

OS Maps: Landranger 195; Explorer OL15

	This Walk	Cumulative	This Walk	Cumulative	Grading	Timing
Ascent	1,597ft	113,758ft	487m	34,674m	Moderate then Strenuous	3.25 hours
Distance	7.1mi	616.2mi	11.4km	991.7km		

For detailed directions see our Walking Guide no. 68, Kimmeridge to Worth Matravers.

This Section mostly hugs the coast running along high cliff tops. Because of the Kimmeridge Clays that are a feature of this Section of the coast, in places the Path can be claggy and slippery after wet weather. There is a particularly steep cliff at Houns-Tout. Towards the eastern end, this length is dominated by St Aldhelm's Head, a flat-topped headland surmounted by an old chapel, which gives extensive views. This is a tough Section with a remote character.

Directions

Bus-walks are not easily undertaken on this Section. Circular walks using the Coast Path, based on inland villages such as Kimmeridge or Kingston, are possible.

The Coast Path from Kimmeridge Bay eastwards is straightforward, although care may be needed where small lengths have slipped, cracked or may be close to the cliff edge. Just beyond Kimmeridge, the Clavell Tower has been relocated 27 yards/25 metres inland and an improved Coast Path installed. There is a very steep climb up to Houns-Tout, followed by a steep descent of 167 steps. The Path then turns inland to avoid dangerous terrain at Chapman's Pool. Look out for a unique stone block sign pointing the way to Hill Bottom at the bottom of the descent. Beyond the hamlet of Hill Bottom the Path turns sharp right and climbs steeply out of the valley. You may wish to pause and reflect at the Royal Marines Memorial, before tackling a descent and climb of two more long flights of steps before reaching St Aldhelm's Head. There are excellent coastal views here to both east and west. The Path then descends to old quarries at Winspit. (For those aiming to end at Worth Matravers, which is about a mile/1.6 kilometres inland, take the track to the left at the valley bottom at Winspit. The village has a pub with simple meal options and café.)

Durdle Door. Photographer Callum White

OS Maps: Landranger 195; Explorer OL15

	This Walk	Cumulative	This Walk	Cumulative	Grading	Timing
Ascent	657ft	114,415ft	200m	34,874m	Strenuous then Moderate	3.25 hours
Distance	6.5mi	622.7mi	10.5km	1,002.1km		

For detailed directions see our Walking Guide no. 69, Worth Matravers to Swanage.

The western part of this Section is dominated by St Aldhelm's Head, a flat-topped headland of limestone surmounted by an old chapel. There are extensive views, along the coast to both east and west. Leaving the valley at Winspit, the cliffs become increasingly marked by the remains of old small-scale quarrying activity. The route then passes through the Country Park at Durlston Head before rounding the headland to enter Swanage.

Directions

Numerous footpaths cross the cliffs to the Coast Path from the outskirts of Swanage and the inland village of Langton Matravers. The Poole-Swanage Breezer no.40 bus runs throughout the year, and this assists in enabling bus-walks which combine these link paths with the Coast Path.

(For those starting in Worth Matravers village, walk past the cottages in London Row, then follow the Path over a field to the track which leads down the valley to Winspit Quarry on the Coast Path.)

From Winspit there is a fine high level walk to Durlston Head. Signing in Durlston Country Park is limited; keep on the low level Path all the way round Durlston Head, then coming up on the north side, take the second turning right (the first is a cul-de-sac to a quarry). Durlston Castle has now been converted to a Jurassic Coast Gateway Centre and includes refreshment facilities.

After leaving Durlston Castle, follow a broad stony Path north through the woods for some 760 yards/700 metres to a junction in the Path. Follow the Path straight ahead over the bridge (this section includes a number of steep steps and slopes) before joining Bell View Road at the top of some steps and through an iron gate. Alternatively, for a flatter route, before the bridge follow the Path to the left for some 125 yards/115 metres to reach Durlston Road at a new ornate wooden gate. Turn right and in 185 yards/170 metres turn right again into Belle Vue Road. Follow the road north-eastwards to the grassed open space leading to Peveril Point. In bad weather or at high tides, use the roadway and then down to the footpath at the end of the coastal buildings, otherwise use the foreshore. Continue along Swanage's sea front promenade. Swanage has all facilities.

OS Maps: Landranger 195; Explorer OL15

	This Walk	Cumulative	This Walk	Cumulative	Grading	Timing
Ascent	492ft	114,907ft	150m	35,024m	Moderate	3.5 hours
Distance	7.5mi	630.2mi	12.1km	1,014.2km		

For detailed directions see our Walking Guide no. 70, Swanage to South Haven Point.

This is an excellent and scenic Section. The southern, Swanage end comprises of increasingly high cliffs, culminating in the length between Ballard Point and Handfast Point, with its offshore stacks. This is an exhilarating length, with superb views over Poole Bay to Bournemouth and across the Solent to the matching cliffs of the Needles on the Isle of Wight. The northern end passes along a long sandy beach before arriving at the mouth of Poole Harbour, an enormous enclosed water area and the second largest natural harbour in the world.

Directions

A bus service links Swanage with South Haven Point, making a bus-walk a good option. There are also popular local circuits using the Coast Path in the Swanage-Ballard Down-Studland area. If needed, check that the Sandbanks to Studland ferry is running as there is a lengthy alternative route for onward journeys to and from Poole and Bournemouth. See page 29 for ferry information.

Swanage has all facilities. The Coast Path passes along the town's sea front, following the main road (Ulwell Road) at the north end by the telephone box, where it bears left and on ahead into Redcliff Road at a one-way system. At a shop and post-box turn sharp right into Ballard Way – do not be put off by "Private Estate" signs. Continue forward into the chalet estate and follow signs for the Coast Path, to emerge on a grassed area on the cliff edge. Turn left and follow the Path to reach the footbridge and steps that come up from the beach. Except at very high tides or in severe weather, it is possible to follow a beach route rather then the Ulwell Road to get to the footbridge. From the sea front continue on past the Bull & Boat restaurant, along the sand (or raised walkway) and past some beach huts. You have to scramble over some groynes until you reach some steps that go up from the beach to meet the footbridge on your left. Don't cross the footbridge, but go right and up some steps.

The Path climbs out to Ballard Down, then the obvious high-level route continues out to Handfast Point and the much-photographed rocks of Old Harry, before turning west towards Studland. The Path from Old Harry is flat with good views across Studland Bay. After about ¾ mile, there is a finger post pointing right to 'Alternative Coast Path South Beach'. If tidal conditions permit and this route is taken when you reach South Beach, go north along the beach to reach a track just in front of the café, which then leads back to the road. At the road turn right to reach the Bankes Arms.

Following the official Coast Path, continue on to reach the road and toilets on your right. Turn right and follow the road up past the Bankes Arms. Just opposite the NT car park entrance (on the left) is a path on your right (next to a house), that heads towards the coast. At the coast go left and walk around the grounds of 'The Pig on the Beach' to reach Fort Henry, where WW2 leaders watched preparations for D Day. Around Fort Henry the Path leads to the car park at Middle Beach. Turning right takes you towards the beach and the slope onto Middle Beach.

The last section is on the sand and is best done when the tide is low or going out so that you walk on firm sand. Walk down the slope, and onto Middle Beach (seasonal cafe and toilets). Walk along Middle Beach, over the concrete slipway and onto Knoll Beach (at high tide there is an alternative behind the toilets and beach huts). Soon after Knoll Beach is the naturist length of Studland Beach. Finally walk round the point and into Shell Bay and South Haven Point and the ferry.

If you wish to avoid the naturist section, there is a path through the Studland Nature Reserve (called the Heather Walk) from Knoll Beach to Shell Bay. However, you may still encounter naturists who use the dunes above the beach.

The ferry operates all year daily every 20 minutes, from Shell Bay (South Haven Point) to Sandbanks. If you intend to use the ferry at this time, check the Association's website or the ferry company's website. For ferry details see page 29.

Postscript

For those who have been with us all the way from Minehead, be it in one go or in bits and pieces over a period, a final few words seem appropriate. Alfred Wainwright, at the end of his work on the Pennine Way, said; "You have completed a mission and satisfied an ambition. You have walked the Pennine Way, as you have dreamed of doing. This will be a very satisfying moment in your life. You will be tired and hungry and travel stained. But you will feel great, just great." Just substitute the South West Coast Path for the Pennine Way and Wainwright's words will doubtless ring true. You will be glad and proud that you have walked and finished Britain's longest and finest footpath. As Wainwright said of the Pennine Way, it's a longer step than most take in their lifetime!

OS Maps: Landranger 194; Explorer OL15

	This Walk	This Walk	Grading	Timing
Ascent	2,290ft	698m	Moderate	8 hours
Distance	17.1mi	27.5km		

For detailed directions see our Walking Guide no. 71 South Dorset Ridgeway West Bexington to Osmington Mills .

This is a very scenic walk, parallel to the coast and a varying distance inland. For most of its length, quite extensive coastal views are obtained beyond a green and rural foreground. Substantial lengths follow chalk ridges and these give impressive views north as well. Coastal features such as Portland and Chesil Beach are clearly seen, as are the flanks of the enormous Iron Age Maiden Castle inland. This is a quiet route, often feeling quite remote, and with usually no refreshments on its length it requires preparation. It is, nevertheless, a superb experience.

Directions

First bus services link both ends, Swyre (for West Bexington) and Osmington, (for Osmington Mills) with Weymouth, making a bus-walk possible, especially using Weymouth as a base.

The Dorset element of the Coast Path is unique in having an official alternative route for part of its length. This was referred to by name of the "Inland Coast Path". It is, however, now known as the South Dorset Ridgeway (SDR) and the signposting uses that name almost throughout. The waymarking has also been replaced and incorporates the name of the South Dorset Ridgeway. The length of the Section makes it an ideal long day's walk. However, be aware that other than one seasonal mobile refreshment van if the timing is right, no facilities are found anywhere along the route other than at the two ends, so it is necessary to be well prepared. A detailed route description is given below.

Leave West Bexington car park by the milestone marked "South Dorset Ridgeway Osmington Mills 17" and turn inland up the road. Where the road bears left continue forward up the stony track, signposted SDR. Recent weather conditions have resulted in some deep, uneven ridges in this track.

Near the top of the track take the right-hand fork signed "5¾ Hardy Monument". Before reaching the layby on the B3157 road, there is a bench from which there is a panoramic view of the coast. At the layby, go over the stile to the left of the field gate and follow the Path to reach the Limekiln. At the Limekiln bear left following the signed Path. After passing through a pedestrian gate go straight ahead (rather than bearing off to the left and up to the signpost just visible in the distance). This takes you past a footpath off to the right signed "East Bexington & Beach 1", should you wish to make a detour. If not, follow the signed SDR to reach a National Trust sign for Tulk's Hill, adjacent to a kissing gate and field gate alongside the B3157. This time cross the road and go over the stile, signposted "Hardy Monument 4 1/2". Follow the Path and a series of steps through the Abbotsbury Castle prehistoric hill fort, passing the trig point with superb views in all directions, including Hardy Monument in the distance. At the end of the hill fort, go through a kissing gate and follow the Path down to and across a minor road. Go through a metal pedestrian gate to follow the Path in an easterly direction along the ridge of Wears Hill and the crest of White Hill, following the signed Path. Be careful not to follow any signs indicating routes down to the village of Abbotsbury in the valley below and its adjacent hilltop chapel.

At the east end of White Hill, bear north-east as signed and leave the field in the north-east corner through a gate on to a minor road. Continue north-east along this road for some 50 yards/46 metres and then turn right as signposted. Follow the narrow and rough bridleway along the wire fence above the scrub to a path junction; where the bridleway bears right take the yellow waymarked footpath to the left through the gate. At the end of this short section take a headland Path north-east. At the far side of the field, the track then leads approximately 50 yards/46 metres to a further gate and waymark. Immediately adjacent to the next field gate is a prehistoric stone circle, a scheduled ancient monument. Continue forward on the track, leaving a small wood to the left, to reach the road between Portesham and Winterbourne Steepleton. Go across the road into a field, signed "Hardy Monument 1". Continue eastwards across a field and along the side of other fields. At a small wooded area before Black Down Barn (ruin) turn north at a signpost to Hardy Monument. Climb through the woods to the monument. In the 'summer' season it may be possible to find a mobile refreshment van here.

To continue, find a roadside signpost 30 yards/32 metres east of the car park entrance. Cross the road and descend eastward on a narrow path. Reaching the same road again and the track opposite turn left along the road, then in another 30 yards/32 metres turn right as signposted. Jubilee Trail discs are now evident. Now there is a good ridgeway path for some 3 miles/4.8 kilometres, with excellent views seaward. Note at Shorn Hill (ref.GR 633..866) traffic lights in place for road / heavy plant crossing. At a point some 550 yards/500 metres after passing under the second set of HV power lines, take the gate north of a large tumulus to stay on the north side of the fence running along the ridge. On reaching the B3159 road, marked by the Borough of Weymouth boundary stone, continue across as signposted and towards the A354 road. Cross the bridge over the A354 and follow the signed Path alongside the A354, until it bears off to the left towards Bincombe Down.

Continue eastwards, then before the farm, with its adjacent radio mast, take care to go through the gate on the right, marked with a blue arrow. After crossing the field, leaving two tumuli on the left, reach a metalled road and turn right. At the junction at the corner of Came Wood turn right at the SDR signpost. At the end of the Path join a metalled lane and at the road junction turn left, signposted "South Dorset Ridgeway". Drop down the road into the village of Bincombe and where the road turns right, take the track forward leaving the small church on the right. Where the Path splits take the left-hand fork, marked with a blue arrow and acorn. After the overhead HV power lines, pass through a small signposted wooden gate and then proceed forward through one field, into the next to a footpath sign. Here turn left, and there is a choice of routes around Green Hill.

For the best option, at a waymark post turn sharp right down a steep grassy slope to a stile at a road ahead. Cross the road to go over another stile, to follow a grassy path that contours around the south and east sides of Green Hill. On reaching a road at a gate and stile turn left, and in 50 yards/46 metres turn right through a gate signposted "Osmington 2¾". The Path is now easy to follow with extensive views to seaward over Weymouth and Portland. On passing a ruined building on the left the route reaches a broad track; here turn right, signposted "Osmington", and after about 200 yards/185 metres go through a gate as signposted. Shortly afterwards pass a trig point on the right, and at the next field gate bear left and follow the field boundary along White Horse Hill. Just beyond the next gate fork right, signposted "For Osmington".

Descend to Osmington and follow the signs through the village. On reaching the main road (A354 to Weymouth) near the Sly Fox Inn (now closed), turn left and in about 250 yards/230 metres turn right at a signpost, over a footbridge and stile. Follow the field boundary on the left through two fields – at the top look back to see the Hardy Monument in the distance and the White Horse on the hillside. Go over the stile to the footpath sign, then turn half right to cross the field at an angle to a further stile. Cross it and turn left along the hedge side to the bottom. This is the official end of the SDR.

At the end of the field there is a very short length of enclosed Coast Path to the road; turn right along it descending to Osmington Mills for refreshments.

Rachel Hadley-Leonard
2022 completer and fundraiser

In 2022, Rachel walked the entire 630 miles, solo, in one through-hike, following the SWCP guide's 52 day itinerary. Rachel raised almost £5,000 for the SWCPA, the RNLI and the YHA.

"

The South West Coast Path, whether completed over 52 days or 52 years, gives you the opportunity to discover unrivalled landscapes. From the tiny villages nestled into coves, across the broad remote headlands to the larger coastal communities that punctuate the path, the ever-changing sea, the mesmerising rocks, the steep sided combes, the towering cliffs, the salty air and the wonderful communities who reside along the way, all make for one of the country's richest walking experiences. Every corner brings a gasp, and a new delight.

Parts of the path are tough, but in truth, the toughest days are often the best days, as they bring a profound sense of achievement alongside total respect and appreciation for the stunning views and scenery encountered along the way.

The South West Coast Path is so much more than a path, it's a personal journey. The mind and the body become free. Whether you walk 6 miles or 630 miles, once walked, the path will remain forever in your heart, and you will always want to return. Enjoy every step.

"

The businesses listed here are our 'Way Makers'. They make the great South West Coast Path experience possible, and give back to the Trail. Please support them if you can. More info at www.southwestcoastpath.org.uk/waymaker

> If you enjoy staying, eating, drinking or doing an activity with a business along the Path, please let them know about our Way Maker scheme so we can share their brilliance!

- **GR** Grid Reference
- **DP** Distance from the Path
- **N** Nearest Town/Village with facilities
- **[3]** Number of Rooms
- **Dogs Welcome**
- **Evening Meal Available**
- **Wifi**
- **Parking**
- **Grocery Shop On Site**
- **Private Transport to the Path**
- **Laundry Facilities**
- **Caters to Specific Dietary Needs**
- **Early Breakfast Available**
- **Packed Lunch Offered**
- **[£] Budget**

Bed & Breakfast and Hotels

NAME	OTHER INFO
Quentance Farm Bed & Breakfast and Self Catering Salterton Road, Exmouth, EX8 5BW ☏ 01395 442733 ✉ palleandrose@hotmail.com ⊕ www.quentancefarm.co.uk	**GR:** SY036820 **DP:** 1.75 miles **N: BUDLEIGH SALTERTON** OFFERS ONE NIGHT STAYS [3] 🐕 📶 🚗 🍽 ☕
The Lawns B&B 11b Westfield Road, Budleigh Salterton, EX9 6SS ☏ 07864392631 ✉ info@the-lawns.co.uk ⊕ www.the-lawns.co.uk	**GR:** SY062822 **DP:** 0.4 miles **N: BUDLEIGH SALTERTON** [3] 📶 🚗
Royal York & Faulkner Hotel The Esplanade, Sidmouth, EX10 8AZ ☏ 01395 513043 ✉ stay@royalyorkhotel.co.uk ⊕ www.royalyorkhotel.co.uk	**GR:** SY126872 **DP:** 0 miles **N: SIDMOUTH** OFFERS ONE NIGHT STAYS [72] 🐕 🍴 📶 🚗 🍽
Belmont House Dolphin Road, Beer, EX12 3EN ☏ 01297 24415 ✉ belmonthousebeer@gmail.com ⊕ www.belmonthousebedandbreakfast.com	**GR:** SY228892 **DP:** 0 miles **N: BEER** OFFERS ONE NIGHT STAYS [5] 📶 🚗
Westleigh Bed & Breakfast Fore street, Beer, Seaton, EX12 3EQ ☏ 01297 23247 ✉ info@westleighbeer.co.uk ⊕ westleighbeer.co.uk	**GR:** SY229892 **DP:** 0 miles **N: BEER** OFFERS ONE NIGHT STAYS [2] 🐕 🍴 📶
Dorset House Pound Road, Lyme Regis, DT7 3HX ☏ 01295442055 ✉ info@dorsethouselyme.com ⊕ www.dorsethouselyme.com	**GR:** SY337923 **DP:** 0 miles **N: LYME REGIS** OFFERS ONE NIGHT STAYS [5] 📶 🍽 ☕
Ammonite Cottage Bed & Breakfast 6 Silver Street, Lyme Regis, DT7 3HR ☏ 01297445955 ✉ maryelizabeth1951@btinternet.com ⊕ www.ammonite-cottage.co.uk	**GR:** SY339921 **DP:** 0 miles **N: LYME REGIS** OFFERS ONE NIGHT STAYS [1] 📶

NAME	OTHER INFO	
Lucerne View Road, Lyme Regis, DT7 3AA ☏ 01297 443752 ✉ stay@lucernelyme.co.uk ⊕ www.lucernelyme.co.uk	**GR:** SY339923 **DP:** 0.25 miles **N: LYME REGIS** OFFERS ONE NIGHT STAYS 4 ☂ 🚗 🌙 ☕	
The George Hotel George Street, Axminster, EX13 5DW ☏ 01297 33385 ✉ georgeaxminster@southcoastinns.co.uk ⊕ www.georgeaxminster.southcoastinns.co.uk	**GR:** SY297985 **DP:** 5 miles **N: LYME REGIS** OFFERS ONE NIGHT STAYS 14 🐕 ☂ 🚗	
The Mariners Hotel Silver Street, Lyme Regis, DT7 3HS ☏ 01297442753 ✉ enquiries@hotellymeregis.co.uk ⊕ www.facebook.com/TheMarinersHotel	**GR:** SY337923 **DP:** 0 miles **N: LYME REGIS** OFFERS ONE NIGHT STAYS 14 🐈 🍴 ☂ 🚗 📷 🌙 ☕ 🍴	
Rose Cottage B&B Main Street, Chideock, DT6 6JQ ☏ 01297 489994 ✉ enquiries@rosecottage-chideock.co.uk ⊕ www.rosecottage-chideock.co.uk	**GR:** SY423927 **DP:** 1 mile **N: CHARMOUTH** OFFERS ONE NIGHT STAYS ☂ 🚗 🛒 🌙 ☕	
Mervyn House Chideock, DT6 6JN ☏ 01297 489578 ✉ callbrig@gmail.com ⊕ www.chideockandseatown.co.uk/accommodation/ mervyn-house	**GR:** SY422928 **DP:** 0.3 miles **N: SEATOWN** OFFERS ONE NIGHT STAYS 2 ☂ 🚗 🛒 🌙 ☕	
Chideock House B&B Main Street, Chideock, DT6 6JN ☏ 01297 489242 ✉ annachideockhouse@yahoo.co.uk ⊕ www.chideockhouse.co.uk	**GR:** SY422928 **DP:** 0.75 miles **N: SEATOWN** OFFERS ONE NIGHT STAYS 3 🐕 ☂ 🚗	
Patricia's B&B 21 Rodden Row, Abbotsbury, Weymouth, DT3 4JL ☏ 07821 899247 ✉ pat21rr01@hotmail.co.uk ⊕	**GR:** SY578852 **DP:** 1.6 miles **N: ABBOTSBURY** OFFERS ONE NIGHT STAYS 2 ☂ 🍴	
Wheelwrights 14 Rodden Row, Abbotsbury, DT3 4JL ☏ 01305 871800 ✉ suenigel@wheelwrights.co.uk ⊕ www.wheelwrights.co.uk	**GR:** SY578852 **DP:** 1.6 miles **N: ABBOTSBURY** OFFERS ONE NIGHT STAYS 1 ☂ 🚗	
Seagull House B&B 18 Castle Road, Portland, DT5 1AU ☏ 07876286147 ✉ frances_wilson66@live.com ⊕ www.facebook.com/SeagullHouseBB	**GR:** SY684740 **DP:** 0 miles **N: ISLE OF PORTLAND** OFFERS ONE NIGHT STAYS 2 ☂ 🚗 🌙 ☕	

NAME	OTHER INFO		
Harbour Lights Guest House 20 Buxton Road, Weymouth, DT4 9PJ 01305 783273 enquiries@harbourlightsguesthouse.com www.harbourlightsguesthouse.com	GR: SY673779	DP:	0.1 miles
	N: **WEYMOUTH**		
	9 📶 🚗 🍎		
St Johns Guest House 7 Dorchester Rd, Weymouth, DT4 7JR 01305 775523 stjohnsguesthouse@gmail.com www.stjohnsguesthouse.co.uk	GR: SY297985	DP:	0 miles
	N:		
	OFFERS ONE NIGHT STAYS		
	9 📶 🚗 🍽 ☕ 🍎		
Alexandra Hotel 27-28 The Esplanade, Weymouth, DT4 8DN 01305 785 767 reception@alexandraweymouth.com alexandraweymouth.com	GR: SY680788	DP:	0 miles
	N: **WEYMOUTH**		
	OFFERS ONE NIGHT STAYS		
	19 📶 🚗		
Chiltern Lodge 8 Newfoundland Close, Worth Matravers, BH19 3LX 01929 439337 densor@btopenworld.com www.facebook.com/Chiltern-Lodge-Bed-and-Breakfast-413119618791180	GR: SY975777	DP:	1 mile
	N: **WORTH MATRAVERS**		
	OFFERS ONE NIGHT STAYS		
	2 🍽 📶 🚗 🍽 ☕ 🍎		
Kingston Country Courtyard West Street, Kingston, Wareham, BH20 5LR 01929 481066 enquiries@kingstoncountrycourtyard.com www.kingstoncountrycourtyard.com	GR: SY962793	DP:	2 miles
	N: **KINGSTON**		
	OFFERS ONE NIGHT STAYS		
	25 🐕 📶 🚗		
Alford House B&B 120 East Street, Corfe Castle, BH20 5EH 01929 480156 info@alfordhouse.com www.alfordhouse.com	GR: SY962816	DP:	3 miles
	N: **KINGSTON**		
	OFFERS ONE NIGHT STAYS		
	3 📶 🚗 🦮 🍽 ☕ 🍎		

Self Catering and Hostels

NAME	OTHER INFO		
The Granary, Larkbeare Grange Talaton, Exeter, EX5 2RY 01404 822069 granary@larkbeare.net www.larkbearegranary.net	GR: SY067976	DP:	12 miles
	N: **SIDMOUTH**		
	2 🐕 📶 🚗 📷		
Higher Wiscombe Southleigh, EX24 6JF 07772 630104 info@higherwiscombe.com www.higherwiscombe.com	GR: SY180933	DP:	3 miles
	N: **SIDMOUTH**		
	16 🐕 📶 🚗 📷		
1 Chapel Mews Chapel Street, Sidmouth, EX10 8ND 07415212196 info@1chapelmews.co.uk www.1chapelmews.co.uk	GR: SY125872	DP:	0 miles
	N: **SIDMOUTH**		
	2 📶 🚗		

NAME	OTHER INFO		
Holyford Farm Cottages	GR: SY236923	DP:	1.5 miles
Holyford Lane, Colyford, Colyton, EX24 6HW	N: **SEATON**		
☏ 01297 552983			
✉ stay@holyfordfarm.co.uk			
⊕ www.holyfordfarm.co.uk	6 🐕 📶 🚗 🎣		
Charmouth Coach House	GR: SY360935	DP:	0 miles
Westwell House, Old Lyme Road, Charmouth, DT6 6BQ	N: **CHARMOUTH**		
☏ 07984966264			
✉ jgroadrunner@yahoo.com			
⊕ www.charmouthcoachhouse.co.uk	1 🐕 📶 🚗 🛒		
Lyme Holidays	GR: SY359934	DP:	1 mile
Merlyn, 3 Greenhayes, Bridport, DT6 6BJ	N: **CHARMOUTH**		
☏ 01297 441222			
✉ lymeholidays@yahoo.com			
⊕ www.lymeholidays.com	🐕 📶 🚗 📺		
Ammonite Cottage	GR: SY469928	DP:1.5	miles
5 Seymour Place, East Street, Bridport, DT6 3LR	N: **WEST BAY**		
☏ 01308 459342	OFFERS ONE NIGHT STAYS		
✉ emilyaltham@yahoo.co.uk			
⊕ www.ammonitecottage.wordpress.com	2 🐕		
Graston Farm Cottages	GR: SY503899	DP:	1.5 miles
Annings Lane, Burton Bradstock, DT6 4NG	N: **BURTON BRADSTOCK**		
☏ 01308 897603 / 0777 8261796			
✉ info@grastonfarm.co.uk			
⊕ www.grastonfarm.co.uk	18 🐕 📶 🚗		
The Seaside Shepherd's Hut	GR: SY532865	DP:	0.05 miles
14 Chalets, Beach Road West Bexington, DT2 9DG	N: **WEST BEXINGTON**		
☏ 01308 897566			
✉ seasidehut@gmx.com			
⊕ https://bit.ly/2r0FdAl	1 📶 🚗 🍳 ☕		
Chesil Retreat Holiday Cottage	GR: SY667763	DP:	0 miles
9 Whitehead Drive, Weymouth, DT4 9XT	N: **WEYMOUTH**		
☏ 07779 283596			
✉ hello@originalcottages.co.uk			
⊕ www.facebook.com/profile.php?id=100076482794043	2 📶 🚗 📺		
Upton Grange Holiday Cottages	GR: SY742831	DP:	1 mile
Upton Farm, Upton, Ringstead, Dorchester, DT2 8NE	N: **RINGSTEAD**		
☏ 01305853970			
✉ info@uptongrangedorset.co.uk			
⊕ www.uptongrangedorset.co.uk	📶 🚗 📺		
YHA Swanage	GR: SZ031785	DP:	0 miles
Cluny, Swanage, BH19 2BS	N: **SWANAGE**		
☏ 0345 371 9346	OFFERS ONE NIGHT STAYS		
✉ swanage@yha.org.uk			
⊕ www.yha.org.uk/hostel/yha-swanage	🍴 📶 🚗 📺		

Campsites and Holiday Parks

NAME	OTHER INFO
Ladram Bay Holiday Park Ladram Road, Otterton, Budleigh Salterton, EX9 7BX ☎ 01395 568398 ✉ info@ladrambay.co.uk ⊕ www.ladrambay.co.uk	GR: SY095852 DP: 0 miles N: **BUDLEIGH SALTERTON** OFFERS ONE NIGHT STAYS [450] 🐕 🍴 📶 🚗 🛒 📺 ◎
Oakdown Holiday Park Gatedown Lane, Weston, Sidmouth, EX10 0PT ☎ 01297 680387 ✉ enquiries@oakdown.co.uk ⊕ www.oakdown.co.uk	GR: SY167902 DP: 2 miles N: **SIDMOUTH** OFFERS ONE NIGHT STAYS 🐕 🍴 📶 🚗 🛒
Coombe View Campsite Coombe View Farm, Branscombe, EX12 3BT ☎ 01297 680218 ✉ coombeviewfarm@branscombecamping.co.uk ⊕ www.branscombecamping.co.uk	GR: SY200902 DP: 1.5 miles N: **BRANSCOMBE** OFFERS ONE NIGHT STAYS 🐕 📶 🚗
Eype House Caravan & Camping Park Eype, Bridport, DT6 6AL ☎ 01308 424903 ✉ business@eypehouse.co.uk ⊕ www.eypehouse.co.uk	GR: SY447911 DP: 0 miles N: **WEST BAY** OFFERS ONE NIGHT STAYS 🐕 📶 🚗 📺
Highlands End Holiday Park Eype, Bridport, DT6 6AD ☎ 01308 426947 ✉ enquiries@wdlh.co.uk ⊕ wdlh.co.uk/holiday-parks/highlands-end	GR: SY449926 DP: 0 miles N: **WEST BAY** 🐕 📶 🚗 🛒 📺 £
Sweet Hill Farm Campsite Sweet Hill Road, Portland, DT5 2DS ☎ 07792 689591 ✉ enquiries@pitchup.com ⊕ www.pitchup.com/campsites/England/South_West/ Dorset/Portland/sweet-hill-farm	GR: SY684699 DP: 0.5 miles N: **ISLE OF PORTLAND** OFFERS ONE NIGHT STAYS 🐕 £
Portesham Dairy Farm Campsite 7 Bramdon Lane, Portesham, Weymouth, DT3 4HG ☎ 01305 871297 ✉ enquiries@pitchup.com ⊕ www.pitchup.com/campsites/England/South_West/ Dorset/Weymouth/portesham-dairy-farm-camp-site	GR: SY601854 DP: 1.5 miles N: **WEYMOUTH** OFFERS ONE NIGHT STAYS 🐕 📺 £
Sea Barn Farm Camping Fleet, Weymouth, DT3 4ED ☎ 01305 782218 ✉ enquiries@seabarnfarm.co.uk ⊕ www.seabarnfarm.co.uk	GR: SY626805 DP: 0.3 miles N: **WEYMOUTH** OFFERS ONE NIGHT STAYS 🐕 📶 🚗 🛒 📺
Tom's Field Campsite & Shop Langton Matravers, Swanage, BH19 3HN ☎ 01929 427110 ✉ tomsfield@hotmail.com ⊕ www.tomsfieldcamping.co.uk	GR: SY995785 DP: 1 mile N: **LANGTON MATRAVERS** OFFERS ONE NIGHT STAYS 🚗 🛒

Eat & Drink

NAME	OTHER INFO		
The Point Bar & Grill 14 Pilot Wharf, Exmouth, EX8 1XA ☏ 01395227145 ✉ bookings@thepointbg.com 🌐 www.thepointbarandgrill.com	**GR:** SX993806	**DP:**	0 miles
	N: EXMOUTH		
	🐕🍴📶🍽️		
Dukes Market Place, Sidmouth, EX10 8AR ☏ 01395 513320 ✉ dukes@sidmouthinn.co.uk 🌐 www.www.dukessidmouth.co.uk	**GR:** SY126872	**DP:**	0 miles
	N: SIDMOUTH		
	OFFERS ONE NIGHT STAYS		
	🐕🍴📶		
Masons Arms 3 Myrtle Cottages, Seaton, EX12 3DJ ☏ 01297 680300 ✉ masonsarms@staustellbrewery.co.uk 🌐 masonsarms.co.uk	**GR:** SY203888	**DP:**	0.4 miles
	N: BRANSCOMBE		
	OFFERS ONE NIGHT STAYS		
	🐕📶		
The Hideaway West Walk, Seaton, EX12 2TY ☏ 0129724292 ✉ thehideawayseaton@gmail.com 🌐 www.facebook.com/Thehideawayseaton	**GR:** SY240898	**DP:**	0 miles
	N: SEATON		
	🐕📶🍽️☕		
Rock Point 1-2 Broad Street, Lyme Regis, DT7 3QD ☏ 01297 443153 ✉ rockpointinn@staustellbrewery.co.uk 🌐 rockpointinn.co.uk	**GR:** SY341920	**DP:**	
	N: LYME REGIS		
	OFFERS ONE NIGHT STAYS		
	9🐕📶		
Poco Pizza 29 Marine Parade, Lyme Regis, DT7 3JF ☏ 01297598591 ✉ pocopizzalyme@gmail.com 🌐 www.pocopizza.co.uk	**GR:** SY338917	**DP:**	0 miles
	N: LYME REGIS		
	🐕🍴🍽️		

Information

NAME	OTHER INFO		
Exmouth Tourist Information 45A The Strand, Exmouth, EX8 1AL ☏ 01395 830550 ✉ exmouthtouristinformation@gmail.com 🌐 www.visitexmouth.org	**GR:** SY000809	**DP:**	0 miles
	N: EXMOUTH		
	🐕📶		
Budleigh Information Centre 14 Fore Street, Budleigh Salterton, EX9 6NG ☏ 01395 445275 ✉ info@visitbudleigh.com 🌐 www.lovebudleigh.co.uk	**GR:** SY064818	**DP:**	0 miles
	N: BUDLEIGH SALTERTON		
	🐕📶		

NAME	OTHER INFO	
Beer Village Fore Street, Beer, EX12 3JH 📞 07817934903 ✉ beervillageuk@gmail.com 🌐 beervillage.co.uk	**GR:** SY229822　**DP:** 0 miles **N: BEER** OFFERS ONE NIGHT STAYS 🐕🍴📶🚗🛒	
Seaton Tourist Information Centre Marshlands Centre, Harbour Road, Seaton, EX12 2LT 📞 01297 21388 ✉ info@seatonjurassic.org 🌐 www.seaton.gov.uk/your-visit	**GR:** SY246899　**DP:** 0 miles **N: SEATON**	
Lulworth Estate Visitor Centre Heritage Centre, Main Road, West Lulworth, Wareham, BH20 5RQ 📞 01929400352 ✉ info@lulworth.com 🌐 www.lulworth.com	**GR:** SY822800　**DP:** 0 miles **N: LULWORTH COVE** 🐕🚗	
Swanage Information Centre The White House, Shore Road, Swanage, BH19 1LB 📞 01929 766018 ✉ welcome@swanage.gov.uk 🌐 www.visit-dorset.com	**GR:** SZ030789　**DP:** 0 miles **N: SWANAGE** 🐕📶	

Activities

NAME	OTHER INFO	
Fifty Degrees Clothing 4A Fore Street, Budleigh Salterton, EX9 6NG 📞 07968736475 ✉ info@fiftydegrees.co.uk　🌐 www.fiftydegrees.co.uk	**GR:** SY064818　**DP:** 1 mile **N: BUDLEIGH SALTERTON** 🐕📶	
Seaton Tramway Harbour Road, Seaton, EX12 2WD 📞 01297 20375 ✉ info@tram.co.uk　🌐 www.tram.co.uk	**GR:** SY246900　**DP:** 0 mile **N: SEATON** 🐕📶🚗🎦	
West Bay Discovery Centre Chapel on the Beach, West Bay, Bridport, DT6 4EN 📞 01308 427288 ✉ info@westbaydiscoverycentre.org.uk 🌐 www.westbaydiscoverycentre.org.uk	**GR:** SY463903　**DP:** 0 miles **N: WEST BAY** 🐕📶	
Fine Foundation Wild Chesil Centre Dorset Wildlife Trust, Chesil Beach Centre, Weymouth, DT4 9XE 📞 01305206191 ✉ chesilbeach@dorsetwildlifetrust.org.uk 🌐 www.dorsetwildlifetrust.org.uk	**GR:** SY668756　**DP:** 0 miles **N: WEYMOUTH** 🐕🚗	
The Etches Collection Museum of Jurassic Marine Life, Kimmeridge, BH20 5PE 📞 01929 270000 ✉ info@theetchescollection.org 🌐 www.theetchescollection.org	**GR:** SZ011788　**DP:** 0 miles **N: KIMMERIDGE BAY**	

Getting Around

NAME	OTHER INFO		
Devine Cars	GR: SZO11788	DP:	I mile
469 High Street, Purbeck, Swanage, BH19 2NS	N: **SWANAGE**		
☏ 07730418046			
⊙ ddevine12@hotmail.co.uk			
⊕ www.yell.com/biz/devine-cars-swanage-8092967			

Abbotsbury. Photographer James Loveridge

Give Back To The Trail

As an owner of this guide, you no doubt already recognise the South West Coast Path's value: it provides health-giving happiness to millions of people every year, connects hundreds of coastal communities, helps the region's economy thrive and is one of our most precious wildlife corridors. It is a vehicle for change that can help us repair the disconnect between people and nature.

Despite its profound positive impact, less than 1% of people who use the National Trail give back to it regularly, so as the charity which cares for the Path, we are asking for your help to share the message that it needs support: it simply cannot live on love alone.

Our climate is in crisis: the consequences of this include increasingly severe storms, rising sea levels and coastal erosion – the effects of which can already be seen along the South West coast. Over the past few years, our charity has had to invest over £2 million in the Trail to keep it open and accessible. We've faced continuous funding cuts, despite increasing usage of trails nationwide, and maintenance costs rising by approximately 40%.

It now costs on average £1,500 per mile, per year to care for the Path.

If we can't continue to meet the level of investment needed the National Trail will cease to exist as it does now, a continuous, unbroken route. The health and wellbeing of the millions of people that use the Path is being threatened, along with the abundant wildlife whose homes it provides, and the thousands of workers and businesses whose livelihoods depend on it.

Here are the top three reasons to support the South West Coast Path;

Health and wellbeing

A wealth of research shows there are many physical and mental health benefits that come from walking, spending time in green spaces and next to water. A study with the University of Exeter has also shown that the health and wellbeing benefits of the Path alone saves the public health services £75 million every year.

Environment

The Coast Path corridor connects an extraordinarily diverse mix of habitats such as grassland, heathland, moorland, woodland, sand dunes, mud flats, coastal cliffs and saltwater marsh – all of which support biodiversity.

Economy

Thanks to the SWCP and its walkers, who come from all over the world, year-round, over £520 million is generated for the local economy every year, supporting 11,000 local jobs and livelihoods.

To tackle the challenge of protecting the Path head on, we are calling on walkers like you to support us in our 50th year as a charity. Whether that is joining us on our Trailblazer Walk, donating to our 50th anniversary campaign, or taking part in a fundraising challenge either out on the Path or virtually, from closer to home.

Please see **southwestcoastpath.org.uk/50** for all the latest news of what's going on and **southwestcoastpath.org.uk/donate50** to support us.

The South West Coast Path plays host to many large-scale running and hiking events and tours throughout the year. You may well pass by (or be part of!) groups taking part in these sorts of activities as you make your way around the Trail, particularly at weekends.

Event and tour organisers who use the Coast Path can give back to the Trail on which they depend through our 'Coast Path Friendly' scheme. We ask organisers to make their activity 'Coast Path Friendly' by contributing £1 per participant towards our work caring for the Trail, as well as adhering to the National Trails guidance for considerate event management. In return they receive a Coast Path Friendly digital badge to demonstrate their support, and can communicate to their participants and audiences that they are giving back to the Trail in this way.

Organised events and tours help to make accessing the freedom and beauty of our Path easy and fun for people of all ages and backgrounds. However – they can impact the Trail. Coast Path Friendly is a way to mitigate these impacts.

Increasing public concern for our environment has meant that many organisers are eager to support this initiative. The whole National Trail family is now encouraging organisers to give back in a similar way across all Paths that carry the acorn.

If you participate in paid-for activities on the Trail – be that charity walks, trail-running challenges, hiking holidays or similar – please look for the 'Coast Path Friendly' badge, and support organisations that display it on their website. If your favourite doesn't yet have the badge – encourage them to be 'Coast Path Friendly'! More details and a calendar of Coast Path Friendly events can be found at southwestcoastpath.org.uk/friendly-events.

CPF Malcolm Whales Foundation Walk

At the SWCPA we want as many people as possible to have access to the beauty and landscape of the South West Coast Path and to experience the health and wellbeing benefits of coastal walking. We know that some people have no problem in getting out and about on the Path, but we also realise that others may not have the same opportunities.

With this in mind, we undertake 'Equity of Access' projects and over the last few years have worked with local organisations in several pilot projects, which has led us to expand this work to a bigger, funded project. These look at how to encourage non-users of the Coast Path to get out and explore. It might be that some people need more information, more support or more confidence to get out on to the Path.

Coast Path Connectors

Thanks to funding from National Lottery Heritage Fund in 2023/2024, we will be leading our new Coast Path Connectors Project which aims to open coastal walking to a range of new audiences.

We will have five hubs along the trail in West Cornwall, Plymouth, Torbay/South Devon, North Devon and Dorset. These areas have been identified as those most in need. We will be expanding our volunteer capacity to include a new type

of volunteer, a 'Volunteer Community Ranger' who will be trained up to support community and health and wellbeing organisations in accessing the Coast Path. We will recruit and train the volunteers to act as walk leaders, points of contact and advocates for the Coast Path in their local communities.

We will be expanding on existing partnerships and collaborations with organisations that already work with key audiences with the aim of breaking down barriers which prevent access. The project will focus on improving wellbeing and building confidence in walking for people so that they can visit the Path independently in the future. The volunteers will also show people the heritage and nature in their local area with the hope of sparking interest and a love of walking which will continue after the end of the project.

For more information visit: southwestcoastpath.org.uk/coast-path-connectors.

Mount Edgcumbe. Photographer Dom Moore

Coast Path Connectors Project

SWCPA Volunteers

Dedicated volunteers walk and survey the Coast Path to make sure it's kept to the high quality standards we expect of a National Trail, helping direct funds to where they are most needed.

Volunteer for us

You can also choose to support us by volunteering and giving your time either out on the Path as a Local or Area Rep or by helping us with our marketing and communications, fundraising and events. Whatever your skills and experience, we would love to hear from you. Find the latest information about volunteering at the charity at southwestcoastpath.org.uk/volunteer.

Be our eyes and ears, as well as feet on the ground

Please let us know if you spot a maintenance need or want to suggest an improvement to this much-loved National Trail. Our volunteers regularly inspect the Path, liaising closely with Local Authority and National Trust teams who work hard to manage it to a high standard. It really helps to also have feedback from people using the Path. If you see a broken signpost, think that a way marker may be missing, identify stiles or gates in need of repair, or encounter potholes and excessive mud please use the Report a Problem page on our website **southwestcoastpath.org.uk/report-problem** contact us on **01752 896237** or email **hello@southwestcoastpath.org.uk** and we'll make sure that the information gets to the right person.

Shop and show your support

Our online shop has a variety of practical books and maps to help guide you along the Coast Path, gifts for you and your loved ones and clothing to wear. Show your support for the Path by visiting southwestcoastpath.org.uk/shop or call 01752 896237 to place your order.

All products and prices were correct at the time of going to print (December 2022).

▲ NEW! South West Coast Path Passport £6.50

Stop off at selected Way Maker businesses and collect your 'hand crafted' stamp in your Passport, to create a unique lasting record of your time on the Path.

▲ NEW! South West Coast Path Roundel £5.00

Show your support with our new, eco-friendly, waterproof, wooden Roundel. Complete with a hole to thread onto a lanyard or hang from a rucksack. *Please note – roundel does not come with lanyard or cord.*

◀ Small or Large Oak Finger Posts from £22

Beautifully crafted, solid oak finger post with National Trail acorn and 'South West Cost Path Minehead - Poole 630 Miles'. Can be personalised – call the office for more information. Measurements: 255mm x 50mm x 25mm.

From Land and Sea also donate 10% from the sales of any products with the SWCP design on, sold through their website **fromlandandsea.com**, back to the Association.

▲ Maps and Books

Our comprehensive range of Maps, Guides & Books will help you plan and walk along the Path, whether it be for a fun day out incorporating a circular walk, or a longer linear distance adventure.

▲ NEW! Assorted Greeting Card 8-pack £7.50

Photographic greetings Cards showcasing scenes along the Path, blank inside making them perfect for any occasion. Size 148mm x 148mm with envelopes. Cards FSC certified – Paper harvested in a responsible way.

Take a piece of the Coast Path home

Photographer Kate Hliznitsova

Whilst out on the Coast Path, you'll probably sample some unforgettable local produce and discover artists and makers inspired by the Trail's unique environment. Now you can take a little bit of the Path home with you and share it with friends by checking out the Coast Path Producers who also support us as Way Makers through our online shop. southwestcoastpath.org.uk/coast-path-producers.

Donate

Photographer James Loveridge

Walking the whole of the South West Coast Path will see you cross:

230 bridges
880 gates, climb over
436 stiles
Pass more than **4,000** Coast Path signs
Go up or down over **30,000** steps

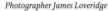

All this is vital infrastructure but it takes a lot of time and money to keep it in good shape. Help us to continue to keep the Coast Path open and healthy for generations to come by visiting southwestcoastpath.org.uk/donate-now.

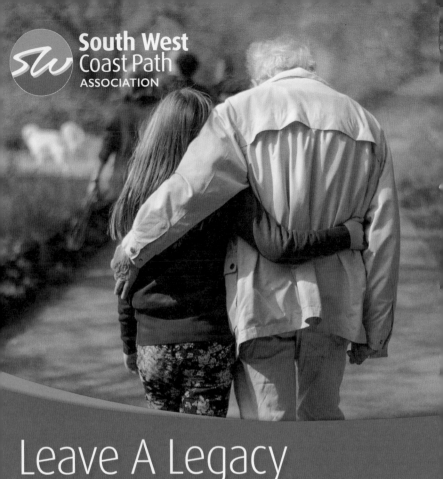

South West
Coast Path
ASSOCIATION

Leave A Legacy

The Path holds many treasured memories of our loved ones and the journeys we have taken together through life. Leaving a gift in your Will ensures that the journey continues after you've gone, and helps our vital work in ensuring that the Path continues to be a safe, accessible and special place for your loved ones to remember you.

If you're able, please consider the Association when making plans for your legacy, and trust that we will use any donation, however small or large, to champion and protect this unique 630-mile Trail for years to come.

**Find out more about leaving
a gift in your Will visit
southwestcoastpath.org.uk/legacy**

Registered with
FUNDRAISING
REGULATOR

Registered Charity No: 1163422